—FOR—
HOME &
COUNTRY

FOR HOME & COUNTRY

With a special message from
H.M. QUEEN ELIZABETH II

WAR, PEACE AND RURAL LIFE AS SEEN THROUGH THE PAGES OF THE W.I. MAGAZINE 1919-1959

COMPILED BY
PENNY KITCHEN

EBURY PRESS
LONDON

Published by Ebury Press
an imprint of Century Hutchinson Limited
20 Vauxhall Bridge Road
London SW1V 2SA

Editor: Gillian Haslam
Designer: Jerry Goldie

Typeset by Adelphi Graphics (Phototypesetters) Ltd, London
Printed and bound by Butler & Tanner Ltd, Frome, Somerset

British Library Cataloguing in Publication Data
For home and country: war, peace and rural life as seen through
the pages of WI magazine 1919-1959.
1. Great Britain. Rural regions. Social Life, history
I. Kitchen, Penny   II. Home & Country
941'.009'734

ISBN 0 85223 855 X

Contents

HM Queen Elizabeth talking with WI demonstrators at the WI Life and Leisure Exhibition, London, 1984

BALMORAL CASTLE

I send my best wishes to the National
Federation of Women's Institutes in their
Seventy-Fifth Anniversary Year, and to all
my fellow WI members, who derive so much
pleasure and benefit from its many
activities. The role of the WI in
encouraging home skills and traditional
crafts, and its important work for women's
health, the improvement of rural services
and the safeguarding of the environment, are
as important as ever today, and I hope that
the Institutes will continue to flourish in
the future.

ELIZABETH R.

1990.

Addressing the AGM Royal Albert Hall

Introduction

Home & Country, the magazine of the National Federation of Women's Institutes, began life as a 'dear little journal' of eight pages and a circulation of 2,000 in March 1919, edited by its instigator Miss Alice Williams who was also the Honorary Treasurer of the WI at that time. The National Chairman, the formidable Lady Denman, was her only enthusiastic supporter on the WI Executive Committee and guaranteed the venture with the grand sum of £10. Miss Williams' confidence was well-placed, however, and Lady Denman's £10 was never needed.

It had been four years since Mrs Madge Robertson Watt, representing the Canadian WI, had set up the first institute in rural Wales which was to be the pattern for thousands more. Before returning to her native Canada, she had the satisfaction of seeing the British sister organisation of the Canadian WI flourish, culminating in the formation in 1919 of an institute, at Queen Mary's request, on the Sandringham estate. She described this momentous event in the first two issues of the magazine and a link was formed between WI members and the Royal Family which exists to this day.

In the days before wireless, and certainly television, for all, *H&C* brought countrywomen a digest of pertinent legislation and the world's news along with the features. Whatever concerned rural women concerned the magazine – poor housing and low agricultural wages, ways to stretch the housekeeping, family health and social problems.

Home & Country recognised the huge influence the cinema would have as early as 1919 and soon carried excellent film reviews alongside the articles on craft and home-making. Advertisers of craft materials saw a burgeoning market as women took up everything from glovemaking to basketry. It wasn't long before there were advertisements telling them how to make money from these skills. Suddenly there were means for rural women to earn a little extra cash from the traditional skills handed down to them.

Naturally, as a 'house' journal, a good proportion of *H&C's* pages were taken up by the activities of the national organisation and of the institutes; advice appeared for delegates speaking at the AGM, for entrants in needlecraft exhibitions and for WI members working in fruit preservation centres.

During the Depression both the news and letters pages were full of suggestions for helping the miners and their families, many of whom were found temporary accommodation and work through the generosity of WIs. When war broke out, this generosity allied to great organisational skills were channelled into receiving the mothers, children and teachers evacuated from the cities. The evacuation was not without its problems and the letters pages were the focus of members' gripes and criticisms, as well as praise and helpful comments.

And of course, the famous jam. The Fruit Preservation Scheme became the WI's best remembered contribution to the war effort and each year the tonnage of the fruit processed was reported in *H&C* along with harvesting hints, complaints concerning sugar supplies and fulsome thanks from government ministers.

Country pursuits such as keeping rabbits, goats and bees and cultivating one's own vegetables came into their own in wartime and for readers new to it all, *H&C* became a veritable DIY manual.

After years of privation, make do and mend and sacrifices for the sake of the country at war, the patience of the WI began to wear thin in the face of government excuses over shortages and shoddy merchandise and by the end of the '40s they passed a resolution criticising the poor quality of household goods. The WI was one of the earliest consumer groups and a voice to be reckoned with.

Environmental issues, too, have always concerned WI members. A resolution was passed in 1925 and another in 1954 in the movement's long-running battle against litter which resulted in the creation of the Keep Britain Tidy Group and a new awareness in the ordinary citizen that littering the countryside was anti-social.

Education and technological advances have altered women's lives dramatically, in many ways for the better, since the 40 years encompassed in the pages of this book. Today *Home & Country* is a flourishing, full-colour magazine, with over 105,000 subscribers. It still comments on consumer, social and environmental problems and reports the serious side of WI business at national and grass roots level (with enough humour to ensure the readers don't take themselves *too* seriously). There is still an emphasis on craft (noticeable by its absence in the '50s when anything home-made was despised) and cookery, but no longer is advice offered on how to make soap or wash dishes!

The coverage of agricultural subjects has lessened, reflecting the fact that far fewer WI members today are directly involved in farming, perhaps only 8% of the total membership of 343,000.

The magazine, like the WI, wants to see an improvement in the quality of women's lives. It is also concerned with the custodianship of the countryside, for the sake of the people who live and work there, coping daily with the erosion of their public services, and for the sake of the nation's children and grandchildren who will inherit the growing problems along with dwindling resources. The organisation's motto, 'For Home and Country', is still as relevant today as it was in 1919.

Penny Kitchen

Home & Country is the magazine of the National Federation of Women's Institutes covering England and Wales. If you would like to join Britain's largest women's organisation, write to the Organisation Department, NFWI, 39 Eccleston Street, London SW1W 9NT or telephone 01-730 7212.

CHAPTER ONE

Women's Lives

HELPFUL HINTS FOR THE BUSY HOUSEWIFE.

W.I. Member.

I.—Daily Routine from 6.30—9 a.m.

Contrary to nearly everyone else, I start my morning's work the previous evening! About ten minutes before going to bed, I take off the serge table-cloth in our sitting-room, shake it well, fold it up carefully and put it at the end of the table. Then I gather up the cushions, shake them too and put them on top of the tablecloth. I then put the chairs seats downwards on the table and roll up any rugs and put them in the passage just outside. Under the table go the fender and fireirons. I put the big pieces of burning coal to the side of the fireplace, and spread out the smaller pieces as much as possible, to prevent their burning away. Then I bring in the ash-box, shovel, blacklead-box with its brushes, and the newspaper, small coal and about ten dry thin sticks, and leave matches by the side—all to hand for the next morning at 6.30 a.m.—not a second later! Then I put out the light and draw up the blind.

Next morning, my preparations for the busy bit before breakfast put me in a good temper right away. I shovel up the ashes, taking care to put the pieces of coal in the coal-box (they go later on the top of the fire), and to make as little dust as possible. Sometimes I put some damp tealeaves amongst the ashes. I brush well into the corners of the bars with the hearth-brush, otherwise my black-leading would have a greyish tinge, instead of being the shiny black we all like so much. Then I mix the black lead (and I do love Nixey's) to a thick " cream " with a few drops of cold water, and rub on a little of it hard with the round brush we buy for 6½d. at any ironmonger's. I give more hard rubs with the first long brush, some quick light polishing strokes with a softer brush and perhaps a final polish with a piece of old velvet or rag.

Now I crumple up the newspaper I had put out the night before into small balls and put about eight of them into the grate, very gently and quickly, one by one, then I lay on the sticks crossways and just as gently I lay on bits of coal. Now I clear away the ashes and blacklead things, light the fire (with one match) and open the window top and bottom to make a draught so that the fire may burn quickly. Then the big bits of half-burned coal go on and the kettle for breakfast. Out come the broom and dust-pan, and I begin sweeping as far as possible from the door, always keeping my eye on the broom and using long strokes, I sweep towards me, going well into the corners and greeting all the ledges of the skirting-boards with my broom bristles. I frequently take the fluff off the broom as I work. Next I sweep the hall in just the same way and while the dust is settling, I sweep the rugs out of doors. Then, I do the dusting, beginning at the highest things and the top of the door, I work methodically all round the room, keeping my eye

table and chair having four legs !

But quick and good dusting soon comes with practice and by 7.30 I am ready to lay the breakfast-table. Yes, the cups, saucers, plates, knives and forks were left on a tray in the scullery after washing-up at supper-time. So, while the bacon is cooking, I only have to add the bread, butter, sugar, and milk to the tray. After making the tea, I fill up the kettle at once and add a little coal to the fire ; we do not want to wait for the washing-up water, do we ? The meal over, I put away the clean things and the bread and sugar into the cupboard, wipe the greasy plates and knives with soft paper, rinse out the cups, and steep the milk jug in cold water. I wash the spoons and forks first and dry them at once, they shine so much better if dried while still hot from the water. Then I wash the cups, saucers, small plates and the knives ; I add more very hot water to the bowl before doing the greasy bacon plates. I rinse out the dishcloth in hot soapy water, a little soda can be put into the water, and peg it out to dry if the weather permits. Now I clean the knives and put some slack on the fire. Then I go upstairs as quickly as possible, to the bed-making and dusting there.

THREE WISE FOOLS.
A Tale with a Moral.
BY THE PRESIDENT OF BACKWELL W.I.

ONCE upon a time in almost pre-historic days, there lived three wise fools, and they met together nightly in the comfortable parlour of the tavern to discuss the affairs of the nation in general, and their own in particular. They were a sleek and well-fed company, having good wives at home, and they knew it ! Now as they sat and smoked and sipped, it chanced that one of the three spoke thus— " Gentlemen, as you know full well, a woman's place is in the home, and she should find her work and recreation therein, but perchance there should arise a race of women so dead to all sense of duty as to wish otherwise, it behoves us therefore to so arrange our houses that she lacks both time and energy to seek other work. She is a docile creature and patient, and if we hide our scheme with a show of much giving she will be grateful. We will give her a kitchen range, a thing of many flues and of iron, that she must, perforce, rise early to remove the soot from many corners, and blacklead the surface, which she will surely do, lest she become a reproach unto her neighbours. Her soul loves bright things, so we will adorn the stove with steel to be polished daily. It shall be built into the wall, quite why, I know not, but methinks it will be better so." For a while they smoked in peace, and then the second, a lusty fellow much given to the chase, thus spake : " Her legs will also require some exercise. For that reason let her not have a sink near her stove, so that, perforce, if she but needs to pour away the water from the tea-pot, ere she brew the tea, she must run to the scullery at no small distance. There should moreover, be a step or two down to the scullery, and one up to the larder, and one or two between the kitchen and the parlour, methinks I have heard, in bearing heavy trays, even one step so placed adds to the exercise of limbs. In her laundry let there be no tap to her copper, being a creature of little resource she will bale it to her life's-end, and think not to syphon it out." Now the third had married a young wife not over fond of the kitchen, and fearing lest she should find time to gad about, thus spoke : " Why not blacklead the parlour grates, give her brass rods, handles and taps that need much polish, ornament her rooms with crevices, mouldings and many ledges for the dust, her stairs with twisted banisters. She doth love a cupboard, give her many, small and dark about her rooms, that she may run many steps to find her goods." So they planned and schemed, and as they wended their way home down the dusty street arm linked in arm (for the good landlord's punch was strong) they thought clothes should need much brushing, why not wear trousers an inch or two too long, turned up to form a pocket for the dust ?

In due course these good men died and left behind them many sons whose motto was : " What was good enough for my father is good enough for me and my womenfolk."

Now the moral of my tale is thus—let those that pay the piper pick the tune ; and the woman pays, if not in cash in kind. Should she not plan the home ?

"You little Spendthrift"

"Listen! Jim! These £3 worth of woollies cost me 13/-."

"What? That lot thirteen bob?"

"Yes—all on my wonderful Cymbal Knitter. Easy as anything—I've turned out this jumper since tea—All these are for us. Then, Jim, I start on my first £10 order!"

"£10 order?"

"Yes, Mrs. Evans and her friend saw some of my work to-day and gave me a £10 order on the spot. They were astounded at the quality of the work, and said they would have to pay double my prices in the West End. *And I make £4-10-0.* But, Jim, this is the best news. Even if I don't want to sell to friends and shops I am sure of a regular income each week from the Cymbal Company. Here is their guarantee to buy at good prices all the work I care to send them for three years."

What about you, dear reader? There's no room to explain here how you can have a regular extra income of your own and have beautiful things to wear for next to nothing, so we have provided the coupon below for you to use. You have everything to gain and nothing to lose by posting it.

JUMPERS
—and Jumper Suits as sold for 20/- to 30/- made for 4/6 in 2 hours.

BABY'S WOOLLIES
—leggings, coats hats, etc., as sold for 17/6 to 35/- made for 3/6 in 3 hours!

GOLF HOSE
—in any mixtures as sold for 6/6 to 10/- per pair made for 2/9 in 30 to 50 minutes.

Readers in London should call at the demonstration Salon at 90 Borough High Street (just over London Bridge)

A Happy Baby is Breast-fed

HAPPY babies make happy mothers, and happy babies are those who enjoy the great advantages of having the food which Nature has provided for healthy growth.

Maternal milk is germ-free and of correct composition. Authorities have proved that the breast-fed baby has many more chances of growing strong and healthy than the artificially-fed baby. No substitute is equal to maternal milk for safeguarding a child against nutritional diseases, such as rickets, and building a sure foundation for future health.

Doctors, nurses and mothers daily testify to the remarkable qualities of "Ovaltine" for producing a rich supply of maternal milk. Not only does this delicious beverage promote adequate lactation, but it assists the mother in maintaining her strength while nursing, and ensures a quick return to normal health.

"Ovaltine" is pure, concentrated nourishment, prepared from ripe barley malt, creamy milk and eggs. The essential food elements and vitamins are present in correct nutritive ratio and in an easily digested form. "Ovaltine" is entirely free from preservatives.

'OVALTINE'
TONIC FOOD BEVERAGE
Enables Mothers to Breast-feed their Babies

Prices in Gt. Britain and Northern Ireland, 1/3, 2/- and 3/9 per tin.

DETAILS OF EXPENDITURE OF A HOUSE-KEEPING ALLOWANCE OF £2 5s. 0d. A WEEK.
(For working man and wife.)
Mrs. BLACKWELL, Member of Baslow W.I., Derby (Prize winner in competition).

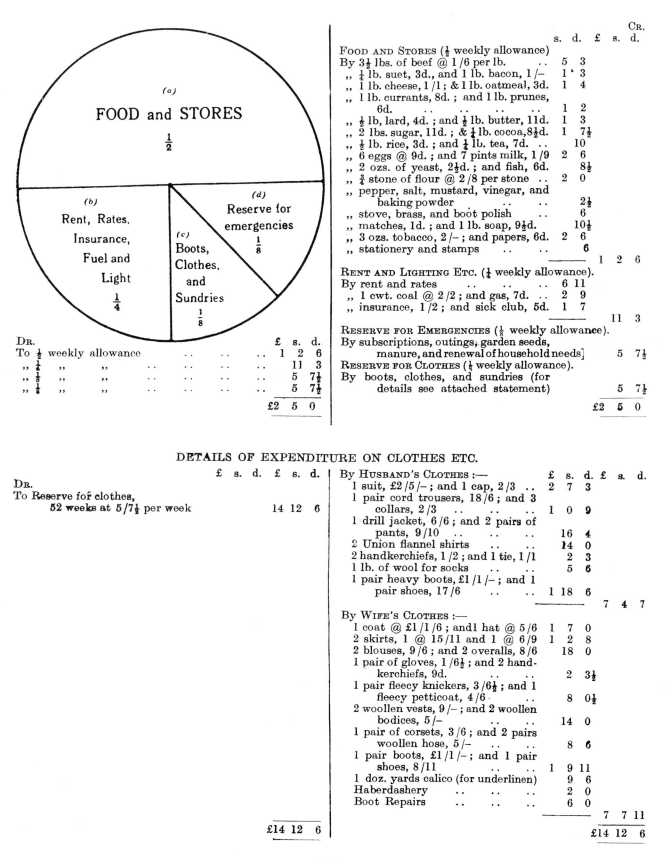

FOOD and STORES $\frac{1}{2}$ (a)

Rent, Rates, Insurance, Fuel and Light $\frac{1}{4}$ (b)

Boots, Clothes, and Sundries $\frac{1}{8}$ (c)

Reserve for emergencies $\frac{1}{8}$ (d)

	£	s.	d.
DR.			
To $\frac{1}{2}$ weekly allowance	1	2	6
,, $\frac{1}{4}$,, ,, ...		11	3
,, $\frac{1}{8}$,, ,, ...		5	7½
,, $\frac{1}{8}$,, ,, ...		5	7½
	£2	5	0

	s.	d.	£	s.	d.
					CR.
FOOD AND STORES ($\frac{1}{2}$ weekly allowance)					
By 3½ lbs. of beef @ 1/6 per lb. ..	5	3			
,, ¼ lb. suet, 3d., and 1 lb. bacon, 1/–	1	3			
,, 1 lb. cheese, 1/1; & 1 lb. oatmeal, 3d.	1	4			
,, 1 lb. currants, 8d. ; and 1 lb. prunes, 6d.	1	2			
,, ½ lb, lard, 4d. ; and ½ lb. butter, 11d.	1	3			
,, 2 lbs. sugar, 11d. ; & ¼ lb. cocoa, 8½d.	1	7½			
,, ½ lb. rice, 3d. ; and ¼ lb. tea, 7d. ..		10			
,, 6 eggs @ 9d. ; and 7 pints milk, 1/9	2	6			
,, 2 ozs. of yeast, 2½d. ; and fish, 6d.		8½			
,, ¾ stone of flour @ 2/8 per stone ..	2	0			
,, pepper, salt, mustard, vinegar, and baking powder		2½			
,, stove, brass, and boot polish ..		6			
,, matches, 1d. ; and 1 lb. soap, 9½d.		10½			
,, 3 ozs. tobacco, 2/– ; and papers, 6d.	2	6			
,, stationery and stamps		6			
			1	2	6
RENT AND LIGHTING ETC. ($\frac{1}{4}$ weekly allowance).					
By rent and rates	6	11			
,, 1 cwt. coal @ 2/2 ; and gas, 7d. ..	2	9			
,, insurance, 1/2 ; and sick club, 5d.	1	7			
				11	3
RESERVE FOR EMERGENCIES ($\frac{1}{8}$ weekly allowance).					
By subscriptions, outings, garden seeds, manure, and renewal of household needs]				5	7½
RESERVE FOR CLOTHES ($\frac{1}{8}$ weekly allowance).					
By boots, clothes, and sundries (for details see attached statement)				5	7½
			£2	5	0

DETAILS OF EXPENDITURE ON CLOTHES ETC.

	£	s.	d.	£	s.	d.
DR.						
To Reserve for clothes, 52 weeks at 5/7½ per week				14	12	6
				£14	12	6

	£	s.	d.	£	s.	d.
By HUSBAND'S CLOTHES :—						
1 suit, £2/5/– ; and 1 cap, 2/3 ..	2	7	3			
1 pair cord trousers, 18/6 ; and 3 collars, 2/3	1	0	9			
1 drill jacket, 6/6 ; and 2 pairs of pants, 9/10		16	4			
2 Union flannel shirts		14	0			
2 handkerchiefs, 1/2 ; and 1 tie, 1/1		2	3			
1 lb. of wool for socks		5	6			
1 pair heavy boots, £1/1/– ; and 1 pair shoes, 17/6	1	18	6			
				7	4	7
By WIFE'S CLOTHES :—						
1 coat @ £1/1/6 ; and 1 hat @ 5/6	1	7	0			
2 skirts, 1 @ 15/11 and 1 @ 6/9	1	2	8			
2 blouses, 9/6 ; and 2 overalls, 8/6		18	0			
1 pair of gloves, 1/6½ ; and 2 handkerchiefs, 9d.		2	3½			
1 pair fleecy knickers, 3/6½ ; and 1 fleecy petticoat, 4/6 ..		8	0½			
2 woollen vests, 9/– ; and 2 woollen bodices, 5/–		14	0			
1 pair of corsets, 3/6 ; and 2 pairs woollen hose, 5/–		8	6			
1 pair boots, £1/1/– ; and 1 pair shoes, 8/11	1	9	11			
1 doz. yards calico (for underlinen)		9	6			
Haberdashery		2	0			
Boot Repairs		6	0			
				7	7	11
				£14	12	6

WOMEN POLICE.

F. E. ABBOTT, Inspector Women's Auxiliary Service.

THE title " Women Police " sounded strange in 1914—we could imagine women bus-drivers, collectors and even railway porters, but police—visions of burglars and desperate characters caused us to shake our heads and smile. Yet there are many sides to police work which women are not only better able to handle than men, but where it is most unsuitable to employ the latter. Police women are a protection to the woman offender. Let me give an example to illustrate this : a young girl of good family, but undisciplined, ran away to a provincial town. She stayed at an hotel and obtained goods under "false pretences." A warrant was taken out for her arrest and an Inspector went one evening to the Hotel. The town employed two police women and he ordered one of them to accompany him instead of one of his men as he would have done six months before. A thorough search was made in the girl's bedroom in her presence ; this was absolutely necessary, but imagine two men searching a young woman's bedroom with no other woman present.

The majority of women offenders come into the police courts charged with moral offences, and surely they should be in the hands of women entirely—not even in the legal charge of men. There is a vast field for welfare work for both police men and women, and only those who have worked with the police realise the amount of this kind of work that they do.

Our streets are the chief playground for the vast majority of the children of London and our large industrial towns. The temptations and dangers there are many for the child and the adolescent of both sexes, and there should be in the streets and parks some public authority to exercise a parental and social control akin to that which safeguards the interests of the children and young people of the wealthier classes. A Mother is mainly responsible for the training of the young. A policewoman is better suited, by nature and experience, than is her male colleague, for this particular work in the

SUPERINTENDENT GOLDINGHAM, M.B.E.
Women's Auxiliary Service.

streets. Moreover it is infinitely easier for a policewoman to get into touch with the Mothers in her district. Many a Mother is most grateful for a friendly hint from the policewoman that her boy is loitering about the streets ripe for any mischief and for assistance in getting him into touch with Boy Scouts or the Play Centres etc., or for a hint that a daughter has been seen with undesirable women. In this case too a policewoman can help in finding a safer direction for the girl's energy and recreation by effecting a change of occupation or environment.

Another most important part of a policewoman's duties is her work in the police court and station, that is entire charge of women in the cells and the dock. Whilst working with a provincial force the writer was astonished to find that women in every sort of distress and difficulty resorted to the police station when they discovered that policewomen had been appointed. One of the most painful duties of policewomen is to take down statements of children and girls who have been criminally or indecently assaulted. These pathetic cases should make a very special appeal to all women and under no circumstances should they allow a man to do this work.

I would emphasise one important point—policewomen must be sworn-in. Their work is arduous and difficult. They need this assistance to maintain their prestige and authority, and, most important of all, unless they are sworn-in policewomen cannot have legal charge of women offenders. The arguments brought forward against the swearing-in of policewomen : (1) that their influence over the girls and women would be diminished or (2) that their lack of physical strength is an insuperable obstacle, have been proved, by personal experience, to be fallacious. Moral strength is far more efficacious than people realise, moreover every policewoman can summon assistance with her whistle. It has also been abundantly proved that kindness on the part of the policewoman is more appreciated by unruly girls when they know that it is not a cover for lack of power.

Law and order must be enforced and offenders punished but punishment should not be our chief object, the reformation of the offender is, or should be, our main

COMMANDANT ALLEN, O.B.E.
Women's Auxiliary Service.

purpose. Offenders under arrest are really in the care of the Nation, whose servants the police are. It therefore behoves every citizen to see that the offender has proper handling and an understanding treatment. This responsibility is very specially that of the women, the Mothers of the Nation. It is the duty of every woman, so far as she can, to study the subject and to insist on the employment of properly trained policewomen with full powers.

The Women's Auxiliary Service, late "Women Police Service" was started in 1914 by the late Miss Damer Dawson, O.B.E., who had studied this subject on the continent before the war. She started a voluntary service, officially recognised by the Ministry of Munitions in 1916 to train and supply trained policewomen for the explosive factories. At the same time it was supplying trained policewomen to Chief Constables in provincial towns. When the Ministry of Munitions was dissolved the Service was faced with a momentous decision —should it carry on ? If it demobilised there would be nobody to whom Chief Constables could apply for trained women. Moreover, it would mean the scattering of those women who had had the necessary experience for training others. In spite of great difficulties it was decided to "carry on."

The Headquarters of the Service is 7 Rochester Row, S.W.1., and any woman anxious to know what steps she can take towards furthering this great and urgent reform should write to this address to the Commandant, Women's Auxiliary Service.

Women Police Service Report, 1918-1919 ; Women's Auxiliary Service (late Women Police Service) Report, 1920-21 ; 1s. 3d. post free from Headquarters, Women's Auxiliary Service, 7 Rochester Row, London, S.W.1.

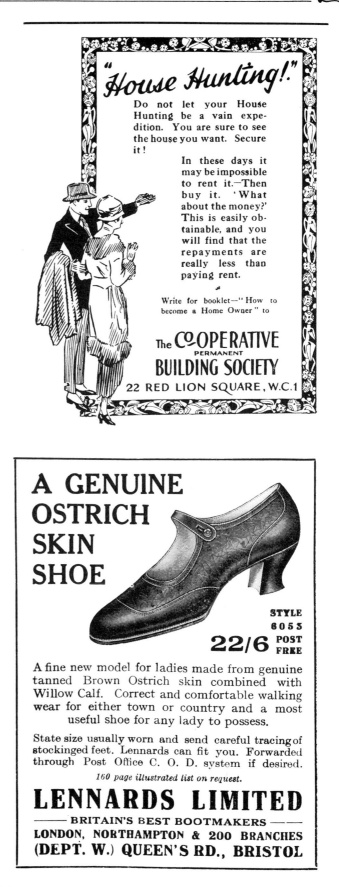

Empire-Builders.

EMPIRE-BUILDERS IN AUSTRALIA

M. WALLER

THE average woman who is thinking of settling in one of our colonies feels a great bewilderment concerning the conditions which may await her, especially if she is going as far away as Australia. I strongly advise any such readers to call at Australia House, Strand, London, to consult Miss Jacobs, as although settlement conditions are very similar throughout Australia, naturally in such a large continent the climate varies tremendously. Therefore clothes suitable for the cool south-east parts are not necessary in the tropical climates of Queensland and the Northern Territory, where too the modern English furniture would crack and perish.

Another call should be made at Caxton House, Westminster, where the S.O.S.B.W., of which Miss Pott, O.B.E., is Chairman, will furnish all approved women and girls with letters of introduction to friendly people and societies near the port of arrival. This will be of great help in matters of employment, accommodation and the many little worries which are met by all travellers. There are numerous societies familiar this side which are banded together officially in Australia under the name of the New Settlers League. I worked with this League for nearly four years in Victoria, under the leadership of Lady Masson and Lady Mitchell, whose interest in migration is well known on both sides of the world. This work, through our branches in other states, kept me in touch with hundreds of British women settlers in town and country.

For a while I took charge of all newly arriving domestics, finding them positions and introducing them to friends and clubs where Oversea girls on their free days meet for tea, chat and games. The greatest care is exercised in the choice of a girl's employment. Girls' references are carefully taken up this side, verified and then mailed to the Australian Migration authorities. I had to examine both these and the references of all prospective employers before making any engagements. Wages vary from £1 5s. to £2 10s. a week according to a girl's ability. Good plain cooking is the chief requirement as many Australian women do their own housework and keep one maid to manage the meals. The accommodation provided for girls is far superior to that in England. I have heard dozens of girls praising their pretty bedrooms . . . "and a silk eiderdown and all," in many cases a little sitting-room and bath room are allotted, as well as far more leisure than is allowed at home. But in return I certainly think the English girls need to quicken their outlook in order to keep pace with the methods of their versatile Australian sisters who are wonderfully adept at getting through their work with the minimum of effort. The Training Hostel for domestics proceeding overseas, which the Government recently started at Market Harborough, will prove invaluable in preparing the trainees to become " all round " workers, not afraid of washing or cooking if they are required to undertake them in the new country.

Before leaving the subject of domestic workers, I would like to pay a tribute to the success of the many I watched blossoming into good health and good citizenship. I kept careful records and can vouch for over 90 per cent. having made good in every sense of the word. Some have found work for themselves when they knew the ways of the country, nearly all have saved money. Several girls have sent for their families to join them and very few indeed have returned to the Old Country once they have enjoyed the fuller life overseas.

When I first went "outback " to visit the women on the new settlements far behind those cities which now stand where forty years back was virgin forest, I was reminded of the words, "Providence being their Guide, they builded better than they knew." I wished those

The Bush.

early-day women could return to see their sons or grandsons in their fine homesteads, where once they lived in tents and "Bag Humpies." An old midwife in Western Australia told me of her work in the mining days of the seventies, when babies were born under a crude tent, which sometimes blew off in the frequent sandstorms. In those days she had to ride to her cases on horseback, often behind the father. The baby's first bath was in a rusty old tin and the water cost a shilling a bucket, being carted miles to the camps.

Many Australians have a "far distant" look in their eyes and I believe it is an inheritance from those mothers who gazed out over the thousands of miles of land and sea which stretched between them and all their loved ones. And this pioneering spirit which animated the first settlers lives on in those families I met way back in the dairy, fruit and wheat blocks, where our new settlers are putting up a brave fight for ownership of their virgin land. Many types of homes are here, from the first shelter of tent or bag humpy, to the neat four-roomed house of Government design. The bag humpy, though, makes a capital temporary home, and I have often unrolled my bed in the kitchen, and spent a good night, sheltered from wind, dust and rain.

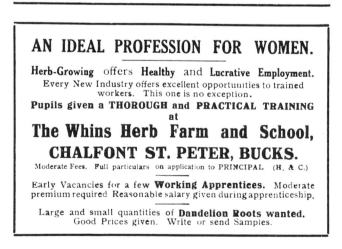
New Settler's House.

The undergrowth is then burnt off, the earth ploughed with a Stump Jump plough, and the first crop sown.

Once that is in, the settler and his wife are able to rest a while and meet their neighbours. Cricket teams are formed, and on Saturday afternoons many a close game is played on the sandy pitch, bare of all grass, where later in the evening the young folks dance in the moonlight to the strains of the gramophone or to the music of the wireless from Melbourne or Sydney. In this community are all ages, classes and types, from the half-trained medical student, the ivory turner, the draper, the 'bus driver, the bank clerk, to the farmer from Lincolnshire, and everywhere I found a quiet courage and a spirit of mutual helpfulness which augur well for the future.

Space forbids any but a fleeting reference to the excellent Bush Schools, Bush Libraries and Bush Hospitals, which, together with the Country Women's Associations, founded on the principles of our Women's Institutes, do so much nowadays to lighten the newcomer's lot. I would like in closing to quote an old Australian farmer's reply to my query as to his opinion of the new settlers' prospects. . . He said, "They have got a stiff fight ahead of them, but they'll win through . . . their women are the right stuff, and it's the women who make the settlement."

The walls are of hessian, treated with a simple waterproofing, stretched round four uprights, with a galvanised roof and door. Partitions make three rooms, and the children's bedroom is usually arranged like a ship's cabin, with beds ranged bunkwise along the walls, a' space-saving notion gained on the voyage over. All the furniture is home-made, and wonderful articles are constructed from packing cases and from kerosene cases from the distant store. Every mantelshelf has its hoard of treasures saved from the old home, and Staffordshire ornaments stand side by side with shell cases from the war, and jars of living flowers veil snapshots of those gardens whence the seed came, thoussands of miles away. The folks love their new gardens, though the water shortage makes it a hard job to keep the plants alive. The women do most of the gardening, as well as helping their husbands to clear the "scrub," as the bush vegetation is called. Most of this is cut down with an axe, though in some cases the contractor's Mallee Roller is called in with its ten horses or bullocks harnessed to a giant iron roller, which crushes down all the growth in its wake.

THE HOME PAGE

A Short Article on Washing Up. The washing up in a house is regarded as the most horrid and tiresome of jobs that have to be done. It comes so regularly, at least four times a day and cannot, like the turning out of a room, be postponed to a more convenient season.

A great deal depends on the preparation you make for washing up and I advise young housewives in particular to give attention to these preliminary arrangements.

The sink should have a draining board on one, or better still, on each side. These boards prevent breakages and any carpenter or handyman will make and fix them for a nominal sum. You should also have an enamel and a wooden bowl, two jam jars, a piece of soap and, most important of all, a brush the size of a nail brush and costing about threepence.

To protect your skirt and the cuffs of your blouse, provide yourself with a mackintosh apron and a pair of cooking sleeves with elastic top and bottom.

Presuming then that you have hot water over the sink or a kettle on a gas ring or stove, collect all the dirty glasses, silver, cups, saucers and plates. Start with the glasses, wash them by hand in the wooden bowl, then turn down on the draining board, next collect the spoons and forks in the enamel bowl and with soap on your brush scrub each article separately, rinse in the enamel bowl first and then in the wooden one, both of which should contain hot water, and lay on the draining board.

Next get a clean cloth and polish the glasses, which will have partly dried, put them on a tray and carry to the cupboard or shelf where they are kept, then wipe the silver, being very careful to dry between each division of the forks holding one end of the article in the cloth, while you rub up the other, then put away in the silver basket, each article in its particular place.

Now empty the water from both bowls, pouring it through a sink dish over the grating on the sink ; in this way you collect all bits, which can be burnt, and the soapy water is good for the drain.

Again fill both bowls with fresh water and start on the cups and saucers, using the brush well soaped and rinsing in the enamel and then wooden bowls, turn down to drain and proceed with the plates and dishes in the same way and lastly with the knives, which should have been previously placed in one of the jars, scrub each blade, holding the handle in your hand and then place in a second jar. Wipe each article. Scrub out the two bowls and turn down to dry after washing out your cloths in the enamel one.

After breakfast there is probably a frying pan and from dinner several saucepans to be cleaned : scrape any fat from them and then wipe with a piece of newspaper ; next fill with water into which a little soda has been added, bring to the boil, rinse round with a saucepan brush (one with a long handle and fibre top preferred), and turn down on a shelf.

Should these simple instructions be carried out you will not find that washing up is either laborious or disagreeable. Your glass, silver and china will be bright and pleasing to the eye and by using a brush in place of a dish cloth, you will avoid meeting with egg and dried mustard from the meal of the day before !   X.Y.Z.

White

"I wouldn't own to a sheet that hadn't had a rinse in blue water!

There are plenty of ways of washing and they mostly get things clean. But if you want the loveliest white, you mustn't miss the last rinse in blue water. It's the only way to get the real white. Just blue water for your last rinse and you've a white like new snow!"

RECKITT'S BLUE *Out of the blue comes the whitest wash!*

THE WOMAN IN THE GERMAN HOME

Evelyn Sharp

In Germany, as to a less extent in England, the housewife is finding it increasingly difficult to make both ends meet. There are five millions unemployed over there, which means that there are twice as many families as in England who are living on insufficient weekly allowances. Naturally, this does not matter so much in the rural districts as in the towns, because country people are more likely to have garden and farm produce to fall back upon ; also, in Germany, agricultural labourers are insured like other workers. But nobody in the working class can be well off in a country that has had to pay heavy taxes for war reparations since 1918 and now in addition has to support the unemployed ; and the same thing is true of the mass of the middle classes too. There are very few German people in any class today who can be called well off.

You would find this difficult to believe if you went to Germany as an ordinary visitor. However poor the people may be over there, they always look clean and tidy. When I remarked on this to a German friend with whom I was walking in a Rhineland town one day last March she smiled and said : "My own hat is four years old and my coat ten years old. Since the war we have all been much too poor to buy clothes ; we clean and turn and re-model them instead." And indeed, her black velour hat and cloth coat with its astrakhan collar were both as modern in shape as my own and looked quite new !

It is the same with the children. You never see a ragged or unkempt child in the poorest kind of school. This may be partly because in Germany every child in every class of society is obliged by law to attend the elementary school up to the age of ten and no mother likes her child to look different from the children of parents who are better off. I am told that the parents themselves are so particular about this that the life of a woman who neglects her child's appearance is made unbearable. Probably, even without this pressure from other mothers, the German mother would still send her child to school well dressed, so high is her standard of neatness ; but I am afraid it often means that extra economies have to be made at home in food and fuel and as soon as the children return from school the tidy garments are taken off and replaced by worn and darned cotton pinafores, which are not much protection against the chilliness of half-warmed rooms.

Apart from poverty, the German woman is suffering greatly from the constant presence of the workless man in the home. If you deprive a German of work, which is second nature to him, he deteriorates even more than we all do when we become unemployed. Continued unemployment makes him irritable and difficult to live with, if it does not drive him to despair. The men know this and many of them do voluntary work in order to keep up their spirits. I found one school, for instance, in a Saxon town, where the unemployed fathers of the younger children had combined with the master to decorate and equip the infants' classroom, because the State was too poor to make its usual grant for the purpose. The result

was a lovely little room provided with toys and exercise books and bright coloured desks and washbasins, looking like the most expensively equipped Montessori classroom. All unemployed fathers have not, however, the spirit or the opportunity to fill their time in this way and their depression adds greatly to the burden of the wife or mother or sister at home.

The cinemas are partly under State control and, certainly in Berlin and perhaps elsewhere, the Government arranges for them to be open at halfprice till four o'clock every day, so that the unemployed may have a warm place to sit in. That causes the picture houses to look fairly full ; but the free libraries are full too and those who go there will be found reading books as well as magazines. In the same way you will find the town theatre fairly well filled, even when, as in the schools, the State can no longer afford to pay as much as usual toward its support. But then, in Germany, the theatre means much more in the life of the people than it does here and I have often found people going without a meal in order to buy a ticket for the opera or play and not only because it is a warm place in which to sit.

In some towns that I visited, the married women are going out to work daily because their husbands' factory has closed down. There is not the same prejudice against domestic service as in England. The difficulty there, I was told by the official at the head of a women's department in the Labour Exchange, is the shortage of employers who can afford to keep servants. In any case, Germany is a more domestic nation than ours and the slatternly woman is rarely to be seen even in the poorest back street ; certainly, I did not meet a girl there who looks down on domestic service, though she would not always prefer it. The same official told me that the out-of-work factory girls could generally be persuaded to take the training courses provided voluntarily by religious or philanthropic organisations, if domestic posts could afterwards be found for them, and this was made possible in many cases in Holland where there is a demand for German maids.

The cost of living has gone down in Germany as it has done here, but this applies much more to clothes, which the people cannot afford to buy, than to food. A woman who is head of a Government welfare department, gave me terrible instances of the hunger in middle-class families where there is no unemployment money coming in, for example, a widow with children when she visited them had had nothing to eat for five days except sauerkraut (a sort of pickled cabbage). Of course such instances may be found anywhere during the present world-wide trade depression ; but what makes the German situation different and rather worse is that this new wave of unemployment and distress has come on the top of twelve years of poverty and suffering. It is the last straw. "We cannot bear any more, something must happen," said one young woman to me and I felt that all German women were speaking through her.

The young people are rising up everywhere in anger

and bitterness ; their childhood has been starved of much that makes childhood happy and now their youth holds out no better prospects. They may make a revolution, many of them want to, and a revolution may lead to another war. That is why the state of Germany is not just a German question ; it is everybody's question and especially the women's, for no woman can want another war if she thinks seriously about it, any more than she wants to think of any woman in any country being asked to bear what the German woman in the home is bearing now. For hunger and cold and the unhappiness of children and young people, are things that hurt as much in one country as in another and our responsibility for them, wherever they occur, is our common human heritage.

– 1931 –

A SMALL FARM AND GARDEN SCHOOL has been opened at the Grey House, Sevenoaks, for about twelve girls of the Backward, Borderline, or Nervous type. Also a few ladies received.' Practical training in all branches of Gardening given, also in Poultry, Rabbit, Bee and Goat keeping. The School is intended for girls of gentle birth, whose Parents or Guardians find themselves unable to pay the usual high fees. The Home, in connection with the Farm School, aims at providing a refined and happy family life, with training in indoor occupations, such as Hand Machine Knitting, Plain Needlework, Rug Making, Basket Weaving, etc.—For terms apply to Mrs. Pearce-Clark.

– 1919 –

WASHING UP—A SCIENTIFIC APPROACH

Major Philipson-Stow has written this article from the masculine angle. Comments from our readers are invited. EDITOR.

I HAVE been asked to write a few notes on my attempts to make washing up easier, quicker and more efficient in terms of labour. Let me say that my efforts have been solely directed to minimizing what is to me a necessary evil, because I am naturally lazy.

At various times during the war I assisted in washing up under conditions that no industrial management or workpeople would tolerate. I decided on my release from the Forces to make the job as easy and pleasant as possible at home, quicker and more efficient in terms of labour.

FIRSTLY there must be sufficient room. A draining board on both sides of the sink—one side for dirty, the other for clean—large enough for all the glass, china, silver, etc., without precarious balancing which spells breakages.

SECONDLY, plenty of hot—and I mean hot—water, 140° Fahrenheit or over, preferably soft or softened. Soap or soap flakes. Three bowls, two enamelled, 12 to 14 inches diameter, and one oval wooden or *papier maché* and a good mop on handle.

THIRDLY, two good quality, clean, dry cloths, one linen for glass and silver, one thicker for china, etc. The enamelled bowls are for clear water, one for soaking and one for rinsing ; the wooden bowl for washing. I like a good lather in the washing bowl.

Spoons and forks should first be put in the soaking bowl and left while the glass and other silver are washed. The water is too hot for the hands, so washing is done with the mop in the washing bowl. (Note : glass must not be plunged suddenly in water as hot as this, it must be washed almost entirely with the mop, sluicing water over it.) The glass is then put to drain on the " clean " draining board. The silver is next dealt with in the same way except that this is rinsed in the rinsing bowl before draining. Then come the spoons and forks, and after that the glass and silver is dried. If the water is really hot, most of the moisture will have evaporated and little more than polishing with the cloth is required.

The china follows—I do not use a plate rack, but I think a folding one for use simply to drain the plates pending drying would be an improvement—and finally the knives. I do not find it necessary to use a special cloth for drying the knives if reasonable care is exercised. If there are any specially greasy or oily things to wash, such as salad bowls these should be left till last.

One or two final observations. Be methodical. Always work from right to left or left to right. Always do things in the same order. Keep your sink, bowls, draining boards, etc., clean, and rinse and dry your cloths regularly. Most important of all let me repeat is the *HOT* water. It halves the work.

Finally, if you like your silver to look nice give it a rub with the leather every time after drying it.

G. PHILIPSON-STOW

– 1946 –

Attitude to Age

MARY EMBREY

PREOCCUPATION with age—not only among women but nearly as much among men—is almost a national trait. The Victorians, bearing in mind that the longer portion of life remains when youth is past, very sensibly decided in favour of making age an advantage.

Everything was done to emphasize the years. Girls put lace caps on their heads and shawls round their shoulders when they were thirty because these were the dignified badges of advancing age. Young men grew whiskers and looked ponderous in the twenties and, judging by their portraits, were elderly by forty. Fashion favoured the older woman. Severely cut dresses, buttoned up to the neck and simple hair-dressing were kind to her and did their best to subdue the glowing youth of her daughter. The years were like gold in the bank—the more you could count the more fortunate you were. All this added up to the elderly smugness and self-satisfaction which was the least attractive characteristic of the period. Wisdom was worn like a cap regardless of whether it fitted. "Mamma knows best" did not by any means have any substance to support the claim, but was unarguable.

Perhaps it was a revolt from the Victorian deification of age which started the swing in the other direction. Then came the first World War introducing consciousness of "age groups". The young became respected, acquiring the tragic dignity of death. For the first time, too, age appeared as a barrier. The bitter years of unemployment that followed strengthened the barrier and before long "too old at thirty" had become a catchword. The over-thirties even banded themselves together, as Old Age Pensioners do today, to persuade employers that there was work in them yet.

The second World War corrected that nonsensical state of affairs and proved conclusively that age has nothing to do with efficiency or its lack, except where rapid reactions are required or the capacity for intense physical effort. Fighter pilots and commandos had to be very young men. Perhaps it was because such young men were heroes to the schoolboys of the war years that they were led, as soon as they were grown up, to put an exaggerated value on their own youth about which many became as self-important as their Victorian forebears had been about their age.

Today's Errors

Today the accent is on youth and the same errors appear in reverse. Youth demands admiration simply because it is young just as yesterday age demanded respect simply because it was old. Youth thinks it has the monopoly of wisdom just as age once did. The truth, of course, is that good sense, a sense of proportion and a sense of humour, which are the ingredients of wisdom, are not the prerogatives of any particular age group and are, in fact, singularly lacking in all this business of age consciousness.

And this brings me to the reaction of women to the matter. Young women, unlike their male contemporaries, do not seem to regard themselves as superior beings simply because they are under thirty. If they escape this tiresomeness it is largely due to the fact that hardly do they become conscious of the advantages of youth than they start to be agitated about its passing! Their twenty-fifth birthday, at latest, seems to be the date line for an anxious scrutiny lest there be a line or a wrinkle or perhaps a solitary white hair.

Older women fight the years with more gallantry than sense, for nothing more emphasizes age than the trimmings of youth. The casual clothes that look delightful on casual young women can be deplorable on the woman who should have developed some degree of poise and sophistication and should reflect this in every line from hair-do to well-shod feet. The whole cosmetic art which gives contemporary women such an advantage over earlier generations is often used to imitate themselves when young instead of emphasizing the particular charm and good looks of their maturity.

Maturity is the watchword. Let us imitate—if imitate we must—the French woman who is a girl for a very short period and a mature woman for the rest of her life.

– 1953 –

THE NATION'S CINDERELLA

RENÉE HAYNES

The feminist movement, which began some hundred and fifty years ago, has always had two sides to it, two pieces of work to do. The first—which has received the most publicity, up to now—is to show and to prove that women are in no way " inferior " beings ; that they can be as public-spirited citizens, as responsible legislators, as independent thinkers, as efficient administrators, as learned scholars and scientists, as their brothers. That this piece of work has to a great extent been done is shown by the fact that women, self-respecting and free, can and do now vote in elections, sit in Parliament, act as justices of the peace, run newspapers, organize businesses, enter and teach in universities, play their part as scientists, doctors, lawyers, and serve in the armed forces of the Crown. It has not yet come to complete fruition, or we should find women receiving equal pay for equal work —as they do in Turkey—and being allotted equal compensation for equal injuries received in the service of their neighbourhood and country during air raids; but much has been achieved. One of the results can be seen in the increase of the social services during the twenty years of peace that followed the enfranchisement of women. A similar development, incidentally, marked the public life of New Zealand, where women have long exercised political power, and where a social service state grew up bit by bit, not from any argumentative desire to put this or that political theory into practice, but because this or that measure of child-care, or medical attention, or industrial accident compensation, seemed to be practical, useful, and necessary to the general good.

The second piece of work to be done by the feminist movement was for a long time entangled with the first, and is only now beginning to shape itself as a distinct and different task. It is to show that women doing their own traditional and specific job of running a household and bringing up a family should be considered as important, as responsible and as much worthy of respect as women doing the kind of job that can be done equally well by either sex; and that their work is just as vital as the other kind, if not more so. A little has been achieved. A hundred years ago a married woman was not allowed equal rights of guardianship with her husband over their children; and a tyrannical man could, if he had a mind to it, forbid her to see them. (My own great-great-grandfather and his wife used to lend their drawing-room so that a woman whose husband had spent all her money and then quarrelled with her might come by stealth to see her own young children, brought there surreptitiously by a faithful nurse.) Seventy years ago, the married woman had no control over her own property, earnings and savings. These things have been set right; but much remains to be done, for even now, both in her status and in her activities, the married woman working in her own house at " unpaid domestic labour " (as the census papers put it) tends to be the national Cinderella.

She is not allowed to retain her own nationality, but must take that of her husband and may in time of war find herself classified in her own country as an " alien ". She is not allowed to contribute to, or to benefit by, National Health Insurance; and usually gets to the very end of her tether and becomes really ill before getting medical treatment. However hard she works inside her home, she is not entitled to call a single penny her own; and being able to call pennies your own is very necessary to self-respect. So much for herself. Her work is in every sense vital, for it is concerned with keeping life going, caring for a live husband and live children, making and mending clothes to keep life warm in them, cooking and serving food without which life would stop, maintaining the cleanliness needed for healthy living; and it carries an enormous weight of first-hand meaning absent from the work of anyone else except farmers and creative artists. You can see the point of doing it; it is not like putting one screw in one piece of machinery again and again and again all day. But because it brings in no money, it also brings in very little understanding and respect; so little, indeed, that the planners of the evacuation scheme could—and did—calmly assume that the housewife need not be paid anything for the time, energy, labour and skill spent in cooking, washing, ironing, mending, " minding " and doing housework for three or four extra children. They did not ask school buses to run free services with unpaid drivers; or farmers to charge nothing for milk and vegetables, or cobblers not to send in accounts for mending evacuated children's shoes. Housewives, playing their part (mostly with affection and efficiency) nevertheless asked themselves—and the billeting officer—the reason why they alone should be forced by law to work without pay. But answer came there none. A good deal is

PASS ON YOUR COPY OF "HOME & COUNTRY"

K.A.

written about the decline in family life and the fall in the birth-rate; perhaps the wave of feeling over the evacuation may draw some attention to the position of the housewife, which lies near the root of these things.

There are two ways of restoring value, importance, and self-respect to the housewife in her work. The practical first is already being handled by the Women's Institutes. It lies in giving comradeship and zest in comparison in that work; in reviving old skills and creating new ones—quilting, pickling, canning, dyeing, renovating ; and in running the small-scale co-operative markets which were beginning to flourish before the war and are more than ever flourishing now. The theoretical second—the consideration of better laws—is being brought increasingly before the public mind; it is of intense importance come war, come peace. Miss Eleanor Rathbone's Penguin book on Family Allowances urges on its innumerable readers reasons for the payment of such allowances to mothers for the benefit of their children; and one great political party has lately included them in its programme. Mrs. Spring-Rice's moving study, *Working Class Wives*—also a Penguin—brings evidence of the urgent need that they should be included in the National Health Insurance Scheme. The Married Women's Association is pressing all parties to consider this point and others; which include the provision that wives should be legally entitled to consider a certain proportion—however small—of the family income their own.

It will be interesting to see what happens.

2G

1. Mrs. N. E. Little (standing), Miss Beatrice Mackenzie (left), and Mrs. G. L. Parnell, three of the small band of enthusiasts from the central working party. Mrs. Parnell was responsible for supervising the work throughout the counties.

2G. F.A.N.Y.S.

3I. Women's Voluntary Service.

....

THE PLAN below has been lettered for reference and the 18 picture medallions, which are all worked in tent stitch, show the following scenes. Some of these are reproduced on these pages.

3I

A, A.R.P.; B, Evacuees; C, Porters; D, Hospital Transport; E, Clippies and Policewomen; F, Canteen; G, F.A.N.Y.S.; H, Nurses; I, W.V.S.; J, W.R.N.S.; K, W.I. Fruit Preservation Centre; L, Housewife; M. N.F.S.; N, Forestry; O, Rest Centres; P, Radar; Q, Camouflage; R, Postwomen. Large Panels (left), The Land; (centre), The Services; (right), Industry.

4C

5K

4C. Women Railway Porters.

5K. A W.I. Fruit Preservation Centre.

6. Miss M. C. Foster at
work on one of the
large panels represent-
ing Women in Industry.

7J. W.R.N.S.

8R. Postwomen.

9N. Forestry work under-
taken by the Land Army,

10L. The ordinary housewife
and the inevitable
queue.

HISTORY IN EMBROIDERY

During the last four years skilled W.I. needlewomen throughout England and Wales have been at work on an embroidered hanging to record in beauty, for the enjoyment of future generations, the work of women in wartime.

Miss Sybil Blunt, a well-known Winchester artist, planned the design so that it could be embroidered in separate pieces and joined together later at Winchester.

It was, of course, essential that the work should be of an overall high standard and accuracy, and that each part should match every other part, wherever it was worked. To achieve this, two-day schools in the canvas stitches decided upon were held in 1946 for a representative from each county, who then taught other members in her county, and eventually about four hundred selected embroiderers diligently plied their needles, some doing a few stitches only, others large portions.

The hanging measures 15 ft. 3 in. by 9 ft. and weighs 47 lb. The foundation is of single mesh canvas, 100 in. wide; 35 lb. of moth proof wool have been used for the 2,000,000 stitches in the work. The large centre panel includes a quotation from "Memory Hold the Door" by John Buchan, and the following amusing and apt quotation from Shakespeare's Henry VIII is worked at the foot of the hanging : " . . . the madams too, Not used to toil, did almost sweat to bear The pride upon them, that their very labour Was to them as a painting . . ."

The completed hanging, in its final magnificence of design, colour and workmanship, has well rewarded the skill and enthusiasm of all those who took part. As an example of W.I. co-operative work it took pride of place at the W.I. Exhibition of Handicrafts at the Victoria and Albert Museum.

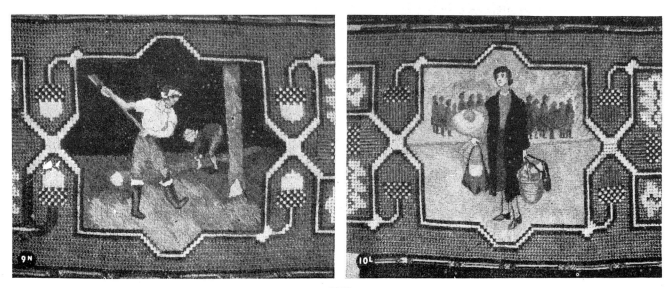

There's always a Singer Sewing Centre near you to serve you, where you can obtain every sewing aid from
a reel of cotton to a modern lightweight sewing machine, and expert advice on all your sewing problems.

SINGER SEWING MACHINE COMPANY LIMITED, SINGER BUILDING, CITY ROAD, LONDON, EC1

CHAPTER TWO

Village Life

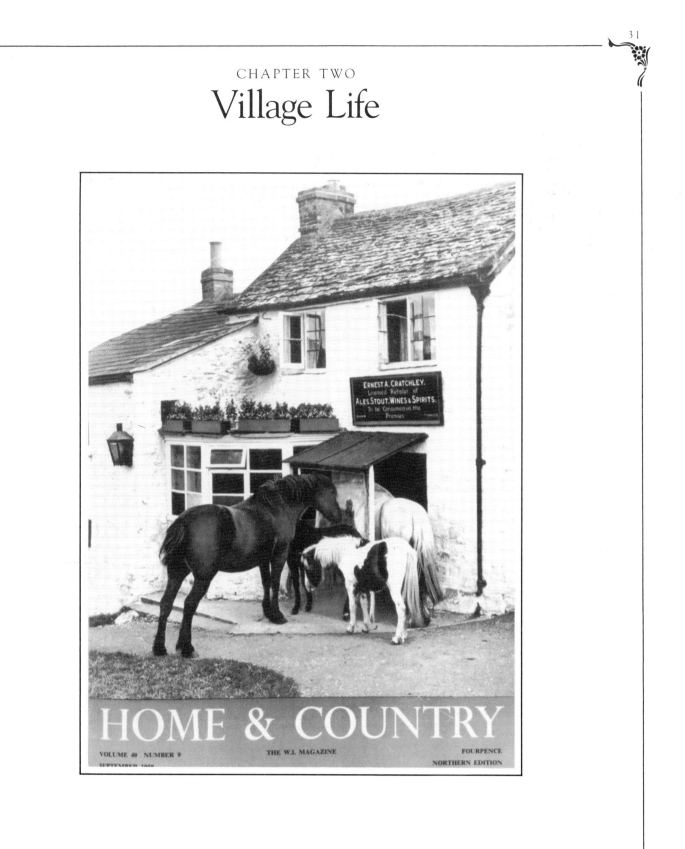

HOME & COUNTRY

VOLUME 40 NUMBER 9   THE W.I. MAGAZINE   FOURPENCE

SEPTEMBER 1958   NORTHERN EDITION

THE CINEMA IN THE VILLAGE.

By MARY C. HORNE.

A GREAT Statesman, well-known in connection with Agriculture, is reported to have said, " We shall never get the people back to the land, or, having got them, keep them there, unless we have a Cinema in every village." The statement, we are told, was received with smiles ! These smiles were probably of a mixed kind. " Bread and Circuses ! " Bread ! yes, we must have *that.* And, strange though it may seem, the way to that essential may be by way of Circuses, or the up-to-date equivalent, Cinemas.

A Cinema in every village may be impossible of realization. But it would be an ideal state of things if no village might be found where the inhabitants could not, by taking a little trouble, say a walk of two or three miles, share in the pleasure of seeing the latest thing in the " Topical News," the recent air race, the most popular boxing rivals, the wonders of the latest invention, the marvels of Nature, life in other countries remote from their own, and the most thrilling Drama and mirth-evoking Comedy. Would it be a waste of money ? Far from it. From the nation's point of view, is it not better to spend something on retaining, when we get them, healthy fathers of families on the land, rather than let them wander off, with heavy hearts, but with steadfast hopes and determination, to people other lands—our Colonies or others—growing rich out of our parsimony? And from the individual point of view, if amusement and recreation absorbs the money which would otherwise be spent in the enrichment of brewers, publicans and railway companies, the local exchequer, controlled by the people themselves, will scarcely be regarded as an unjustifiable experiment. Wealth need not leave the village. Profits, if there are any, can be used for the encouragement of sports, games, clubs, or the financing of village industries. This, it may be objected, is drawing upon a vivid imagination, and could only in rare instances come to pass. The expense is prohibitive.

It is to remove some misapprehension that this article is written.

There are many problems which will have to be faced before we can effectually restore a rural population. Housing, transport, railway rates, all have to be dealt with in a practical manner.

But it is " not by bread alone " a man lives. There is the need for self-expression felt by every intelligent being. One who has lived all her young life in a village, one possessed of a high degree of optimism, of energy above the average, and of a real love of country pursuits, can only write with the deepest conviction of the need to deal with this question of " how to occupy the spare time." More leisure, with shorter working hours, will only tend to greater discontent, unless provision is made for mental stimulus. The outlook on life in country places may be deeper and more philosophic as a result of communing with Nature. But many will go " to make a living " to whom the communing with Nature presents no attraction. And not for them alone, but for others, it must inevitably be a real and trying limitation arising out of circumstances that the outlook will tend to become narrowed as regards the doings of men.

To obviate this will be one of the indisputable claims of the Cinema, which few will be found to ignore.

The first essential is *the place* where films might be shown. The Parish Room might be adapted at some small outlay. Where there is a porch at the end opposite the stage, or place for screen, the requirements of the local authorities might be most suitably met by piercing the end wall and so getting a small exterior operating chamber. Failing this, an iron fire-proof operating room, collapsible and portable, can be obtained for £18.

If it should be found advisable to erect a hall for the purpose, provision will naturally be made for the separate operating chamber, and exits opening outwards. But the demand for " Huts," so-called, gives rise to a fear that the beauty of the village may be sacrificed. The Village Green, sacred to quoits, geese, and infant cricketers, must not be profaned by club-house, " ideal " or otherwise. If it is a little way " down the lane " all the better. Why deprive the young people of the pleasure of " setting each other a bit of the way ? " If by moonlight, all the more romantic ; if by bulls-eye lantern, all the more amusing. Some homes may be two or more miles from the Cinema—but what matter when people are young ?

The cost of equipment and installation is usually that which brings to a halt any much-desired and half-formed scheme.

This matter has received the most careful attention of the Cinema Re-Creative Circle, whose aims are briefly stated as the " uniting in a definite and concerted effort, on practical lines, all clergy, teachers and social welfare workers, in order to harness the unbounded force of the Cinema in the interest of right thinking and noble living."

Where there is electric light available the outlay for machine and necessary accessories, apart from the equipment for connecting the light, can be covered by £30. A small portable machine suitable for a room accommodating 500 persons being specially manufactured for the Cinema Re-Creative Circle. The equipment for connecting with the current would run to about £15 or £20. The alternative for country places, where there is no electric current available, and where the expense of a generating plant would be prohibitive, would be the use of Limelight equipment and an outfit, which would cost about £60. By outfit we imply everything necessary including the screen. This is capable of showing a picture of ten or twelve feet, and the apparatus would conform to the requirements of the Cinematograph Act.

The next item, a big one, and a great puzzle to the uninitiated, is the films. What to show ? Who will choose ? What will they cost ? These are questions which immediately arise. A carefully selected list will be sent to enquiriers enclosing postage to Head Office : The Cinema Re-Creative Circle, 52, Haymarket, London, S.W.1. New lists of films on every required subject will be issued from time to time.

Advice as to operators, programmes, cost of hiring films can be supplied, and suggestions as to programmes and lecturers to accompany will form part of our service to the community.

It comes to your village

With all their boasted advantages, town folk are no more fortunate than you when they buy Tea.

You can buy the same Brooke Bonds Edglets as they use, just as fresh, at the same price, in your village shop.

And what a splendid tea it is ! You use a little *less* than usual to the pot and obtain just that little *more* of flavour, aroma, and enjoyment which makes all the difference.

Brooke Bonds Edglets is pure leaf edge tea, free from excess tannin. Our own motors deliver it fresh every week to your village shop. Buy it there.

Ask in your village for

Brooke Bonds Edglets

quarter **8**^d pound.

(Sold only in packets.)

If you cannot readily obtain Brooke Bonds Edglets, write to Brooke Bond & Co., Ltd., Goulston Street, London, E.1. They will see that you are supplied.

CO-OPERATION IN THE VILLAGES.

By MABEL EDWARDS WEBB.

WE are often asked " What is Co-operation ? " " What does it really mean ? " " How do we set about getting it ? " All sorts of explanations are offered, more or less complicated, and when people do not understand an explanation, they get discouraged, and go no further.

Now, let us suppose there is a great quantity of fruit grown near a village, and Mr. Brown driving through thinks to himself that if he opens up a small jam-making, bottling and canning factory he will make an excellent thing of it. Well, Mr. Brown looks out for premises he can convert into a factory, gets to work, buys the fruit as cheaply as he can, and sells at the best prices possible, and at the end of the season he is thoroughly pleased with the result.

The difference between the cost of fruit, labour and the expenses goes into Mr. Brown's pocket in the way of profit, and the benefit is his only. *This is private enterprise.*

But suppose instead of Mr. Brown starting jam making, bottling and canning, fifty of the villagers had decided to undertake it. They would meet together, and knowing that money was necessary they would start in a humble way, and each contribute a small sum of money. That is to say they would form a society and become shareholders in the little business. They might say that they would give £1 each. Perhaps, to some of the poorer ones that would be too big a sum to find straight off. So they would buy a £1 share and give towards it one, two, three or more shillings, just what they could afford, promising to pay up the rest of the money later on.

Rules would be drawn up and a committee of management appointed who would set to work. They would get premises, buy the necessary bottles, jars, cans and fruit. They would give the time necessary when the fruit was ready, and get a great amount of preserving done. They would sell the jam, bottled and canned fruit at a price reckoned by adding all the outlay necessary to produce the finished article and adding a reasonable profit. The balance of this profit, after payment of five per cent. interest on capital, would be returned at the end of the season to the working members as a bonus to be decided by the Committee. The bonus, or dividend, could be added to the shares not fully paid up until the full amount was paid. Then they would qualify for interest. A portion of the profit should be kept in the bank for next year's operations.

These villagers would have done the work, taken all the risks, and they would share the profits and advantages.

THIS IS ONE FORM OF CO-OPERATION.

And it is this wonderful system of working together for mutual benefit that won for the industrial co-operators of this country the sum now lying to their credit of fifty million pounds. The simple motto of the co-operative movement explains better than anything else why co-operation has done so much to better and brighten conditions —to uplift, to educate. The motto is—

All for Each—and Each for All.

– 1919 –

PUBLICATION RECOMMENDED.

Rats and How to Destroy them, by Mark Hovell, F.R.C.S. Price 10s. 6d. Publishers, John Bale, Sons & Danielsson, Ltd., 83-91 Great Titchfield Street, Oxford Street, London, W.1. Country people are specially interested in the attempts (some of which have been organised by the Government), to get rid of the pestilential rat which not only destroys an incalculable amount of food stuffs in stack, granary and mills but acts as a plague carrier. The book is well written with bits of information thrown in regarding pleasanter things than rats. The practical directions as to the best means of rat destruction are of great value. An organised and successful effort to free a neighbourhood from rats would be a piece of community service sure to win public recognition. The book should be in every village library.

– 1925 –

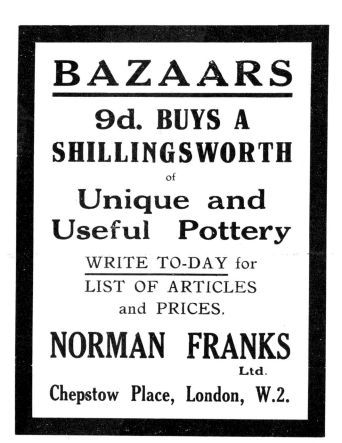

ROMANCE OF AN OLD FORGE

Margaret Taylor

In the time of good Queen Victoria it stood at the corner where three roads meet. Perhaps we should call them lanes today; they had tall, straggling hedges, where in summer festoons of briar rose and masses of honeysuckle filled the air with fragrance. A big elder tree grew at the eastern side of the forge and many wind-bowed firs and horse chestnuts made a dark green background to its weather-beaten timbers.

In those days, in the dim wintry twilight, a little girl might have been seen creeping shyly inside and standing in a dark corner as near as she dared venture to where the smith was swinging his sledge-hammer. Peggy had long dark brown curls nearly to her waist. She wore a cherry-coloured coat which reached to the tops of her black buttoned boots and a tiny cap of squirrel-fur, she looked as unlike the child of today as possible.

The forge had a great fascination for her. The roaring of its huge fire, the thousands of sparks when the hammer beat the iron, that strange odour of horse flesh and burning leather all delighted this little girl. The smith resembled Longfellow's famous character :

> "His hair was thick and black and long,
> His face was like the tan."

Sometimes he would spy her in the semi-darkness and call out in his jolly voice : "Eh, little maid, run home ! You'll be late for tea." Then Peggy, recalled to earth, would seize her satchel of books and race away.

There were hard winters in those days. Sometimes the snow on the Green would be as high as Peggy's head. More welcome then than ever appeared the scarlet flames and the delicious warmth inside that old building.

* * *

Some ten years later we called it "Lover's Corner," and here a bonnie young maiden used to linger with a tall man at her side.

"Don't let us go home yet, Fred," she would whisper to her lover, "Cook was so good-natured today that she promised to put the clocks back half-an-hour. My aunts will never guess the time ! Isn't the old Forge a picture in the moonlight ? It's too beautiful. Listen ! There's the nightingale. He seems to sing us a love song."

* * *

This all happened long ago. The other day a very matronly and demure Peggy came back from a foreign land to visit her old home. She was accompanied by a boy and girl, who demanded eagerly on the first day, " to go and see the old forge where Mummie and Daddy used to meet and listen to the nightingales." Alas ! it is all so strangely changed that it hardly seems the same place. There is no forge. A very new-looking garage stands in its place. Big motors find a home where once sparks flew upwards and red and blue petrol pumps fill the place where the elder tree once flowered. Instead of fields and hedges there are mansions with gorgeous gardens. Little white buses tear down that aforetime shady quiet lane and big red tramcars whiz across the Green. It is years since the nightingales flew away and one looks in vain for wild-rose or blackberry. All is changed. Surely Romance must be dead.

Perhaps not ! The other night two young folks met at the "Corner." They held each other's hands as they waited for the bus and a joyous lovelight shone in their eyes.

They did not look at all like those lovers of olden times ; but I think they had the same heart-happiness. Romance can never die. It can even bloom beside a petrol pump !

Managing an Earth Closet

SOME country folk say "If you haven't any drains in the house there aren't any drains to go wrong". Which of course is quite logical. But, and there is a very big but, an earth closet can be the most unpleasant thing in the world if it is not managed correctly. It is no harder to manage it the correct way than it is to mismanage it.

Four things are essential to its proper running: two buckets, dry earth, a plot of land some ten feet square and a pile of waste vegetable matter.

The two buckets are most important, one being used for urine and the other for night-soil. Under no circumstances must these ever be mixed, for it is the mixing of these which causes all the unpleasantness. The night-soil should be covered immediately with a shovelful of fine dry earth, and, if the closet is not fitted with a dry earth hopper, a pile of earth should be kept near the closet door with a shovel near at hand to convey it to the bucket. This earth should be kept under some form of covering to ensure it being kept reasonably dry.

The urine pail should be emptied every day, the night-soil pail, however, can be left for two, or even three days before being emptied.

The disposal of the contents of the pails is carried out on a small piece of land set aside for this purpose. Here a good supply of waste vegetable matter such as garden refuse, grass cuttings, straw, hay, nettles, leaves, etc., should be available. The first thing to do on this composting plot is to make a pile of this vegetable matter, and a little distance away make another small heap, about six inches high. Each day the urine pail is emptied on the large pile of vegetable matter and the night-soil pail is tipped out on the smaller pile and immediately covered over with a layer of the urine soaked vegetation from the big pile.

The urine pile must be restocked with fresh material as it becomes used up, the night-soil pile of course getting bigger as each bucketful and urine soaked vegetation is added.

After the elapse of a few weeks the night-soil pile will require turning. This is done by forking it to a new site alongside and a new pile started adjoining it. The turning process is not an unpleasant task, for if the heap has been properly constructed there is no smell, or anything objectionable at all. A second turn will be necessary three weeks after the first. By this time the second pile is ready for its first turn. Six weeks later the first pile will be ready to use on the garden as first rate compost, it can either be dug in or used as a mulch. No better fertilizer exists.

As air plays such an important part in fermentation it is most necessary to see that the piles never become depressed or trodden upon, and in constructing the piles care must be taken to keep all the material open and loose. This is not so important when the pile reaches its anaerobic state, that is, some three weeks after its final turn. The piles should also be kept damp—not wet—and if moisture is required, as it is at times in the summer, then the urine pail should be used for this purpose.

Although all the foregoing might sound complicated and to entail a lot of work, actually it is not so and the time taken is but a few minutes a day. The turning of the piles taking about ten minutes every few weeks.

As flies are *not* attracted to a properly constructed compost pile, the presence of any flies attempting to breed on the heaps, or if any unpleasant smell is in evidence, then this is a sure indication that something has gone wrong—the pile is too wet, not enough air or insufficient vegetable matter. A turn will generally put matters right.

Soiled bedding from rabbit houses, chickens, ducks, etc., make excellent material for the vegetable pile. In fact there is nothing short of metal and glass which will not compost. CECIL D. BACHELOR

Water, Water, Everywhere

E. DIXON GRUBB

Mr. Dixon Grubb is the author of one of the standard textbooks on water supplies used by the National Fire Service. He has also written a book on Local Government. Here he discusses the influence of restricted authority on our rural water supplies. This has been the subject of many A.G.M. resolutions in the past. What is going to be the answer?

MANY of us remember the days when each village had its own separate well or spring. We mistrusted the tasteless sterility of pipe-borne water. The picturesque procession of cottagers with buckets slung, milkmaid fashion, from their shoulders, seemed a natural proceeding.

That attitude has gone. A plentiful supply of pure water has become a necessity of modern life. The danger of infection from a polluted well, and the waste of time spent in carrying water are just as important to villagers as to townsfolk.

But the resources at the disposal of rural districts are often inadequate. In many cases, spring and borehole rights have been acquired by a neighbouring town, to the detriment of those living close to the source of supply. Most of us can cite examples of people living on one side of a boundary who have abundant water, while those across the way suffer continually from shortage, simply because they are in a different district !

There is ample water to meet the needs of the whole country, provided it is properly distributed. If the artificial barrier created by the district boundary can be removed, the mains can be inter-connected and hardship will be avoided. There will be no need to talk about restricting the use of water, if leakages from mains and service pipes are remedied.

At the present time there are more than eight hundred and fifty separate water undertakings in England and Wales. Some serve populations of less than a thousand, while others supply more than a million consumers. There are more than five undertakings which supply less than ten thousand consumers, to every one which supplies more than a hundred thousand. Every one of them resists any encroachment upon its source of supply.

As may be imagined, the standard of efficiency varies. The labour and instruments required to locate underground leaks involve spending money; and the smaller the undertaking, the greater the tendency for the certainty of immediate expenditure to overshadow the prospect of ultimate saving. I have actually experienced cases where the investigation and cure of leaks in service pipes, has shown that more than a third of the water supplied to the district was running to waste. Such conditions are far more common than is generally supposed.

But waste is not confined to small authorities. So long as the sources of supply continue to be owned by separate undertakings, those communities which have acquired springs which yield more water than they require will have no inducement to avoid waste.

Until the boundary problem is tackled, there can be no lasting cure of the water problem. In theory, the local authorities are responsible for the provision of adequate supplies for domestic use; but they cannot supply what they have not got. Some run their own water undertakings, others rely upon water companies; but the problem is the same in both cases. Isolationism is an outworn creed.

Before the war, there was much talk about a grid water scheme. Nowadays, instead of being treated as a separate proposal, the idea has become the background for more ambitious proposals. All the utility services for the community are grouped together under the name of Local Government; and the fate of the grid water scheme will be settled by the steps which are being taken to bring the machinery of Local Government up to date.

The artificial boundaries which used to interfere with the work of fire brigades were overcome by the formation of a National Fire Service. The influence of the penny-rate complex upon Civil Defence measures was avoided by the appointment of Regional Commissioners with over-riding powers. Both services have been superb under war conditions. So has the army. But that does not mean that we would like to live under martial law all our lives. An amazing revival of interest in Local Government is sweeping the country.

That is why the solution of the water problem is likely to depend eventually upon the opinions formed by individuals and groups, of which Women's Institutes are typical.

– 1944 –

WELL LAGGED

Courtesy: " Leamington Spa Courier "

At this time of year we have, if we are sensible, lagged our exposed water pipes by wrapping hessian, rag or straw round them. We know, if we are wise, where our main water stop tap is in the house and in frosty weather we turn it off each night, flush all water closets, and in outside W.C.s we turn off the stop tap where there is one. As an extra precaution many households institute a nightly drill to see that wash basin and bath plugs are put in place so that there is less danger of icing up.

But Warwickshire Federation have pointed out to us that these precautions do not apply to a number of cottages where people have to rely on the village pump for their water supply and thought readers would like to see how the village of Hampton Lucy has thatched its pump instead of lagging it with unsightly rags. Straw-lagged and straw-hatted (an every-day reminder of one of our most skilled crafts), the pump stands near the village church to give water to the village even after icy nights.

– 1954 –

WINNING SET OF EPITAPHS FROM DURSLEY, GLOUCESTERSHIRE

Here lies Ann Mann ;
She lived an old Maid
And she died an old Mann.

(Bath Abbey.)

Here lies Father and Mother, and Sister and I';
We all died within the space of one short year ;
They be all buried at Wimble, except I,
And I be buried here.

(Nettlebed, Oxfordshire.)

The wedding day appointed was,
And wedding clothes provided ;
But ere the day did come, alas !
He sickened and he die did.

(Bideford Churchyard.)

Beneath this stone our baby lies
He neither cries nor hollers.
He lived just one and twenty days,
And cost us forty dollars.

(Burlington Churchyard, Mass.)

Sacred to the memory of Anthony Drake,
Who died for peace and quietness sake ;
His wife was constantly scolding and scoffin',
So he sought for repose in a twelve-dollar coffin.

(Burlington Churchyard, Mass.)

In memory ov
John Smith, who met
wierlent death neer this spot
18 hundred and 40 too. He was shot
by his own pistill ;
It was not one of the new kind,
but an old fashioned
brass barrel, and of such is the
Kingdon of heaven.

(Sparta Diggings, California.)

Here lies the body of Mary Ann Lowder ;
She burst while drinking a seidlitz powder ;
Called from this world to her heavenly rest,
She should have waited till it effervesced.

(Burlington Churchyard, Mass.)

This spot is the sweetest I've seen in my life,
For it raises my flowers and covers my wife.

(A churchyard in Wales.)

Here lies the body of Joan Carthew,
Born at St. Columb, died at St. Cue ;
Children she had five,
Three are dead, and two alive ;
Those that are dead choosing rather
To die with their mother than live with their father.

(St. Agnes, Cornwall.)

My wife is dead and here she lies,
Nobody laughs and nobody cries :
Where she is gone and how she fares,
Nobody knows and nobody cares.

(Painswick Churchyard, Stroud.)

Beneath this steane lyes our deare child who's gone from We
For evermore unto eternity ;
Where, us do hope, that we shall go to He,
But him can n'er come back again to We.

(A churchyard in Wiltshire.)

As I am now, so you must be ;
Therefore prepare to follow me.

Added by his widow and executrix :

To follow you I'm not content,
Unless I know which way you went.

(Woolwich Churchyard.)

HOW I KNOW WHEN RAIN IS COMING

A COUNTRY LASS

WE do not need weather forecasts nor barometers in my part of the country.

Through generations of unchanged belief all the signs of coming storm are known to us, a pale yellow sun-set, rays slanting downward from the sun, or " sun drawing water " as we call it, rainbow in the evening and a halo round the moon. Still worse weather is heralded by a " sun dog " or halo round the sun.

Animals can tell me when to expect rain and storm. Cattle and horses become restive in Summer and tear about the fields, teased by horse flies which bite more fiercely just before rain. Sheep cluster together under trees and, in wintry weather, all animals instinctively seek a sheltered spot before the storm.

Pigs run about excitedly grunting and carrying straw in their snouts. Cats often indulge in wild antics, as if pursued by something unseen, or else turn their backs to the fire and wash their faces assiduously. Dogs will often refuse food, but eat grass and dig holes.

The donkey brays and as country folk say

When the donkey blows his horn
'Tis time to cock the hay and corn.

Rabbits come out to feed early instead of in the late afternoon. Moles rise to the surface, ready to feast on the worms and insects that rain will bring.

Toads are seen hopping and crawling over the grass. Frogs change from greenish yellow to russet brown and spiders creep from their webs at the approach of rain.

Birds give many clues to the coming weather. Seagulls fly inland at the approach of storm, marking the coming change by their loud excited clamour. Rooks behave strangely, as observed by Edward Jenner, of vaccination fame, who wrote an amusing poem giving forty reliable signs of rain.

And see yon rooks, how strange their flight.
They imitate the gliding kite,
Or seem precipitate to fall
As if they felt the piercing ball.

The painted wood-pecker or " yaffingale " as we call him, makes the welkin ring with his harsh " laugh." Swallows and swifts fly low, peacocks scream and ducks quack loudly.

Trees turn back their leaves for the coming rain. Many flowers are accurate barometers and close tightly if the day is going to be wet. Thus the little scarlet pimpernel, known for generations as the " poor man's weather glass," will close its petals when rain is expected, but, after one or two wet days, the petals become water-soaked and remain open.

Other flowers that keep closed if the day is going to be wet are the convolvulus, marigold, hawkweed, water-lily, chickweed and lettuce flower.

But, in watching flowers for weather signs, it must be remembered that when the blossoms are beginning to fade, they lose the power of responding to heat and light and either remain open or keep tightly closed.

A·GRINSTEDE·RHYME·OF TIDINESS

Of minor virtues I confess
My heart inclines to tidiness.

How many a happy homestead can
Be wrecked by an untidy man !

How many an honest merchant's life
Is marred by an untidy wife !

Untidy children may learn sense
Through Nurse's kindly influence;

But were I King there should be laws
To curb untidy visitors.

How little anybody loves
The folk who always lose their gloves,

And who unpack their bags to find
They've left their comb and shoes behind.

I hate a sweet disorder'd dress,
I loathe a garden in a mess,

And how I execrate the lout
Whose used bus tickets float about,

While picnic litterers on the spot
I would have hanged—and also shot.

In fact, if I should rule the race
England would be a tidy place,

And who would break the laws?—not you!
These are the things you'd NEVER do.

P. de G.

KALENDARIUM RUSTICUM

MAY

THE countryman's heart is revived (if this Month prove seasonable), With the hopes of a happy Autumn ; if it prove cold, it is an Omen of good for health, and promises fair for a full Barn.

Forbear cutting or cropping Trees you intend shall thrive till October ; kill Ivy.

If your Corn be too rank, now you may Mow it, or feed it With Sheep before it be too forward; weed Corn: In some places Barley may be sown in this Month.

Now sow Buck-Wheat or Brank ; sow later Pease.

Also Hemp and Flax may yet be Sown.

Weed Quick-sets ; drain Fens and wet Grounds ; Twifallow your Land ; Stub or root out Goss, Furze, Broom or Fern ; and Grub up such Coppices or other Shrubby woody places you intend should not grow again.

About the end of this Month mow Clover-grass ; St. Foyn, and other French-grasses.

Garden and Orchard. Plant all sorts of Winter greens.

Sow the more tender Garden-Seeds ; as sweet Marjoram, Basil Thyme and hot Aromatick Herbs and Plants : set Sage and Rosemary.

THE VILLAGE DUMP

A True Tale of Self Help

THE STORY begins with the sad misfortunes of two very respectable maiden ladies who lived in a village. They were sisters of uncertain age and of Victorian upbringing, very circumspect in all their ways. One was a Sunday School teacher, and both were members of the Women's Institute. They lived in the middle of the village, on the main road.

One Sunday morning, to their unspeakable horror, they discovered that a heap of damaged stout bottles had been deposited outside their garden wall during the night. As it was a Sunday, they did not like to ask anyone to work for them, and they feared to remove the bottles themselves because they had very respectable neighbours who would be shocked to see them carrying stout bottles.

The two poor things spent a miserable day peeping through their windows at the passers-by to observe who noted the bottles, and early next morning one of them went to a man to implore him to take away the cause of their trouble.

" Lor' bless 'ee, Miss," he said, " I'll come in a jiffy, or folks might think you'd drunk the stout yourselves and chucked the bottles over the wall."

The poor maiden lady shuddered, and when her sister was told she nearly fainted.

The man gathered up the bottles in a wheelbarrow.

" Now, where be I to put 'em ? " he asked.

One sister looked at the other sister and said she didn't know ; the other one said: " Why not down in the little shed by the river where all our bottles have gone before ? "

" That be chock-full," said the man.

" Couldn't you clear it out ? " asked the first sister.

" But where be I to put all this lot ? " said the man.

The sisters consulted together, and they thought of the people in the village who had less ground than themselves, yet must have many tins and bottles. They said: " We will lay the matter before the Institute, which will no doubt see that a rubbish dump is provided for our village."

They wrote to the President, who said: " It is a matter for the whole Institute to discuss."

All the members were gathered together, and they talked and they talked. At last one of them declared: " It is not work for us women; the men should do it."

THEN THE Secretary said: " Let us send a deputation to the Parish Council," and a member whispered: " Perhaps the Men's Club might help." The Treasurer suggested meekly she was sure the Rector would do what he could. A member of the Committee thought a deputation had better be made up of the best looking members of the Institute; they would be the most likely to get their way with the men.

The President murmured nervously it would be difficult to decide who were the best looking members. One of the Committee said: " Looks aren't much use without brains," another exclaimed: " Brains ain't a scrap of good wi'out sense." Then there was much shrill discussion, and at one terrible moment the President feared the proposed dump would wreck the Institute.

Finally they divided into groups—the best looking in one, the cleverest in another, and the wisest in a third. Then two were chosen by lot from each group, and a deputation of six set out to visit the Parish Council. It was decided the two clever ones should speak.

The Parish Council was frightened. The Chairman said that if the Council did anything it meant a halfpenny rate, which would anger the parish and they would never be elected as Parish Councillors any more.

Then the deputation went to the Men's Club, where they made the good-looking members speak, but these annoyed the men right away by telling them they never did anything, and now they were going to be made to work. This was meant playfully; but the men were offended, and said: " We ain't goin' to be dictated to by no Women's Institute, there—that's straight, our Club be only for amusin' of ourselves."

Then they went to the Rector, and here the wise ones spoke. The Rector listened attentively. He was grieved to hear of the trouble of his parishioners with their pots and tins, and shocked at the pile of stout bottles outside the gate of his worthy Sunday School teacher. He said he must consult the Bishop, and this he did. The Lord Bishop of the Diocese replied that his duty was to the souls of his parishioners, not to salmon tins and beer bottles, the contents of which filled their bodies.

WHEN THE Institute was told that the deputation had been a failure, the members were angry. Then the President rose, and said: " Fellow Members, listen to me. Let us determine to show the men that we women are more powerful and useful then they. Let us plan the Dump ourselves."

And so they did, and the honour and glory of the Institute was much increased thereby.

NOTE. *The above story is based on facts. A scheme for unburnable rubbish has been started in two Dorsetshire villages which originated in the incidents related. Last year there were 124 subscribers in a population of 900, and a balance in hand of £2 after all expenses were paid. Occupants of houses of a ratable value of £20 per annum or under pay a yearly contribution of 1s. 6d., those above, 3s. There are two villages. A lorry visits each in alternate months. The owner of the pit in which the rubbish is dumped is paid £1 yearly.*

Three Games for the Social Half-hour

Knocking the Cushion : A cushion is set up on end in the middle of the room. Members join hands in a large circle and walk round, each one trying to get one or other of her neighbours to knock over the cushion. Anyone who does so is out.

Circles: Members join hands in a large circle and move round until the leader calls out a low number, for example, three. They then join hands in circles of three and dance or walk round, according to age; any one or two members left out sit down. Another low number is called when new circles are formed of the number called; probably a few more members will be out. This goes on till only two are left as winners.

Blindfold Orders: This game is played in pairs, one giving the orders and the other carrying them out blindfolded. Several members are sent out of the room while the Institute decides on some action to be performed, such as taking a pencil from the table and handing it to the oldest member present. One member is then called in and blindfolded, and her partner gives the necessary orders to enable her to carry out what has been decided on; this should be done in as few sentences as possible. Each one outside is called in and blindfolded in turn and a different member gives the orders, the pair who are successful with the fewest orders being the winners.

WHY NOT KEEP BEES ?

—its such a profitable hobby

Do you realize that there is a most valuable source of pocket money going to waste on your very doorstep ? Hundreds, thousands, of pounds of nectar produced by flowers of all sorts—fruit blossom, charlock, clover, sanfoin, lime trees, heather : the list could be extended indefinitely—are waiting to be collected by bees and turned into honey. And honey is not only a wonderful food for home consumption but is readily saleable. **Furthermore, in the event of war, it will prove a most welcome substitute for the sugar which we cannot get.**

Why not " cash in " on this source of potential wealth by keeping a hive or two of bees ? For, besides being profitable, bee-keeping is a most fascinating hobby and quite easy. And it costs very little to make a start. Send a postcard today for our booklet " Profitable Bee-Keeping."

Taylors OF WELWYN

LARGEST PRODUCERS OF BEE-KEEPING REQUISITES IN EUROPE

AWARDED SILVER MEDAL
ROYAL AGRICULTURAL SOCIETY SHOW

TAYLORS "COUNTRY LIFE" OUTFIT

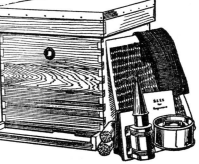

Comprising one of our standard W.B.C. pattern hives complete with all fittings ; a stock of specially selected and healthy bees ; smoker, bee veil, queen excluder, feeder, etc. Price £7 15s. or without bees £4 15s. carriage paid.

TAYLORS "COTTAGE" OUTFIT

Comprising one of our commercial pattern hives fitted for producing section honey ; a nucleus of specially selected and healthy bees, smoker, bee veil, queen excluder, etc. Price £4 15s., or without bees £3 carriage paid.

An Elegy on Elms

(A disease is destroying large numbers of English elms)

OH, well-aday for you, our quiet friends !
If you should perish, what should make amends ?
England and Elms—the two words run together
Like sun and happy thoughts in summer weather,
When one without the other cannot be.

What child of England, driven to foreign realms,
Brooding on home, but pictures English elms
In the green meadows, or along the lane
The homeward path he yearns to tread again ?
Or sees their branches 'gainst the winter sky
Snow-laden, woven in delicate tracery ?

Beeches are noble ladies, oaks are kings,
Birches are fairies with green silken wings,
Alders are wise and sad, and pollard willows
Are gnomes and sprites among the misty shadows
Threatening us thro' the mists the river sends:—
But oh ! the elms, the elms are all our friends !—
As dear to us as to the kine who browse
In their cool shade or munch their lowest boughs.

Oh, stealthily it swept across the seas
And crept along the land, that dark disease,
And on our trees it laid its withering hand:—
And now, where'er you go throughout the land,
You find a tree with branches sickly yellow
And one that should have been its flourishing fellow
Thick with ten thousand leaves, all green and quick,—
It points to heaven a leafless, lifeless stick.

Strangers have come from many a foreign shore
And some who claim to have lived with us before,
And to our landscape only have been lost
Through long continuance of untimely frost.
Hemlocks and thuyas and the cypresses
In every garden plot they take their ease
And o'er the woodlands, high and ever higher
The Noah's Ark tree points its growing spire:—
And they are welcome—these new foreign trees,—
But not the best, and not the host of these
Could they our land with verdure overwhelm
Would comfort us for our familiar elm.

If elms should perish, what should greet the spring
With crimson clouds on sunny evening ?
What trees at Hallowe'en would light the land ?
Oh, not as trees, as very saints they stand
Shining in glory like the holy ones
With raiment borrowed from the setting suns !
And now the wind, whirling the leaves around
Has laid the lovely garment on the ground.

If elms should perish quite from shore to shore
England would be the land we know no more.   A.F.

– 1938 –

Barn Owls
AND THE OXFORD ZOO

THE photograph below of two barn owls, taken at Oxford station some time ago, may be of interest as a memento to those who have enjoyed visits to the Oxford Zoo. It shows two young barn owls on their way to the gardens at Kidlington. These gardens are to be finally closed this month when the inmates, which at present include three barn owls, will be transferred to the "new Whipsnade" now being prepared near Dudley.

Barn Owls.
Photo by H. C. Frost.

Barn owls, it may be noted, are among the most beneficial of all animals : one pair has been known to destroy over 600 rats in a year. It is, therefore, a matter for concern that the species should be declining very rapidly throughout most of the Southern and Midland counties of England. A recent census showed that there were only about 30,000 barn owls in the country and that their numbers were decreasing at an approximate rate of 1,000 a year.

Every year barn owls get into the headlines for attacking human beings. At nesting time the birds are apt to be very suspicious of anyone having designs on their eggs or young, and pairs which inhabit suburbs and have thus a certain familiarity with and contempt for man, often attack innocent passers-by merely because they happen to have walked near a nest. In the vast majority of cases, however, the owls' attacks are quite harmless and it would certainly be most unjust to destroy a barn owl because it was jealous for its offsprings' safety.
                                                        J.D.U.W.

– 1936 –

Children's Supplement

"HOME AND COUNTRY" December 1936

RIDE-A-COCK-HOSS!

When first I went to Banbury
  I was but two years old!
Upon my rosy fingers were
  Bright rings of shining gold:
I wore a lacey bonnet,
  And a harebell-blue silk gown,
And on a wooden rocking-horse
  I galloped through the town.
A ring on every finger
  And a bracelet on each hand—
I rode through Banbury, which was
  Next door to Fairyland.

There were a score of cottages,
  Diamond-paned and small,
A shop, an inn, and one grey
    church
  Its spire so very tall
It looked just like a darning-needle
  Piercing through the blue;
And all the streets were cobble-
    stoned
  When we went riding through,
Clip-clopping loudly on our way—
  Adventurers were we,
Out to explore gay Fairyland
  Next door to Banbury.

There was a lake in Banbury
  With rushes growing round,
And patches of forget-me-not
  Brightening up the ground;
And every cottage garden there
  Was gay with hollyhocks,
With gillyflowers and marigolds,
  With white and crimson phlox.
And a fine lady rode her horse
  On every sunny day
From Banbury towards Fairyland—
  Just half-a-league away.

When last I went to Banbury
  I was no longer two,
I wore no golden chains and rings,
  No gown of harebell-blue.
I journeyed there by railway train,
  I wandered up and down,
And factories reared ugly heads
  Above the little town.
I shut my eyes against the truth—
  But knew it, to my cost—
That Banbury was growing up
  And Fairyland was lost.

        IVY O. EASTWICK.

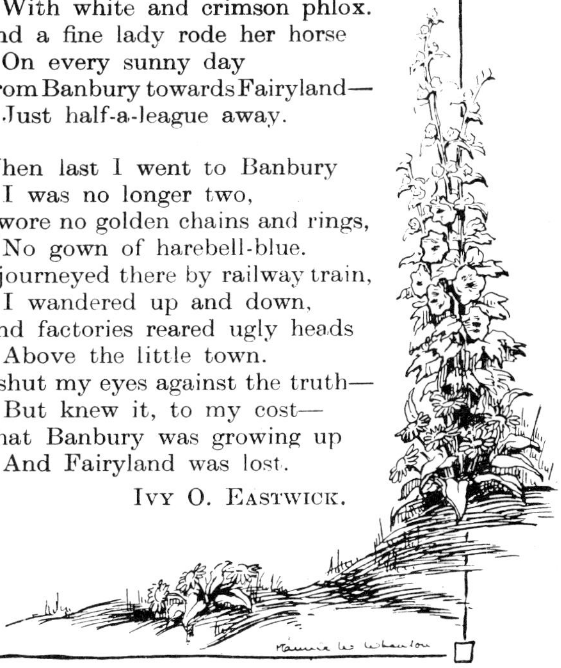

TREES

The Fir tree is a soldier bold,
  So straight and tall he stands ;
The Oak a mighty sage of old
  With gnarl'd and crooked hands.

The Ash tree weaves a net of lace
  With leaves against the sky ;
The Poplars seem to run a race
  To reach the clouds on high.

The Plane tree gives us playthings
  And shades the town's hot way ;
The Aspen seems to say things
  In whispers all the day.

The Hawthorn in the winter drear
  Gives hungry birds their food ;
The Holly comes with Christmas cheer
  And all things glad and good.

The Willow has a graceful air
  Above the waterfall ;
But the Birch tree is a lady fair
  And loveliest of all.

CYNTHIA HARVEY

Staffordshire Members enjoy Water!

A MEMBER of Longdon Women's Institute writes: "I have lived in this cottage for over six years. During the first four and a half years we had no water supply on the premises and had to fetch it from a draw well 40 feet deep from a cottage 70 yards away. We had to make three journeys a day, which would take about half an hour. Eighteen months ago the well became very low until the water was unfit to drink, we brought up soil, worms and several reptiles, some alive and some dead. Afterwards we got our water supply by collecting the water in a hole we dug close by a spring in a field about 150 yards away, but this soon failed. We then carried water once a day from a house a quarter of a mile away and, with the help of a canful brought each morning by my milkwoman, we were able to carry on until the water was laid on.

My supply is now from a tap over the sink in the back kitchen. There is no doubt about its purity and now water is always available without having to go outside for it in all weathers. You will understand what a blessing it is to us and we often wonder how we managed before. We are only too pleased to pay the water rate which is roughly 5d. per week."

A member of Armitage Women's Institute writes: "For years on end we have had to get our water from a well. I had to go some distance up the road to fetch all my water for drinking and cooking. In the summer time when I had no rain water, I had to draw all the water for my washing. Often the rope would break and let my bucket down the well, then I had to drag for it and the result was water all muddy and not fit to use for hours.

When the electric light poles were erected one was put just outside our well yard. When we had heavy rain it washed all the creosote off the pole and our water tasted of it, not at all pleasant, especially when I had my mother ill. Then I had to get a bucket or two off a neighbour.

Some eighteen months ago some repairs were done to the property, but best of all we had water laid on from the main, the South Staffordshire Water Supply. Now I have a tap of my own over the sink in the scullery, no more running up the road for buckets of water. It is here ready for use whenever I want it. Lovely, clean pure water to drink and use for cooking and good water to wash with. Now we have a water lavatory, self-flushing and after one has had those dreadful old-fashioned ones for so many years you can imagine how much we appreciate our new water supply.

The cost is 3s. 11d. per quarter water rate, very reasonable. In fact if it were more we should pay up and smile. We often talk about our " old well." and wonder how we all managed to get our water from there as there were seven houses to be supplied and we imagine all kinds of dreadful things that would happen if anybody took our water from the main off us."

" Pure water is the best of gifts that man to man can bring." *Attributed to the Hon. G. W. E. Russell.*

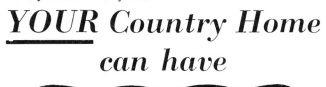

" I could tell you what to do with it if it were a horse, mister." " What's that ? " " Have her destroyed ! "

– 1940 –

Our Village Carriers

SIXTY YEARS AGO, there were no buses plying between small villages and the neighbouring towns. Railway stations were few and far, and " carriers " occupied an important place in village life.

WHEN I WAS A CHILD, packmen still roamed the hills of Wales, selling their goods to the wives of isolated farmers and herdsmen, and telling them the news of the outside world; and in every village there were " carriers "—a man, or maybe a woman, who drove to the nearest market towns to buy for their neighbours, charging a trifle on each commission.

In our village we had two carriers. One was a dear old apple-cheeked woman, nearly seventy years of age, who kept an invalid husband by the aid of her donkey and little cart. She had a small stable in her cottage yard, cleaned by her son who also fed the donkey for her. From there, in all weathers, old Mary Jones would sally forth, dressed in an old fur-lined cloak which the Squire's wife had given her, with a black cottage bonnet and white cap border framing her old face. Round her shoulders was pinned a small plaid shawl, and on her hands she wore an immense pair of the Squire's driving gloves—much too big for her—tied on round her wrists with string. She could speak no language but Welsh, but she was very quick at making out what we wanted by signs.

There were only two very small shops in the village: one, the Post Office, sold stamps and tobacco and very little else. (Telegrams—if there were any—were brought over from the small town nearby by a young man we called " a cad on casters "— i.e. a very high bicycle not often seen in our locality.) The other sold principally red herrings, peppermints, acid drops, and tea, but often said of the last, " We are just out of it, my dear; we'll be having some in next week " !

One day each week, Mary went to the little town—or large village—four miles away, to buy groceries for herself and her neighbours; and sometimes she would go to the doctor's, with various bottles to be refilled.

Our other carrier was a bachelor of uncertain age. He owned a large cart and horse, and went two days a week to the nearest market town—nine miles away—to sell sacks of flour and turnips, or barrels of apples for the farmers; but he did not disdain small commissions for his neighbours. One would say, " Will you sell these two dozen eggs for me, Richard Davies ? " Another would ask him to buy a pound of good Cheshire cheese, " for me husband does love a bit ". Then the Squire's wife would commission him to get a pot of salted butter for the winter. He was equally ready to oblige rich patroness or poor customers. He could not write or read properly (only spell out little words in his Bible), but he never forgot what he was asked to bring, or made any mistake over the prices.

Richard was a strict teetotaller and even when he had a bad accident and was nearly fainting, he refused to have his lips moistened with any brandy: but he thoroughly enjoyed the mince pies the Squire's lady gave him at Christmas—little guessing that there was brandy in them.

He always wore corduroy trousers (clean ones on Sundays), a cloth jacket, and a coloured kerchief round his neck, a cloth cap, and an old-fashioned bowler for best. He saved money, for he was very hardworking; and finally owned a row of houses.

These two were our " carriers "; but there were also our water carriers. One, a middle-aged widow, daily carried drinking water from a well half a mile away for the Squire's family; three buckets a day—one in each hand and one on her head. Every woman had thus to carry drinking water from the wells, and this habit of carrying buckets on their heads gave them a beautiful stately walk.

Patterns for a Summer Outfit

No. **143543**	No. **141413**	No. **126453**
In bust sizes	*In bust sizes*	*In bust sizes*
32-40 inches.	*32-40 inches.*	*42-48 inches.*
(Price 1s. 3d.)	*(Price 1s. 3d.)*	*(Price 1s. 3d.)*

THESE attractive summer dresses and coat are all suitable for making up in linen, cotton, light woollen, or wool-and-artificial silk mixture. The dress and coat pattern (No. 143543) is wonderful value; the dress needs 4⅞ yards of 36 inch stuff in bust size 36 inch, the coat 2¾ yards. The second dress for the younger member (No. 141413) takes 3¼ yards of 36 inch material in bust size 36 inch. The dress for the older member (No. 126453) is distinctly slimming in cut. It takes 5¼ yards of 36 inch material in bust size 44 inch. This is the only dress illustrated with a zip fastening, but such a fastener would look equally pleasing on the other designs.

The patterns cost 1s. 3d. each post free.

Orders, stating the number of the pattern and the bust size required, should be sent to the Paper Pattern Department, HOME AND COUNTRY, *Puddephat's Farm, Markyate, Herts.*

There were also several children who fetched water from the canal for their busy mothers, or for a few pence for those who had no one to help them or were too infirm to carry it for themselves. How often we watched them, with envious eyes, from our nursery windows ! What fun they seemed to have, splashing the water about. Then they settled little round woollen pads on their heads to support their buckets, and, helping each other to lift them, they moved away, laughing and chattering.

Every cottage in the village had a rain-tub attached to it to help save so many journeys for water. But it was not always put to its original use, for once as we were walking along a lane with our governess a man's head peeped over the edge of the water-butt, stared curiously at us for a moment, and withdrew: doubtless a miner who, to save his wife carrying water, was taking his bath in the water-butt. How he got in and out of it we did not stop to see !

Nowadays many of the cottages in our village have water laid on, and with buses going to the town every day we have no need of carriers to shop for us. Yet people who do not know still talk of " the good old days ".

A.G.E.

"COME TO THE FAIR"

by DONALD LOWE

THE entry of summer sees the return of that hardy annual, the village or church fair or fête, with its attending problems of arrangement and decoration. How to approach this task in an artistic yet profitable manner with the materials and money at our disposal, often proves something of a headache to the Committee and erectors. Nevertheless, the task is ours, so to it.

First having acquired the site, a field with high hedges acting as a wind break and a gentle slope to ensure good drainage, we mark or peg out the relative positions of the stands.

Now comes the construction. The first point to consider is the general treatment of the stalls and stands so as to give the fair a definite continuity of style rather than consisting of a number of unassociated units. To do this we must settle on a type of period of decoration, such as Elizabethan, Continental or Modern, to give a few examples.

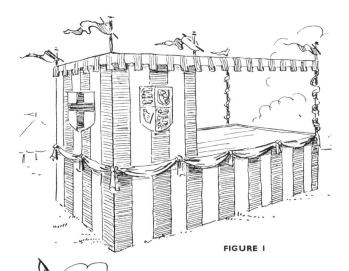

FIGURE I

Let us suppose we have decided on an Elizabethan setting with its simple design and brave colour. We commence with the dais or platform, the stability of which is a most important point. A flat lorry will serve our purpose.

For the decoration we first drive four eight-foot poles or posts into the ground, one at each corner of the driving cab, around which we fasten a screen of fabric or strong paper to hide it completely from view. We then make three wooden frames and cover these with paper (old wall-paper will answer) and fix them against the sides and rear of the flat to screen off the wheels and chassis. Having done this, we now erect two more eight-foot poles, one at each rear corner of the lorry. Our structural work is then complete and we are ready to commence decorating.

FIGURE 2

We paint the side and rear panels and cab screen in broad vertical stripes of red or green and white with distemper colour and complete the effect by hanging drapes of cheese cloth or muslin dyed in a bright colour along their top edges.

Next the poles are painted red and garlanded with festoons such as one uses at Christmas time. From the tops of the poles flags may be flown. Between the pole tops we run a length of strong twine from which we hang a paper pelmet painted to match the screens. When completed, the dais should appear as the illustration in *Figure 1*.

NOW for the stalls. Trestle tables usually serve for this purpose—in themselves anything but objects of beauty, but at least their simple form and construction will give us a frame on which to work. We treat them first by enclosing them with paper to form a solid-looking base for the stall tops to rest on.

Above the stall we erect a dummy awning to take away the low and flat appearance. To do this, obtain four "long mop" handle fittings and screw them in pairs to the centre of each end of the stall, allowing them to cant outwards. Now insert a broom handle in each to carry the pelmet, which is fixed in a similar manner to the one on the dais.

We can now complete the scheme by fastening a further length of the pelmet along the edge of the stall and painting the whole to harmonize with the rest of the set. *Figure 2* will give us some idea of the finished stall.

NO fair is complete without the "Gypsy" and her caravan, so we will attempt to create this popular feature. We shall require a flat cart, a small tent and the usual pieces of timber and paper.

The best position for our caravan is in a corner of the field, the reason for this will be seen later. Run the cart into place with the shafts facing the centre of the field. Between the shafts erect a small

flight of steps leading up to the cart flat. We are now ready to make the superstructure.

The tent is pitched on the flat with the door or flaps opening out on to the steps. This forms the body of the caravan.

Now for the construction of the dummy frontage. Commence by building a wooden frame to form the façade or front of the caravan. This is fixed to the front of the cart and held in position by stays running from the frame to the cart sides. Next, build the door frame and fix in position above the steps. The space between the two frames can now be covered with stiff paper and decorated to look like a Romany caravan. As the tent part of the mock-up is in no way camouflaged, we use the hedges in the corner of the field as a screen. The result of our efforts will be seen in *Figure 3*.

ANOTHER important feature of any fair is the buffet with its small tables and serving counter. The former can be made from up-turned barrels on which are placed squares of hard-board or even pastry boards. Paint the barrels in bands of colour and cover their tops with gay paper. The serving counter is made by placing a number of kitchen tables end to end and decorating them in a manner similar to the dais. Group the whole unit within a staked-out enclosure, draped with strings of flags to give an air of semi-privacy.

As other units, such as entrance ways, side-shows, etc., take their turn, we treat and decorate them in a like manner, always remembering our original scheme with its simple form and flamboyant colouring.

FIGURE 3

CHAPTER THREE
The War Years

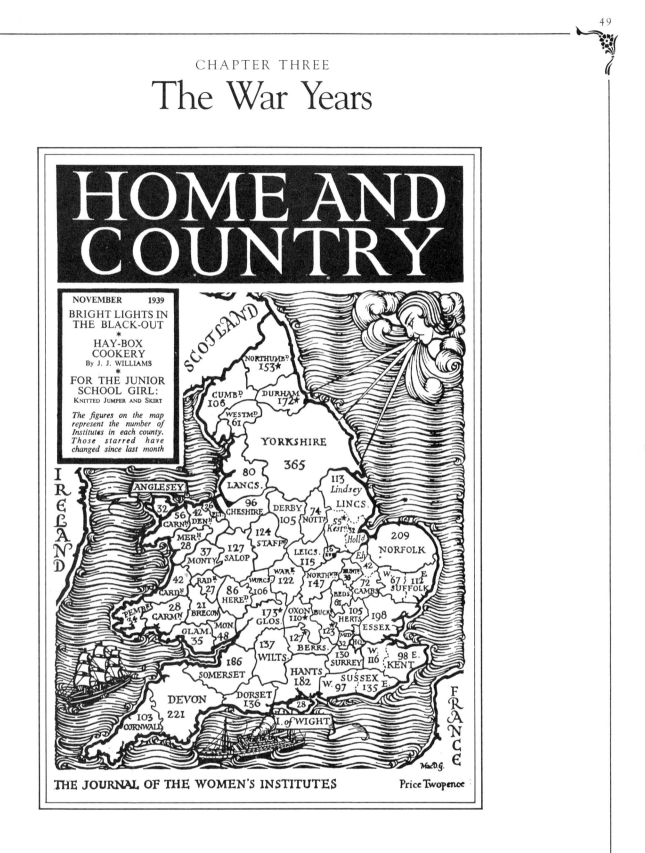

Message to the Women of the Empire

Broadcast by H.M. THE QUEEN *on November 11*

THE last time that I broadcast a message was at Halifax, Nova Scotia, when I said the few words of farewell to all the women and children who had welcomed the King and myself so kindly during our visit to Canada and the United States of America. The world was then at peace, and for seven happy weeks we had moved in an atmosphere of such goodwill and human kindliness that the very idea of strife and bloodshed seemed impossible. The recollection of it still warms my heart and gives me courage.

I speak to-day in circumstances sadly different. For twenty years we have kept this Day of Remembrance as one consecrated to the memory of past, and never to be forgotten, sacrifice. And now the peace which that sacrifice made possible has been broken, and once again we have been forced into war. I know that you would wish me to voice, in the name of the women of the British Empire, our deep and abiding sympathy with those on whom the first cruel and shattering blow has fallen—the women of Poland. Nor do we forget the gallant womanhood of France who are called on to share with us again the hardships and sorrows of war.

War has at all times called for the fortitude of women. Even in other days, when it was an affair of the fighting forces only, wives and mothers at home suffered constant anxiety for their dear ones, and too often the misery of bereavement. Their lot was all the harder because they felt that they could do so little, beyond heartening through their own courage and devotion, the men at the Front.

Now this is all changed, for we, no less than men, have real and vital work to do. To us also is given the proud privilege of serving our country in her hour of need.

The call has come, and from my heart I thank you, the women of our great Empire, for the way that you have answered it. The tasks that you have undertaken, whether at home or in distant lands, cover every field of National Service, and I should like to pay my tribute to all of you who are giving such splendid and unselfish help in this time of trouble.

At the same time, I do not forget the humbler part which so many of you have to play in these trying times. I know that it is not so difficult to do the big things. The novelty, the excitement of new and interesting duties have an exhilaration of their own. But these tasks are not for every woman. It is the thousand-and-one worries and irritations, and carrying on wartime life in ordinary homes, which are often so hard to bear. Many of you have had to see your family life broken up, your husband going off to his allotted task, your children evacuated to places of greater safety. The King and I know what it means to be parted from our children and we can sympathise with those of you who have bravely consented to this separation, for the sake of your little ones. Equally do we appreciate the hospitality shown by those of you who have opened your homes to strangers and to children sent from places of special danger.

All this I know has meant sacrifice, and I would say to those who are feeling the strain: Be assured that in carrying on your home duties and meeting all these worries cheerfully, you are giving real service to the country. You are taking your part in keeping the Home Front, which will have dangers of its own, stable and calm. It is, after all, for our homes and for their security we are fighting, and we must see to it that despite all the difficulty these days, our homes do not lose those very qualities which make them the background, as well as the joy, of our lives.

Women of all lands yearn for the day when it will be possible to set about lding a new and better world, where Peace and Goodwill shall abide. That day must come. Meantime to all of you, in every corner of the Empire, who are doing such fine work in all our Services or who are carrying on at home amidst the trials of these days, I would give a message of hope and encouragement. We have all a part to play, and I know you will not fail in yours, remembering always that the greater your courage and devotion, the sooner shall we see again in our midst the happy, ordered life for which we long.

Only when we have won through to an enduring peace shall we be free to work unhindered for the greater happiness and wellbeing of all mankind. We put our trust in God, who is our refuge and strength in all times of trouble. I pray with all my heart that He may bless, and guide, and keep you always.

Printed in England

– 1940 –

THE QUEEN AND THE PRINCESSES AT SANDRINGHAM W.I.

We are happy to publish this photograph of H.M. the Queen and H.R.H. Princess Elizabeth among their fellow members at the January meeting of Sandringham W.I. H.R.H. Princess Margaret was the guest of honour.

– 1944 –

H.M. The Queen in the Yellow Drawing Room at Buckingham Palace: a portrait by Cecil Beaton

A Message from H.M. The Queen to her Fellow W.I. Members

IT GIVES ME great pleasure to send a message of goodwill to the Women's Institutes throughout the Country.

I know what difficulties the Women's Institutes have had to overcome in meeting Wartime conditions. Members have done much important National Service, including work for evacuees, co-operative work on comforts for Men of the Services, and Hospital supplies; also co-operative buying of vegetable and potato seeds to increase our food supply. I congratulate them with all my heart on this good work.

I hear that the Monthly Meetings have been held often under great difficulties, and that they have maintained their high level and have proved more than ever a welcome source of strength and refreshment to Members and Visitors.

Knowing, as I do, the great value of the Women's Institutes to the life of the community, I send my good wishes, and rejoice in the sure knowledge that, whatever they may be asked to do, my fellow members will not fail.

ELIZABETH R.

Women's Institutes in War-Time

A Message from our Chairman

IN EVERY W.I. members are asking in what way they can best be of service at the present time. Since evacuation began many of us have been too busy receiving children or mothers and helping them to settle in to be able to think of anything else, but now we are thinking about facing a winter of war conditions, of dark nights, and of general stress and strain. How can we who must carry on in our own villages, best serve our country?

In the first place, every one of us can help to keep alive a spirit of steadiness and freedom from panic. Germany is said to count on breaking our nerve. Every person who spreads an atmosphere of cheerfulness and quiet resolution at this time is helping to win the war. We are proud of the cause for which Britain is fighting, and those of us who are not called upon to endure the hardship of actual warfare will be glad to feel that we have comforts to go without, difficulties to contend with in daily life, and that by meeting such troubles cheerfully and helping our neighbours to do so, we are taking our small share in winning the victory which we believe will come, but which will come only if the whole nation is ready to make willing sacrifice.

It is not easy always to maintain courage and cheerfulness in war-time. Our Institute meetings should be centres not only of the many forms of war-work which we shall be asked to undertake, but of neighbourliness among ourselves and among the visitors whom war has sent to live among us. Never have town and country mothers and children had so good an opportunity of getting to know each other. It will be something very valuable achieved if out of evacuation can come a more united nation than before.

I expect that many of you know that I am now Honorary Director of the Women's Land Army and I hope that W.I. members will welcome any Land Army girls who come to their village and will do their best to prevent these volunteers, who are helping so much to maintain our food supply, from feeling lonely or friendless.

Keep the social side of the W.I. alive however hard this may be and even if our usual generous tea has to become only a cup of tea and a biscuit! To laugh together will send us home heartened and cheered for our daily work.

Every W.I. will be put on its mettle to find ways of meeting and programmes which can be carried out without outside help. Perhaps from this will come a development of initiative and self-reliance which will enable us to be twice as effective as before when war ends.

G. DENMAN

A Message from the Minister of Health

ALL OVER THE COUNTRY the local authorities at my request are preparing to make a survey of available housing accommodation, as part of our plans for transferring children and others in an emergency to the homes of those who are willing to take care of them. I hope that every householder will give all possible help to the visitors making the survey. Some of them will be officers of the local authorities and some of them voluntary helpers. They will be going round to collect the information which we need, in order that we in Whitehall may estimate how many people could be properly accommodated without overcrowding either guests or hosts.

If an emergency should come upon us we shall have the greatest need of the help of voluntary workers, such as members of the Women's Institutes, in the country districts to which the children will be sent. It is an immense undertaking to move and re-settle even one million people—especially when they are children. There will have to be an infinite number of special arrangements—for communal cooking and feeding, perhaps for communal laundry work, for crèches and play centres and any other activities. This can only be done if there are willing helpers remaining in the districts to which the children will be sent, and it is for this reason that the services which women can give—both as householders looking after children from the danger areas in their own homes and as workers engaged in these thousand-and-one community tasks—must rank as national service of the first importance. **WALTER ELLIOT**

THE TOWN COMES TO THE COUNTRY

WHEN THE HISTORY of this war is written, one of the most interesting chapters will be devoted to the social changes resulting from the exodus from town to country. This " invasion " of the villages has caused a good many surprises—not all of them pleasant—on both sides. Jane Strong, who knows both town and country, here introduces the townswoman to her country hostess

THE VILLAGES, with the Women's Institutes to the fore, made grand preparations to receive their war-time town guests. Of course all the adults would be nice people, deeply grateful for the shelter afforded them. All the children would be charming—pale-faced and strange, perhaps, but country fare and country air would do them no end of good.

The guests arrived, good, bad and indifferent. Since the arrival, countrywoman and townswoman have endured several shocks before settling down to make the best of things.

The townswoman from the small suburban house has a very different outlook on life from that of the cottage woman. This townswoman for the most part is a thrifty wife, an ambitious mother, and a good neighbour. She is proud of her home and preens herself on its conveniences. Electric light, gas cooker, washing machine, bathroom, hot-air cupboard are, by now, necessities. The shops are round the corner and shopping is an agreeable diversion. She reads the daily paper, generally in the evenings when her work is done, and takes a lively interest in politics and in the Royal family. She goes to the pictures once or twice a week and when occasion offers makes an expedition with a friend to the city shops, not to buy but to look round. This woman, at first, will be appalled by the inconveniences of the old-fashioned cottage and by the quietude of the country. Patience on the part of her hostess and an effort to see her point of view may induce her to give the new life a chance for the sake of her children. Decent towns-folk, whatever their standard, appreciate the kindness they are receiving, and ultimately sensible women will discover common interests.

Letters to the Editor

AIR RAID REFUGEES

DEAR EDITOR, The letter from Woodgreen Women's Institute last month adds another to an already long list sent to the Press since " the Crisis " regarding the billeting of refugees. The writers of these letters have almost unanimously referred to the refugees as being dirty, diseased, disreputable and altogether objectionable. A point that seems to escape these letter writers is that the refugees might themselves be victims—as in a case a doctor reported at one of our local meetings where an infectious disease had broken out in one of the villages just at the time of the crisis.

There may be a lot to be said for bringing pressure to bear on the Government to provide proper facilities for billeting, but to exaggerate the defects of the refugees as an argument to that end does not seem to me to be in accordance with the high traditions with which the Women's Institute has always associated itself.

Yours truly, EMILY WHITNEY,
Easebourne, Midhurst.

DINNER TIME AT ST. IVES
An everyday scene in the communal kitchen for child and adult evacuees organized by the W.V.S. It is in the charge of Mrs. Parker, Treasurer of Huntingdonshire County Federation

OXFORDSHIRE, in the thick of the reception area, is hard at it. **Ascott-under-Wychwood** has a bunch of happy children, but their teacher (who comes from a city school of 800 and has left 600 behind) admits that she has " no use for the country ". **Charlbury,** whose excellent central school can absorb all the children, uses the Scout hut as a twice a week club for visitors to make their own clothes. But **Greys,** whose romantic hall stands among forest trees in the Chilterns, finds that the *walk there* is a real difficulty to pavement-bred visitors. **Kiddington,** a broad-minded Institute, wonders *what* the returned London mothers say about the country ones.

Horspath members, in the most heavily billeted area of all, have attacked their problem with spirit and success. They have a " make and mend " corps, each member undertaking one household of evacuated children. The mothers offered to help, one being specially expert. When all the Horspath children are tidied up the corps will turn itself over to hospital sewing, elderly people or those without evacuees being specially welcomed. Horspath also has clubs for the innumerable boys and girls, London and Oxfordshire, who hold mixed meetings every week. Plays full of local and metropolitan talent are being rehearsed for Christmas. The teachers get manuscript music down from London, and boys and girls alike help with hospital sewing. " London boys can often knit ", adds the reporter with interest. And London girls can act and dance. Your correspondent's earliest Folk Dance teacher was a gifted imp from an East End club, and one of the most thrilling performances she ever saw of " Is this a dagger which I see before me ? " was given by a London slum girl.

The Countryman says: When the members of a Women's Institute were asked what they found most disagreeable in present war conditions someone called out, " Mending evacuee schoolboys' trousers."

ᖇᖇᖇᖇᖇᖇᖇ

Evacuation Notes

London children evacuated to Norfolk are reported to have put on half a stone in weight in a week.

*   *   *

A housewife in the Ipswich district who is able to feed her two young guests for 11s. a week intends to spend the extra 6s. she is receiving on boots and winter clothes for them.

*   *   *

Hundreds of fathers and mothers from the evacuation areas are visiting their children in the reception districts—by train, bus, car and bicycle. Will this social upheaval, one wonders, be the beginning of a serious back-to-the-land movement ?

BRIGHT LIGHTS IN THE BLACK-OUT

MANY INSTITUTES have been getting over " black-out " difficulties by holding afternoon meetings, but as the days shorten, means will have to be found of keeping rooms bright inside and black outside

THE GOVERNMENT is prepared for this war to last three years. When we " black-out " our meeting places therefore it is no use using materials that will last only a few weeks.

Institutes that meet in rooms or halls lit by oil lamps may find that they need thicker and heavier materials than those lit by gas or electric light, since oil lamps are often moved about and may be stood on a table close to the window.

Windows that are not essential to daytime lighting can be covered with a double sheet of thick brown paper, with cardboard, or with black paper—all materials that can be bought cheaply at the multiple stores or any stationer's. It should be stuck flat on the glass with paste, made in the same way as paste for wall papering, or tacked to the framework with drawing pins. Very tall windows can perhaps have the top portion blacked-out permanently, leaving the lower part to be curtained.

Ordinary linen or casement curtains are useless unless lined with a dark material, which may not wash well. Institutes that already have bright curtains would do well to leave them and to make frames of wood to fit the windows, against which they can be held by turn-buttons or some similar contrivance. Dark cloth or paper can be used to cover the frames.

Thick black material can be had by the yard, very suitable, but rather expensive. Then there is a cheap felt, 5½d. a yard, 36 inches wide, not very strong, needs careful handling. A piece of tape placed between the felt and the head of the nails will help to prevent the felt from tearing. For a hall, or where there are a number of windows to cover, roof felting is the best material. This can be bought in 12 yard rolls, 1 yard wide, from 4s. 9d. per roll. The local carpenter will most likely help in making the framework for the village hall windows, using strips of wood or laths. Amateurs will find blind laths easier to use, as they splinter and split less readily.

These frames must be made to fit exactly into the windows. If they will fit only when placed in one particular way, mark which is top and bottom, left and right. Remember you will not be the only one to erect them, and when it is getting dark they are not so easily placed in position.

If thick curtains are used, and when they are drawn, strips of light can be seen along the top and the sides, stick pieces of paper along the edges of the glass ; or, at the top, nail a strip of felt 2 or 3 inches wide on to the framework.

When your black-out preparations are complete, go outside on a *very* dark night when the lights are full on to make sure you have done the job well.   H.G.H.

(On behalf of the N.F.W.I. Organization Sub-committee).

– 1939 –

National Service

W.I. AMBULANCES: *The ambulance presented to the Royal Navy (above) and one of the three ambulances presented to the Royal Air Force by the National Federation of Women's Institutes.*

Let's talk about FOOD

WOMEN everywhere are asking the health values of foods ; which foods can take the place of others, and so on.

Well, here we are at the Ministry of Food, ready and glad to help. Perhaps the following replies, which we have recently sent to correspondents, will interest you, too.

QUESTIONS YOU ASK

Are potatoes really better for us if cooked in their skins?

Yes. In addition to some of the potato being wasted in peeling, cooking tends to extract mineral salts and lessen the health protection of this valuable food. The skin "seals in" the goodness and should be eaten, because it is itself of definite health value.

My child sadly misses his "apple a day" which I cannot now always manage. What can I give instead?

A well-scrubbed raw carrot. Carrots contain sugar which helps to satisfy the desire for sweets, and chewing is good for the teeth. Carrots also contain valuable protective vitamins and are good for the complexion.

My children don't much like meat. Is there any harm in their going without?

The chief value of meat is as a body builder, but the very best body building food for children is milk. As long as they get plenty of milk for building muscles, bones and teeth; potatoes for energy; their ration of fats, and plenty of vegetables, your children should be all right. Have you taken advantage of the Government scheme for free and reduced price milk for children?

I have heard potatoes save suet; how is this?

Potatoes, like suet, are nourishing, warming and energising; though not quite in the same degree. Half the usual quantity of suet and an equal quantity of grated raw potato, added to your usual quantity of flour and mixed with a little water, makes a light crust, thus saving suet to use in something else. You will find many economical recipes in Food Facts Announcements in the newspapers and in the Kitchen Front Wireless Talks at 8.15 a.m. on weekdays.

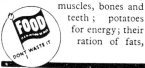

Mary, Mary quite contrary,
Wouldn't learn anything new.
But Martha was wise
Used her wits and her eyes,
Her catering worries just flew

Issued by The Ministry of Food.　　　　(S8)

National Service

Children of Wigtoft (Holland) help to collect scrap and waste paper

Branscombe (Devon): members and helpers sorting waste paper

Mrs. Kennedy Minards, of Canfield Cliffs (Dorset) with some of the scrap collected by W.I. members there which she is carting

The Editor wants good pictures of W.I. members engaged in the many and various pieces of work our movement is undertaking for inclusion in the series now being published under the heading "National Service". Glossy prints (not negatives) should be sent, and they MUST BE very clear in detail—otherwise they will not make good half-tone blocks. Photographs not used will be returned if stamps are enclosed.

Keeping the Family Healthy

WOMEN'S INSTITUTE MEMBERS have carried out a great work in helping with the Government " Dig for Victory " Campaign, and also in preserving surplus foods for use later in the year. Our work does not end in growing and preserving the food. We must see that it is given its proper place in the diet and see that it is properly cooked. We must " cook for victory " as well as grow for it

AT THE PRESENT TIME we all have a part to play in the war effort. A great many Women's Institute members are doing valuable work in Women's Voluntary Services and First Aid Detachments, etc. But the members who are not able to leave their homes, who have their families to look after are, in a quiet way, helping the country in its war effort just as much as the members in uniform, for the health of their families is entrusted to them. Courage and determination are needed to see this war through, and these cannot be maintained without good health.

Health depends to a large extent on the food that is eaten. During the first 12 months of war the housewife's task was a comparatively easy one as very few foods were restricted. Now in the second year of war the housewife's job is growing more and more difficult each day. Many of the foods to which we are accustomed are rationed or difficult to obtain, but fortunately the foods most valuable in maintaining health are home produced—fruit and vegetables, dairy produce and eggs.

The money value of our meat coupons has been cut, but this should not worry us if we purchase the cheaper joints and use plenty of vegetables and savoury dumplings to eke them out. Haricot and butter beans will help as body building foods.

Bacon, our favourite breakfast dish, will go much further if oatmeal porridge is served first and then fried potatoes, bread or batter is served with the bacon. The bacon rinds should be cut off and used for flavouring soups.

With the shortage of fats, the frying pan should be used only when other methods of cooking are not possible. All fat over from frying, however small the amount, should be strained and used again. Suet is unrationed at present and should be used instead of fat whenever possible.

Fresh fruit is scarce, but we shall not suffer if we include plenty of raw vegetables and properly cooked greens in our diet.

The housewife is not expected to carry out the difficult task of feeding her family alone. Scientists have been working for years on food in relation to health, and we have now some of the best brains in the country planning meals and devising new recipes so that our diet may still be nourishing and varied with the limited foods at our disposal. All their findings are available to help the housewife in her task. The Ministry of Food's Chart " The Four Group Way " should be studied when planning meals. Something from each group should be chosen each day.

Women's Institute members are fortunate in belonging to an organization which arranges for lecturers and demonstrators to bring this knowledge to their own villages and present it in an attractive and practical form. The organization also provides an opportunity for members to discuss their achievements and difficulties, thereby gaining from each other's experiences.

Thanks from the Minister of Food

All Institute members will be interested to read these two letters :

To all Chairmen of Fruit Preservation Centres.

DEAR MADAM,

I know that you, and those who helped you with the Fruit Preservation Scheme last summer, will be glad to see the letter which I have just received from Lord Woolton.

May I add my thanks to his—it was a fine piece of work, splendidly carried out by all concerned in spite of, in many cases, very severe difficulties.

The winning of the war depends enormously upon the country population. We must all be ready to undertake any job which comes to hand. We country women are fortunate that, owing to our peacetime Women's Institute organization, we have the machinery through which our efforts can best be used in this time of national crisis.

I know that you will not slacken your efforts this year and that as there will be longer time for preparation, the results will be even better than those achieved last summer.

With my best wishes to you all,

I am,

Yours sincerely,

G. DENMAN

(On behalf of the N.F.W.I. Executive Committee)

December 31, 1940.

Dear Lady Denman,

I have just seen your Agricultural Organizer's report on the results of the co-operative fruit preservation scheme which was carried out last summer at 2,600 centres set up and managed by your Institutes.

I have been very greatly impressed both by the quantity of preserves made and by the enthusiasm and determination with which the members of these centres, whether they belonged to your Institutes or not, undertook the formidable task of saving the exceptionally heavy plum crop, as well as other garden and wild fruit. This was work of national importance demanding administrative ability of a high order at the Headquarters of your organization, and local initiative and co-operation which are a fine example of democratic action at its best.

I know also that the centres are eager to extend and improve upon their performance in 1941.

I should be glad if you would pass on to them this message of thanks for the good work done last season and of encouragement to prepare now for the even greater effort which I hope will be possible next year.

Sincerely yours,

WOOLTON.

An old lady who was in Coventry all through the raids was asked how she managed to remain so unmoved and to sleep so calmly. She answered: " Well, when I go to bed I says my prayers, and I read my piece of the Bible, and then I lays down and I says to myself *To hell with Hitler* ".   DEVON

HOME AND COUNTRY

The Magazine of the National Federation of Women's Institutes

The main purpose of Women's Institutes is to improve and develop conditions of rural life

FROM THE EDITOR'S DESK

By the time these words appear in print, the FRUIT PRESERVATION CENTRES should have started on their great work.   The object of that work is to preserve all privately grown fruit not required for immediate consumption so that it may be added to the national store cupboard for the days of the year when fresh fruit is unobtainable in these times of restricted imports.   The bulk of their produce will be jam—indeed, so far as the early fruits strawberries, black currants, and raspberries are concerned the Ministry of Food has issued an instruction that they may be used only for jam.   Later crops will be made into jam, canned where facilities for canning exist, and in some centres bottled.

The introduction of jam rationing last February appeared at first in the guise of a serious setback to the whole scheme; but, now that we have adjusted our minds to the difficulties it certainly presented, it turns out to be something of a blessing, for it disproves the theory rather widely advanced by persons ill-informed as to the basis of Women's Institute thought, that we were being allowed by the Government to engage in a selfish effort to stock our own jam cupboards without any corresponding benefit being conferred on non-members. These same ill-informed persons freely stated that the introduction of jam rationing would kill the scheme, a statement adequately disproved by events : at the moment of going to press 4,148 centres have been registered, and further registration forms are coming in daily.

Jam rationing certainly caused a momentary confusion—due in the main to the fact that the centres have very small funds at their disposal, and fears for their solvency were felt if their products could not be immediately sold (as they were last year) to provide funds for the next batch of preserving. The Ministry of Food's undertaking to back the scheme and to purchase and collect any jam, jelly, or canned fruit not disposed of through the other recognized channels has solved that difficulty; and now it is clear to everyone that Women's Institute members are engaged on a piece of very valuable national service for the benefit of the whole community—service that, it is satisfactory to feel, is wholly constructive.

"*BOIL AND BUBBLE . . .*
TOIL AND TROUBLE"

These pictures are published as a salute to the good work of 1,659 Centres in 1943

THE PRACTISED HAND

SORTING THE FRUIT IN THE GARDEN

BRINGING IT INDOORS

BOILING THE JAM

FILLING THE JARS

TYING DOWN THE COVERS

VISIT OF THE SUPERVISOR

READY FOR COLLECTION

*Below: Queen Mary at Kimble
Fruit Preservation Centre,
Gloucestershire*

*Right: Fruit preservation at
Thornton-Le-Dale, Yorkshire
Bottom: Sealing the canned fruit*

Left: Despatching jam for the village store

Below: Fruit preservation exhibition at Cheltenham, 1942, showing American canning machine

National Service

THE FIRST AMBULANCE
Picture taken outside the N.F.W.I. Office after Lady Denman had presented the first W.I. Ambulance. With Lady Denman are the Hon. Frances Farrer, General Secretary, N.F.W.I., and Capt. P. H. Bentley, M.C., R.S.C., who accepted the Ambulance on behalf of the War Office.

DOUBLE SERVICE
Mrs. Stebbing, leader of the Bures (W. Suffolk) W.I. Waste Paper Section, with 2 tons 3 cwts. of paper collected and sorted by W.I. members. The three willing helpers shown loaded the lorry before breakfast. The proceeds go to the W.I. Ambulance Fund.

THE JAM FRONT
Helpers filling jars at Bearsted and Thurnham Centre (W. Kent), where over 800 lbs. of jam was made in six days. The good work included canning, and will go on until plum time comes to an end.

– 1940 –

What has Post-War Planning to do with Winning the War ?

There is at the moment some difference of opinion between those who are keen to discuss reconstruction and the building of a better social order and those who say all this must wait until we have *won the war*. People belonging to the last group say we are engaged in a fight for existence that demands all our energies and that no one yet knows what things will be like after the war or what it will be possible to do.

Obviously the Government already feel it wise to make plans for the future. They have appointed several Committees to examine the hundred and one problems that will arise and make proposals for dealing with them. They do not want the heroes to come back and find no homes, fit or otherwise, to live in and no work by which to support themselves. Although we may not be able to carry out much reconstruction while the war lasts we do not want anything to be taking place that will make matters more difficult afterwards. Black markets and worthless food substitutes have shown us that there are people who cannot resist making money by despicable means, who will cheat and rob others in order to get rich themselves.

It is true that we cannot yet do more than tidy up our blitzed cities but we must guard against land speculation and other evils that might prevent them being eventually re-built on finer and better lines.

It is obvious to everyone that post-war Britain is going to be very different. It needs to be. The best minds are agreed that there must be more equality of opportunity, a fairer distribution of wealth, better homes for all.

A certain number of people have already made up their minds that because changes are coming they are bound to be for the worse. Those who have in the past enjoyed higher standards of living and greater privileges fear that all this is slipping away from them. They are not as yet prepared to co-operate in a more genuinely democratic Britain.

Talks and discussions help to make clear to us what are the aims and principles we should have in mind when we do start reconstructing. In this great struggle against evil forces we are keyed up to a higher level, we have more vision, more faith. When victory comes there may easily be a reaction, a longing for ease, a return to more selfish ways of living.

Planning for a " New Order " does help in winning the war because victory depends so much on faith. In November 1940, Mr. Austin Hopkinson asked the House of Commons " What have *we* to set against the passionate belief which leads millions of young men and women to die for the vile creed of Nazism ? Do we believe in anything at all ? " A very wise man, Mr. Eugene Bagger, writes : " A people can fight and conquer only if it has faith, even faith in the Devil masquerading as God." Sir Stafford Cripps has told us recently that " youth in Russia has a burning zeal for its country and its institutions ".

If we are to have a burning zeal for our country's institutions we must know all about them and feel personally concerned in planning their improvement and in carrying out such plans.

We have much to learn from our great Ally, China, where the most wonderful reconstruction is going on right in the midst of war. Although fighting desperately against an enemy vastly superior in equipment and trained men the Chinese are rapidly developing the interior of their country. Students of blitzed universities have tramped hundreds of miles carrying their books and are now passing on knowledge to the uneducated masses. Health services, co-operative stores, are making life infinitely more worthwhile for thousands of humble villagers.

Japan is fighting not an army but an entire population. If our whole nation has that unity it will also be unconquerable.

Women's Institutes have played a splendid part in the war effort. Whatever the call—billeting, salvage, food production, they have responded whole-heartedly. They will deserve even better of their country if they keep alive faith in its future destiny.

And as faith without works is useless let us, like the Chinese, start here and now to make our visions come true.

WINIFRED M. COMBER

– 1942 –

Custodians of a Heritage

THERE are 250 pages of the Scott report. Too many to digest at one time. So this article is limited to a few of its ideas on land and houses.

"Citizens of this country", says the Report, "are the custodians of a heritage they share with all those of British descent. . . . It is a duty incumbent upon the nation to take proper care of that which it holds in trust. . . . The British countryside today owes its characteristic features to the fact that it has been used—in other words it has been farmed."

Yet those people who have "used" the countryside have gradually left it for the towns. 44 per cent of the male agricultural workers under 21 left the country in the 14 years preceding the war. So did 19 per cent of those over 21. According to the Report, there are five reasons for this: low wages, bad housing, lack of water, sewerage and electricity, and unsatisfactory health and social services.

LET us think first about housing as that is the part which concerns W.I. members most nearly. This has been recognized by the Scott Committee which says that W.I.s should be consulted and that women should be appointed members of all housing committees. Members will remember that a resolution to this effect would have been brought forward at the Annual General Meeting if that meeting had not been cancelled. In the opinion of the Scott Committee "W.I.s have proved the organizing ability of countrywomen".

On the vexed question of tied cottages, a question very much the concern of many of us, the majority report feels that for some people, such as stockmen and key employees, tied cottages should be available, but the Report recommends the building of a sufficient number of untied cottages. These should be at a rent within the reach of the agricultural worker.

Houses should be built of good material but not necessarily in the traditional style, for any attempt to prevent the use of new materials and new types of design is futile. The Committee is anxious that while the beauty and variety of the countryside should not be spoilt, no attempt should be made to preserve villages merely as museum pieces. Professor Dennison, writer of the minority report, goes further. He recommends more modern and more intensive agricultural methods. This would result in higher wages and fewer employees, and so would affect the whole housing problem.

HE feels, too, that agriculture should not have the first claim to the land. It is more important, he says, to provide housing space for slum clearance schemes than land for, say, the cultivation of daffodils. We all agree on the need to rehouse slum dwellers. What we want to discuss is the best way to do it.

Professor Dennison tells us that the building of new towns to relieve present over-crowding would probably involve the use of one per cent of existing agricultural land. According to the majority report a garden city in spite of intensive private cultivation, can only produce a fraction of the food which would have been grown on the same land before building began. So we come back to the question, is it better to use the land for houses for individuals or for food for the community ? Food can be brought from abroad. Houses must be provided on the spot.

It seems inevitable that towns in the future must encroach more and more on the country. W.I.s have long pleaded for a central planning authority to be set up to consider the rival claims on land of farm, factory and potential householder. Professor Dennison thinks that a central planning authority should be strictly impartial. The majority report thinks it should have an agricultural bias, since good farm land is limited. Both reports agree on the urgency of central planning. To quote the introduction, "It is our firm belief that a vital incentive to the war effort is the presentation of a clear picture of a better world which, if plans are drawn up . . . can be achieved after the struggle is over."

INSTITUTES have already had many discussions on that better world. Here are some subjects for more debates suggested by reading the Scott Report. The wording is purposely controversial:

1. That before the war, bad housing was the chief cause for the drift from country to town. 2. That new villages should be built in the same material as that of the local traditional style. 3. That good farm land should never be used for any other purpose and that the claims of the farmer should always be considered before the claims of factory and house builder. 4. That the system of tied cottages should be abolished.

CICELY MCCALL

Americans DO Care

DURING THE FIRST EIGHT MONTHS OF THE WAR, Americans imagined the conflict to be a pantomime rather than an honest-to-God struggle between two worlds. They fancied the German and Allied armies grimacing at one another from Siegfried to Maginot lines. Peace rumours chased each other through American newspapers, and it was widely believed that a group of influential British appeasers would momentarily step into the daylight to conclude a makeshift peace with Germany. Suspicion that the war was an imposture explains why American voluntary relief trickled to Europe sparingly, totalling only £70,000 from September 1939 to May 1940.

America's attitude changed suddenly after Denmark, Norway, Holland, Belgium and France were crushed under the Nazi war machine, and especially when German bombers began to wreak destruction and death in Britain. Talk of appeasement and of the phoney war stopped. Millions of Americans ceased taking a box-office view of the struggle and sensed that their own fate is tied to British victory or defeat. While munitions and aeroplanes started streaming across the Atlantic, United States voluntary help in the war's second eight months rose to £3,000,000, to which more than fifteen million Americans contributed. About 80 per cent. of this relief flowed through the American Red Cross.

Neither Germany nor Italy has received any American Red Cross assistance, however. On the day war was declared, the American Red Cross approached all belligerents' Red Cross societies, but the Germans said they needed no American help and when Italy entered the war on June 10, she replied similarly.

It was news of Dunkirk and of the army returning without medical stores that first loosed the big flood of American aid. Then came the story of 30,000 Channel islanders, homeless in Britain, and of evacuated Gibraltarians, of Poles and fugitive French fisherfolk, fleeing to Cornwall in tiny, open boats. But it was the unleashing of air war over Britain in August and the tale of British courage and successful R.A.F. defiance that dispelled the last doubt that this war is a deadly challenge to ideals which Americans, too, hold dear.

Thousands of Americans proved their own earnestness by giving their blood : there were 6,000 blood donors in New York City alone, including General Pershing's son. The first blood plasma was flown to Britain by Clipper in August; in September and October, 3,000 gallons a month were being sent—each gallon sufficing for four transfusions. It was divided here among the twelve civil defence régions and held in " blood banks ". From the New Year, British equipment was able to provide the necessary blood plasma and American supplies ceased.

BESIDES THE RED CROSS, American voluntary help is now canalized in the British War Relief. Neither American organization distributes its supplies directly in Britain; all their medical equipment goes to the British Red Cross, while civilian aid, especially clothes and food, is dispensed through the Women's Voluntary Services. About two million garments have already been shipped and an equal number is on the way. American vernacular labels on some of the clothing have been causing W.V.S. members to scratch their heads, but they quickly learned that union-suits are combinations, slickers are mackintoshes, rubbers equal galoshes and rubber-boots are Wellingtons.

Twenty of 126 American mobile canteens, now being built in England, are already in operation. Six were rushed to Coventry when little hot food was available to victims after the first bombing ; others have gone to Birmingham, Bristol, Southampton, Sheffield and other stricken cities, though their main work is naturally in London.

The American Red Cross is caring for 1,400 children under five in 35 country houses and guaranteeing their upkeep for a year. While 120,000 pairs of new boots and shoes have been sent, American Red Cross cash grants to the W.V.S. for urgently needed clothing total £165,000. Medical aid from America ranges from 156 ambulances—300 more are being shipped—to 300,000 blankets, over 15,000 surgical dressings, ten X-ray units and thirteen complete operating tables delivered and five of the former and six of the latter on their way, over 100,000 hospital garments, like white gowns, over half-a-million yards of material for hospital clothing and vast quantities of drugs, including a quarter-of-a-million sulfanilamide tablets.

American contributions have come from big and little folk. In July American business men in Britain collected £100,000 in a week and presented over a hundred American-made ambulance units to the Ministry of Health. Sam Goldwyn, film producer, gave £20,000. America's Junior Red Cross sent Christmas presents for 210,000 British children.

FROM SAN FRANCISCO comes the story of a nine-year-old boy and six companions, who spent two days collecting scrap-iron in alleys, sold it and handed the 3s. 6d. proceeds to Mr. Bowen McCoy, now executive officer of the American Red Cross in London. A workman trudged 14 miles to San Francisco and back to his suburb to save tram fare and deliver the whole of his two shillings to British relief. With their Saturday sixpences, children in Maybank, Missouri, are buying milk for refugee children from Malta, now billeted in London. Kirk Barnes, of Gladwynne, Pennsylvania, and his nine-year-old pal, Gordon Hargraves, raised £1 from the roadside sale of vegetables, grown in Kirk's garden, and sent it to the British relief fund. Another boy contributed £1, earned by cutting neighbours' lawns.

American Red Cross officials have enjoyed letters from recipients of their supplies. There is no stilted diplomatic courtesy, for instance, in this one:

" Dear Friends in America:

" Thank you very much for The Pretty Frock which you have given me and the nice warm things too. I am eleven years old and my home is in Hull. But we have been sent to the country to be safer. My mother came to see me last week and she says I look very well and am so happy.

" With love from
" Annie Stanley."

FREDERICK KUH
(*Correspondent of the United Press of America in London*)

AMERICAN GIFTS TO BRITAIN

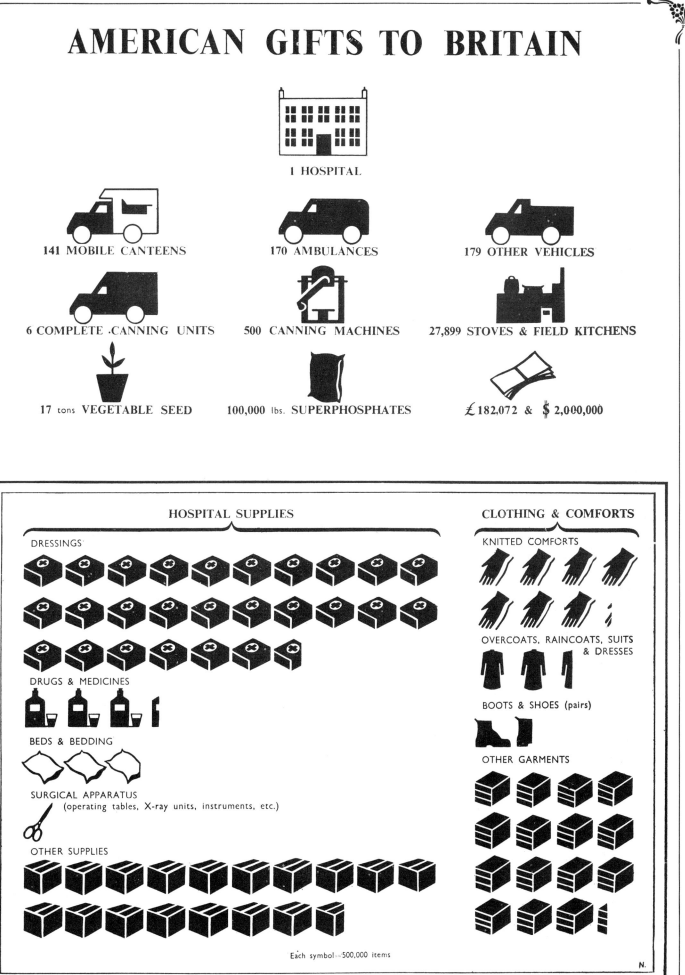

1 HOSPITAL

141 MOBILE CANTEENS

170 AMBULANCES

179 OTHER VEHICLES

6 COMPLETE CANNING UNITS

500 CANNING MACHINES

27,899 STOVES & FIELD KITCHENS

17 tons VEGETABLE SEED

100,000 lbs. SUPERPHOSPHATES

£ 182,072 & $ 2,000,000

HOSPITAL SUPPLIES

CLOTHING & COMFORTS

DRESSINGS

KNITTED COMFORTS

OVERCOATS, RAINCOATS, SUITS & DRESSES

DRUGS & MEDICINES

BOOTS & SHOES (pairs)

BEDS & BEDDING

OTHER GARMENTS

SURGICAL APPARATUS
(operating tables, X-ray units, instruments, etc.)

OTHER SUPPLIES

Each symbol = 500,000 items

N.

his Spitfire . . .

He had dreamed of it—
thought of it—
read of it—
neglected his lessons
for it—
Watched it through the
classroom window.
and now
He'd got it . . .
His own Spitfire!
He had worked hard—
even studied . . .
listened with his eyes
popping, asked
questions, travelled to
Canada—to America
and back home just
to climb into that
cockpit . . .
and now it was his.
He had charged through
clouds with it—
in and out of the sun—
he had climbed
and looped in it—
and done the
victory roll . . .
more than once.
There were several
Messerschmitts and
Focke Wulfs that
would fight no more—
for he had under his
hand—the toughest . . .
the truest . . .
the nimblest . . .
Terror of the air . . .
His SPITFIRE!

*   *   *   *

Every enemy plane he kills is a stroke for our
freedom. *We owe him a great deal—more than we
shall ever repay.* Our savings—which we merely
lend—what are they compared with what he
gives ? . . . Don't measure your savings by what
you can spare—think instead of what you OWE.

Volunteers Wanted!
For Short-term Land Service

Food must be grown in this country, farmers have ploughed
their land, have sown the seed, and they must have in addition
to their regular workers extra hands in the spring, summer and
autumn to cultivate and to carry the crops.

Much of this work can be done by local people working from
home, and I am sure that Women's Institute members will be
amongst the first to offer to give this help, but in some
districts the available local labour will not be enough.

To help to meet this shortage the Women's Land Army
Auxiliary Force for 1940 is being organized at the request of
the Minister of Agriculture, and here again those Women's
Institute members who can leave their homes for a few weeks
can give most valuable service.

Recruits are wanted now for this new force. They are asked
to enrol for at least a month or for longer if they can. Those
recruits who are 18 years or over will get a minimum wage
of 28s. a week. Many of them will work in groups, they may
camp out in tents or in empty houses or they may be billeted
with local families. They will have to pay for their board
from the wages they receive.

Volunteers who can give four continuous weeks' service or
longer during the coming months are asked to enrol in the
Women's Land Army Auxiliary Force either through the
Women's Land Army committee in their county or through:

The LADY DENMAN,
Honorary Director of the Women's Land Army,
Balcombe Place, Balcombe,
Haywards Heath, Sussex.

These volunteers need not be skilled workers: they will be
wanted by farmers to undertake jobs such as planting potatoes,
hoeing the fields, harvesting, picking fruit, or making hay.
The work may be hard, but they will be giving a most vital and
urgently needed form of national service.

– 1940 –

"THERE ARE SOME BETTER MOMENTS"

– 1944 –

CULLED FROM THE COUNTIES

One small Institute enjoys the use of a sewing machine at the dressmaking classes, thanks to the energy of a member who brings it in a perambulator each week.   BUCKS.

*   *   *

Congratulations to Mrs. Stone (Netterton W.I.) whose suet pudding recipe was broadcast by the BBC.   NORFOLK

*   *   *

Corbridge Preservation centre sent its final profit to the Merchant Navy Comforts Service as thanks to the seamen who brought the sugar to make the jam.   NORTHUMBERLAND

*   *   *

The three-minute speakers were all good, especially those who declared themselves incapable of uttering a word.

OXFORDSHIRE

"**Real thrift is not making rather ugly and unnecessary articles with queer materials, but rather a frame of mind, a spirit of true economy combined with a lively sense of invention and resourcefulness.**"
WEST SUFFOLK

*   *   *

Coveney school children bring large potatoes each day for their dinners, and these are roasted under the school grate. Eaten with margarine, cheese, etc., they provide a happy solution to the request " eat less bread ".

ISLE OF ELY

[H. & C. staff thought this was its own exclusive idea ! Many a hot potato has been roasted in the office grate and eaten with great relish in the lunch-hour during the winter months.]

LORD WOOLTON'S COMPETITION
POTATOES FOR FLOUR

In view of the promise made to Lord Woolton at the Fruit Preservation Conference entries are invited for a competition for the most appetizing supper dish for four people, using potatoes as the main ingredient, made on the basis of not more than one ounce of cooking fat to 1 lb. of potatoes.

Conditions.

1.   Each W.I. is asked to hold a competition for the above supper dish at its March or April meeting and send the recipe of its winning entry to its County Federation Office *not later than April* 30.

2.   County Federations are asked to choose the best recipe for the county and to send it to the N.F.W.I. Office, 39 Eccleston Street, London, S.W.1, marked " Potato Competition " in the top left-hand corner, not later than May 15.   The recipe should state the time taken in preparation of the dish and the length of time required for cooking.   The name, address, Institute and County of the member submitting the recipe should be clearly written at the end of the recipe.

3.   The county recipes will be tested and judged by judges appointed by the Ministry of Food.   Their decision will be final.

4.   Lord Woolton will present two certificates to the winners, one for the area north of and including Holland, Leicestershire and Rutland, Staffordshire, Shropshire and Montgomeryshire, and one for the area south of these counties.

5.   The presentation will, it is hoped, take place at the Ministry's experimental kitchen, London, at the time of the N.F.W.I. Annual General Meeting.

Embarkation leave

Sheila carries daddy's gas-mask,
Peter carries daddy's gun.
Mother's chattering on and laughing
As if parting were just fun.

She's put apples in his pocket,
He's got photos in his book,
When he isn't busy fighting,
He'll have time to have a look.

Dad is going to fight for England,
For a world where men are free,
Better times for all but—mostly
He'll be fighting for these three.

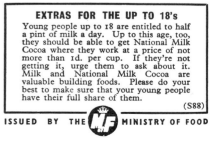

GROWING UP— and building up

The 'teen age is a critical stage of development. The young people are still growing. Longer hours and the harder conditions of business, compared with school, are a further tax. Right feeding is most important at this time.

There is a helpful booklet, just published, called "How to plan meals for children from 12 to 17 years of age." Why not send a postcard for it to the Ministry of Food, Food Advice Division, London, W.1 ?

Meantime, here are some pointers for you :

Breakfast

Always give some builder (milk, or dried eggs, or fish, fresh or canned) and some energiser (porridge, fried potatoes or bread). Rushing out on an empty stomach is bad for everyone; especially for growing youngsters.

Mid-day Meal

Impress upon young workers the need for them to have a real good meal, *including greens or a salad*, at mid-day. If they cannot come home, persuade them to go to their canteen or a British Restaurant if there's one near them. Buns and tea are all very well for 'elevenses' or tea-time, but *not* for the mid-day meal. If you put up packed meals, remember that each meal should include : (1) a builder; (2) a protector, such as fruit, when you can get it, a raw vegetable salad in a container, or salad sandwiches; (3) energy food, which generally looks after itself in bread, pastry, turnover, cake, etc.

> **HERE IS A SUGGESTION FOR ONE PACKED MEAL**
>
> Turnover filled with sausage meat, cooked dried peas, herbs, parsley, and chopped leek or onion. Raw cabbage salad in a screw-top jar. Oatmeal scones and jam.

Evening Meal

Here again, try to get in a builder, a protector, and an energiser. For example, an omelette or scrambled eggs, made with dried eggs is a first-class builder. Add some lightly cooked green vegetables or a salad — some watercress or mustard and cress is excellent — and some fried potatoes or bread and margarine and you have a perfect meal. So easy to prepare, too, and a boon if you have to return from your own work to cook. *For a bed-time drink,* try soup sometimes for a change.

GRIST TO THE MILL

"Purl one, slip one, knit three", dreams the knitter in careful reiteration throughout the night. The sleeping bridge-player mutters and worries over impossible "hands", and lost opportunities to "double". But in Jane's nightmare she sees row upon row of gigantic boxes, each one filled with a heartbreaking jumble of old tins, paper, bones, cardboard, rags and metal. A label on each box says "To be sorted", and dismay falls upon her, for does she not remember, even in her sleep, that she is the collector of salvage for her district, and that *she* must do the sorting ?

Once a month, in rain or shine, Jane sets out in her "7", trailer attached, to badger the housewives in our village and district to produce their waste material. And once every four weeks (or six, or eight, there's no knowing !) comes a man and a lorry to pick up Jane's sorted salvage and take it away to the hungry factories and workshops.

All is grist to Jane's mill except used wall-paper. "I've told you, Mrs. Beck, that I will not take your wall-paper scrapings. They contain something which makes them of no value for the manufacture of *anything*." Considering the number of times I have heard her tell the villagers this, I thought her mild exasperation showed admirable restraint. But Mrs. Beck was unimpressed. "Ay, I ken weel ye've telt me,'. she replied dourly, "but I thowt ye'd mebbe oblige by takin' it a' awa'. Yon kitling fair sneezes when she curls up on 't in t' corner, and the bairns cough fit to bust theirsels when they cut t' bit roses oot t' mak' li'le picters."

"It never occurred to you to *burn* it, I suppose, Mrs. Beck ?" asked Jane, stowing the great sack, with an air of repression, into the back of the trailer.

One farm always has bones for us—not well-boiled, naked bones, with shining smooth surfaces, but greasy, evil-smelling things, to which meat still clings. Some time ago, before we were honoured by visits from the lorry and the man, Jane had to deliver her modest cwt. of bones every month at the premises of the nearest knacker. The first time she went she reluctantly made her way through what seemed like hundreds of carcases and rivers of blood to where she found the man she sought. He looked at her contribution with amusement. "I'll give you 2s. 6d. for that lot, but ", with a twinkle in his eye, " I usually buy them by the ton, you know."

Jane dismisses her bones with a wrinkled nose and " I just make myself remember that each one is a nail in Adolf Hitler's coffin."

Nearly every house produces at least one sack of paper, always mixed with cardboard, of course. It is part of this war-work of Jane's to separate the two when she gets them to her sorting room. One day, nearly everyone we visited gave us paper, and the trailer was piled high with sacks. "Only a wishful thinker would call the mouths of those sacks safely shut," I warned Jane, "and the ropes look none too secure." "We'll risk it," she laughed, so we did, and off we went. On the road over the fell, the harsh helm wind enticed our paper with wild, persuasive fingers, and soon the fell-side was white with flying scraps, dancing with their windy liberator in gay abandon. For one wicked, fleeting moment Jane toyed with the idea of securing what remained of our load, and letting the rest blow where it listed over Westmorland. But Jane is a Guider and has strong anti-litter principles (even on a fell-side), so she gave the order to recover salvage. Now, when one has reached a comfortable middle age, one does not chase paper in a high wind with any degree of grace or dignity, so I was thankful that the setting was not Bond Street. I am glad to say that, since then, Jane's method of fastening the mouths of sacks has improved enormously.

Jane wonders why so many fire-tongs become decrepit before their time. Poor, pathetic things, with dejected grips like flaccid hand-shakes. She has collected some sixteen in a year.

Kind old Mrs. Burn sometimes produces bundles of rags. "Joe, he says t' me, ' ye cud get Tom Murphy t' tak' them clouts and gie ye mebbe twa-three pence for them ', but I telt him we mun hae tanks to beat they Germans, and th' lass mun hae a' my pieces when she ca's."

On the way home Jane loves to dwell on the happy days when she will have lost her job. "We shall be able to use a whole newspaper to light the fire," she says dreamily. "I shall eat toffees and throw the papers with easy nonchalance into the flames. Flopsy shall have her bones and she may bury them all over the garden in dozens if she so desires. As for tins—tins with their nasty, jagged edges and unsavoury insides—they may mount and mount on the ash-heap and who is to mind ? And," as firm hands steer her miscellaneous load through her home gate, and eyes brighten in joyful anticipation, " I shall never again touch a second-hand rag as long as I live."

KATHARINE DOBBS

Where it goes . . .

6 *old bills make* 1 *washer for a shell.*

1 *envelope makes* 50 *cartridge wads.*

1 *9-inch enamelled saucepan makes a bayonet.*

2 *3-pint "tin" kettles make a steel helmet.*

1 *broken garden fork plus a* 10½-*inch enamelled pail makes a tommy gun.*

2 *4-inch flat irons make* 6 *hand grenades.*

6¼ *lbs. rubber makes an airman's dinghy.*

8¼ *lbs. rubber makes a Mae West stole.*

1 *ton of mixed rags makes* 250 *battle dresses and* 13 *Army tents.*

300,000 *tons of kitchen waste maintains* 15,000 *pigs.*

Every pound of bones (except fish bones), after cooking, contains enough fat to provide 2 *ozs. Glycerine which makes double its weight of Nitro-glycerine, a very high explosive; also* 2 *ozs. glue for aircraft work, and the rest is ground down for feeding stuffs for animals and poultry.*

. . . . . DON'T BE SELFISH WITH IT —

SHE STOOPS TO "CONKER"

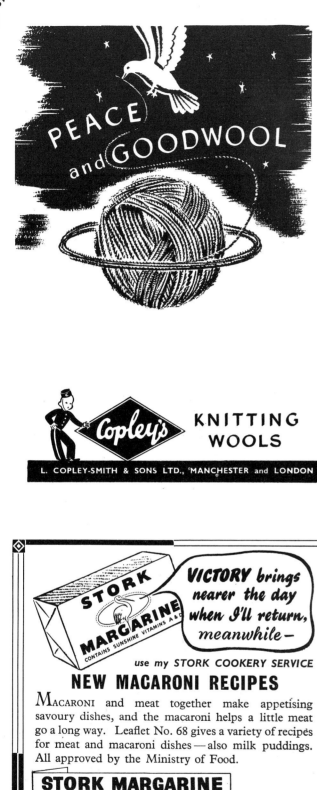
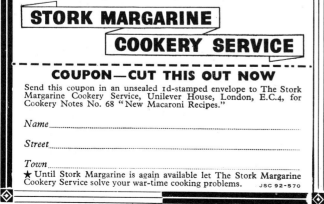
POST-WAR FAMILY ADJUSTMENTS

VE DAY has come and gone and now we are looking forward to VA Day, when we can all share the rejoicing over total victory everywhere. But many families will be having private rejoicings before then, on the happy day when husband, son, sweetheart, wife or daughter returns home after months or even years of separation.

Unfortunately many have found already that these homecomings are not without their difficulties. After the excitement and joy of the first meeting there is sometimes disappointment and resentment. A woman may find that her husband is changed. He has new ideas, new enthusiasms. There may even be a suspicion of criticism in the way that he regards her efforts in the home. He may talk, at what seems unnecessary length, of the food he has been eating elsewhere, of the fun he has had and the things he misses. A daughter returning home from the factory, too, may seem different. She, too, will have acquired different standards, she may show that she finds home life dull and has no wish to share home duties and responsibilities with her mother. The wife and mother who is not prepared for these changes may find herself growing resentful and angry. And her anger may easily find an outlet in words which will call forth equally angry retorts; the joy of the reunion is soured by quarrels and bickerings.

Usually such misunderstandings will be superficial and will pass in a week or two. But in some cases they will last longer and may even be permanent if mutual understanding and tolerance is not shown.

Changes in Outlook

The most important thing is to realize that all of us have changed in the last five years. No one, no matter how peaceful and undisturbed his life, can live for five years without changing to some degree—even though he may merely become more set in old opinions and attitudes. But millions who, during the war, have been away from home for years have changed in the opposite direction. They have been shaken up, both mentally and emotionally. They have met lots of different people—people from the other end of England and even from the other end of the world. They have met new ideas, new ways of looking at things, new customs. They have met people with different religious and political views. They have discovered new ways of enjoying themselves. Some of the new things they have learned you may not approve of. But a thing is not bad simply because it is new; there may be something in some of their new points of view if only you stop to listen and consider. At any rate, do not fall into the error of thinking that because their ideas have changed they are criticizing you. Remember that when we have made a discovery for ourselves we want to share it with our friends—and that is what they are trying to do. They will feel hurt and snubbed if you dismiss all that they say with irritation and resentment.

Boredom after War Excitement

Boredom is another problem that has to be faced. Most of the folk who have been away during the war have been leading, for good or ill, more exciting lives than are possible in peacetime. When they come home they are very likely to complain of the dullness of their life, particularly if they return to quiet country villages. This, too, in most cases will be only a passing phase, but it is very understandable and needs to be met with sympathy. It can have one permanently good effect in that it may stimulate more people to work for the establishment of Community Centres where social activities, dancing, concerts, film shows, whist drives, discussions and lectures can be enjoyed by men and women together in even the most remote corners of the country.

Mutual Understanding

If family life is to be resumed after the war without conflict and distress, it must be on a basis of sympathy and tolerance. Don't expect to pick up the threads just where you dropped them. Particularly where a husband and wife are concerned it may be necessary to go back a bit—to get a little nearer to your courting attitude, where you weren't quite so sure of each other and couldn't afford to take things for granted, but rather set out to please and to win the other's affection. All but the most fundamental difficulties (which would probably have arisen, war or no war) can be overcome where there is affection, sympathy and tolerance.

K. M. CATLIN,
Educational Psychologist, Central Council for Health Education
(on behalf of the Education and Public Questions Sub-Committee).

– 1945 –

Are *You* Telling *Me?*

Major Radcliffe gives some excellent advice to husbands and wives on settling down to home life after demobilization.

"'ERE! Oo's supposed to be telling their experiences?" Those few words beneath a recent drawing in *Punch* drew humorous attention to a very possible source of friction and misunderstanding between husbands and wives who have been parted from one another during the war.

The drawing showed a soldier, surrounded by his war trophies, gazing indignantly at his wife and children, who with intense faces and outspread arms, are clearly far more interested in telling him of their bomb experiences than in listening to his adventures. It is easy enough, as one looks at the soldier's face, to imagine his hurt feelings. For months, perhaps for years, he has been looking forward to this moment, when he would tell the tale of his war adventures to his admiring and breathlessly attentive family, for whose dear sakes he has endured so much. He has in all probability taken endless pains and broken many regulations in order to bring home the war trophies as dramatic illustrations to his tale—and now the great moment has fallen flat—they are neither interested nor listening—they are telling him!

HE WASN'T THE ONLY ONE

It is easy enough, too, to understand and sympathize with the woman's feelings. All through the raids, perhaps, she wrote bravely and cheerfully to her husband, minimizing the dangers in order to save him from anxiety, and now she feels that she cannot wait another minute without telling him all that she has been through while he has been away—or, perhaps, she did mean to let him speak first, and then, because he seemed to think that he was the only one who had really been through it, she just had to burst out with her tale to make him realize things.

Well! There may be nothing very serious in a single episode like this, and we will certainly hope that the couple of Mr. Punch's imagination soon found a happy solution to their dilemma and that no lasting hurt remained. On the other hand, a misunderstanding of this kind could very well be the forerunner of many others, which would lead to bitter recriminations between a husband and wife and prevent them from ever really coming together again. So it is right that the full lesson of the drawing should be understood. That lesson lies, I think, not in the obvious problem of who should tell their adventures first, but in the far deeper one of the difficulty of people appreciating experiences which they have not themselves had.

WE WANT THEM TO REALIZE

It is natural that we should like people to appreciate our efforts, and even more natural that we should like those whom we love to do so. To the returning serviceman, the applause and admiration of his wife means far more than any other person's praise, and similarly the woman longs for her husband to understand all that she has done in his absence, all the more, perhaps, if her part has been the undramatic, but most heroic one, of keeping the home going. This understanding of each other's war effort will be made more difficult when, as will often be the case, both have minimized their dangers and difficulties in their letters in order to keep the other from worrying.

Yet it must be done, and for those who love one another the way should present no insuperable difficulties. Let them, as was wisely suggested in a previous article on the subject, go back to their courting days and find out about one another again by listening and talking to each other as they did when they were first getting acquainted.

Then only will they be able to understand and appreciate properly not only what each has done in the war, but, far more important, what the war has done to each. Strengthened by the knowledge and mutual understanding, and with their love refreshed by the mutual pleasure of courting, they will be fully ready to resume the adventure of married life, gainers rather than losers from the years of separation.

R.A.C.R.

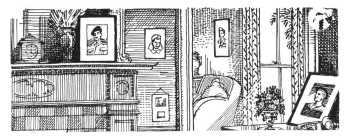

THE PHOTOGRAPHS ARE WATCHING

On the mantelpiece
in the parlour, on the piano,
on the sideboard—
a boy in a beret
a pretty nurse in her white cap,
a youth with wings,
a sailor with H.M.S.
on his hatband:
'Not home yet?'
'No, he's out East.'
'In India.' 'In Germany.'

The war is not over—yet
not over in many and many
a home . . .
Let us not therefore
behave thoughtlessly.
Let us prepare a better
homeland for all and give
thanks that Victory has
brought us the chance to
do what our affections and
our duty require of us.

THE BEACHES ARE CLEARED! These have been hard years for children. They have missed so much that *we* once enjoyed. Let us now build for them a land and a life worth having. When the Jap is beaten there will be much to do and our savings will be vital. For the children's sake

GIVE THANKS BY SAVING

CHAPTER FOUR
Food and Farming

HOME & COUNTRY

MARCH 1955   THE W.I. MAGAZINE   FOURPENCE
VOLUME 37 NUMBER 3   NORTHERN EDITION

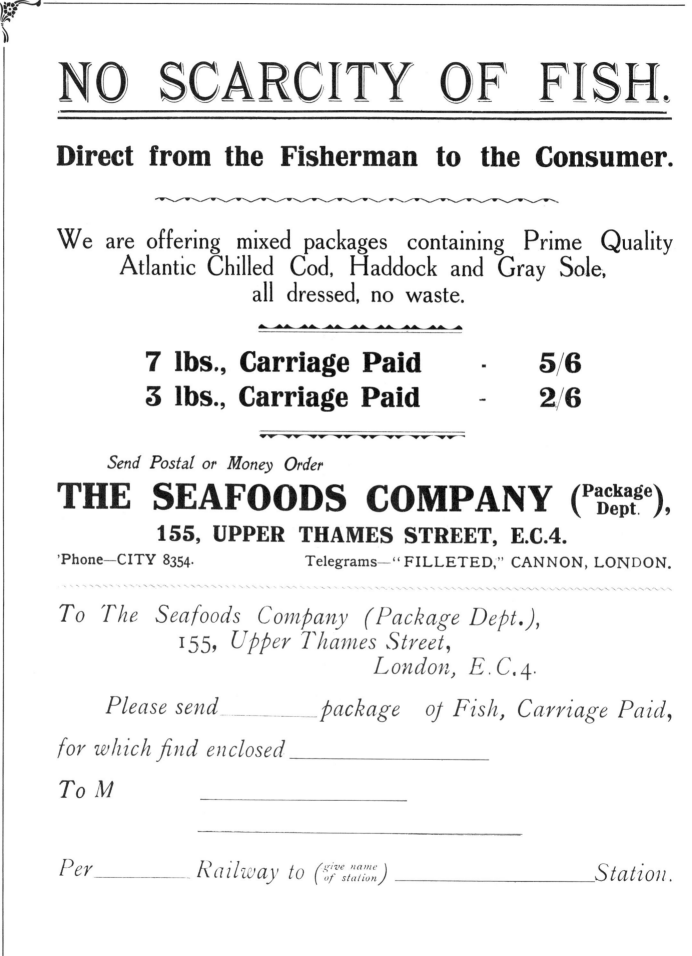

NO SCARCITY OF FISH.

Direct from the Fisherman to the Consumer.

We are offering mixed packages containing Prime Quality Atlantic Chilled Cod, Haddock and Gray Sole, all dressed, no waste.

7 lbs., Carriage Paid   -   5/6

3 lbs., Carriage Paid   -   2/6

Send Postal or Money Order

THE SEAFOODS COMPANY (Package Dept.),

155, UPPER THAMES STREET, E.C.4.

'Phone—CITY 8354.   Telegrams—"FILLETED," CANNON, LONDON.

To The Seafoods Company (Package Dept.),
    155, Upper Thames Street,
                    London, E.C.4.

Please send_____package of Fish, Carriage Paid,

for which find enclosed _____

To M   _____

            _____

Per_____ Railway to (give name of station) _____Station.

THE HARVEST OF THE HEDGEROWS

B. J. WILLANS

Now that the greater part of the community relies for so many table dainties on the tinned and preserved goods supplied by grocers and other stores, there is a likelihood that in a comparatively few years, many of our native fruits and their uses will be neglected and forgotten. This would be a great pity, because wild fruits have flavours and qualities distinct from the cultivated varieties and, though small in size, grow very abundantly in favourable districts.

Not all country dwellers possess fruit gardens, yet they disregard the fact that there is an appreciable harvest to be gathered from the hedgerows.

Early in the summer there is the wild gooseberry in its green state (usually unnoticed except by the children and, later on, by the birds), from which tarts and preserves can be made as tasty as those made from the larger garden fruit. The wild red currant can be found in some districts, but the produce of these bushes is small and scanty. Wild strawberries growing on the hedge banks furnish a dainty dessert fit for a fairy banquet and are sometimes plentiful enough for common mortals' food.

If we roam on the moors, we may fill our baskets or cans with blaeberries (bilberries or whortleberries—the name varies in different counties), and the less well-known bearberries.

In June the hedgerows are white with the sweet-scented blossom of the elder tree which is good for flavouring custards and jellies. The method used is to tie the flowers in a muslin bag and boil in milk or syrup as desired. The rich juiced elderberry makes a delicious addition to stewed apples and is the source of the old-fashioned elderberry wine, still popular in some country households.

Wild cherries, the fruit of the tree which in its bridal-dress of spring blossoms is so charming to the eye, are a good deal below the normal size of those grown in our orchards, but are fully as luscious, as the birds know well.

Children and grown-ups enjoy gathering wild raspberries and nutting excursions into the hazel thickets in autumn and the thorny excitement of " blackberrying." The school authorities in the northern counties often grant the scholars a special day's holiday known as "Blackberry day." Bramble jelly, tarts and wine are the pleasant results of these happy expeditions.

The sloe is used commercially in the production of sloe-gin. Wild plum and bullace make good preserves.

When the crab-apples fall from the tree and have been touched by the frost, the wise housewife makes the crab-apple jelly for her winter tea-table. In Scotland and the north of England, the berry of the mountain-ash or rowan tree is employed to make a jelly that is an agreeable change from the red currant jelly eaten with mutton and venison.

The haws or berries of the hawthorn are used in the same way and, in spite of the meagre quantity of edible matter around the stony core, this fruit in its raw state is often eaten too freely by children.

The wild pear is too austere a fruit to be of any economic value. The carefully prepared conserve of the scarlet " hips " of the dog-rose (for every trace of the hairy inner layer must be removed), is considered efficacious as a remedy for sore throats.

Beneath the hedgerows grow the nettles which in spring and early summer are ready for making nettle beer, while the young shoots boiled, are eaten in the form of " nettle pudding." A wayside plant frequently found in the vicinity of old monastic establishments, is the mercury goose-foot or " Good King Henry," the leaves of which, in some districts, are boiled and eaten like spinach. The plant can be transplanted to the kitchen garden. It is easily identified by the white powdery substance on its under leaf.

In spring " cresses from the brook " may be gathered and a sweet wine distilled from the pale golden blossoms of the cowslips that make beautiful those fields from which later on will be gathered the harvest of mushrooms, the only fungi that the Britisher ventures to add to his menu.

Above: Christmas market in Ningwood and Shalfleet WI, Isle of Wight, 1933

Above: School for Produce Leaders Guild, 1942

HAY-BOX COOKERY

AT THE PRESENT MOMENT many housekeepers, especially country dwellers, are faced with problems never experienced before. They have to arrange for the evacuees under their care as well as for their own households. Let us consider hay-box cookery, an economy practised for years by thrifty Norwegian housewives

TO MAKE A HAY-BOX, secure a strong, well-made box—a Tate's sugar case is to be recommended—in good condition. Line it inside with strong brown paper, cardboard or newspaper. The box must have a well-fitting lid; secure it by two hinges at the back and a staple and hasp in front. If a spare length of American cloth or similar material is available, use it to cover the outside. Now decide what kind of saucepans are to be used. The enamelled camp kettles which have milk-can lids are most convenient as being easy to lift in and out, but the humble jam jar, if covered with a saucer, which should be weighted, is not to be despised. Tin and iron saucepans are *not* suitable for use in a hay-box, as food left in them for some hours is liable to spoil.

Having decided on the kind of saucepans, begin to pack the box, with hay, pressing it tightly down, for some distance up the box. Then place the saucepans exactly where they are to go, and pack firmly all round with hay until the top of the saucepans is reached. Then remove the pans, put weights on the packing, and, after shutting down the lid of the box, leave it for two or three days, when the packing will have sunk somewhat; then add more packing, making it very solid. Some material, such as ticking, should now be drawn tightly over the packing (leaving holes into which to fit the pans) and be nailed to the box. Have a cushion, made of ticking and packed as tightly as possible with hay, to fit the inside of the lid.

Place the finished hay-box close to the range, fire or gas cooker on which the food to be finished by hay-box is brought to boiling point. The pan must be boiling to the centre, must be filled as full as possible without boiling over, and must be transferred as quickly as possible to the hay-box.

FISH IS EASILY COOKED the hay-box way. Take a piece of a solid kind of fish such as hake or cod, weighing about two pounds. Let it simmer gently for about ten minutes on the stove; then put it at once into the hay-box where it can continue to cook for two to three hours. It will not spoil if left in longer. A good beef stew is prepared by cutting up one pound of stewing steak into pieces—not too small. Put it into a pan with an onion cut in slices, two carrots, a turnip, a little rice or tapioca, seasoning, and water to cover. Let the stew cook very gently on the stove for about three-quarters of an hour; then—while very hot—put into the hay-box and let it remain for about four hours.

To boil a piece of beef, allow rather longer time per pound than when cooking entirely on the stove. Half an hour to the pound and half an hour over is a good proportion. Let it cook for half the time allowed on the stove; put it into the box and leave it as long as possible—the longer the better.

THE BREAKFAST PORRIDGE is delicious cooked in the hay-box. Allowing four large breakfastcupfuls of water to one of oatmeal, bring the mixture to the boil overnight on the stove. When the porridge is boiling right to the centre—in about five minutes—put it into the box and leave it all night.

Fruits, soups and stock are particularly good when cooked in the hay-box, the first named retaining all their flavour and goodness. The hay-box is a great economy when using bones for stock, the slow, gradual cooking extracting all goodness from the bones and giving a stock that, when cold, is a thick jelly. Break up the bones, put them into a pan with enough cold water; bring to the boil and put at once into the box.

JESSIE J. WILLIAMS, M.C.A.

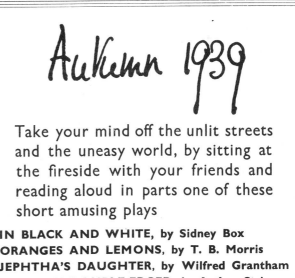

MINISTRY **MoF** OF FOOD

FOOD FACTS

ON THE POTATO FRONT

POTATOES are home grown : we can eat as many as we like without using one inch of cargo space. Potatoes are good for us : they give us energy and bodily warmth and are what scientists call "protective" foods — that is, they help us to ward off infections. And remember—potatoes shouldn't always mean *boiled* potatoes. There's no end to the delicious ways in which they can be served.

Can you Cook Potatoes?

Before you answer "Yes" just read quickly through these questions.

1. Do you always *scrub* your potatoes rather than peel them ? (Nearly one-fifth of the value of the potato is lost if it's peeled.)

2. Do you conserve the goodness of your potatoes by baking or steaming them whenever possible ? (If you haven't a steamer, a colander put over a pan of boiling water and covered with the pan lid will do.)

3. When boiling potatoes, do you boil them only for 10-15 minutes, then drain, cover with a cloth and the lid and then let them cook in their own steam for about 20 minutes, to keep them whole and floury ?

4. Do you keep your baked potatoes nice and floury by bursting them gently when they are done, and returning them to the oven for a minute to let the steam escape ?

Potato Salad

The golden rule about Potato Salad is "Mix warm and eat cold."

Steam some potatoes in their skins, peel and cut them into small chunks while still warm, add a finely chopped raw onion and whatever kind of salad dressing you like best. Mix these together thoroughly with a wooden spoon. When the salad is cold, add a good sprinkling of chopped parsley.

Stuffed Baked Potatoes

Large baked potatoes can be stuffed in a great variety of ways. Here are three suggestions :

1. Cut the potato in half length-wise, scoop out most of the inside and mix in a basin with pepper and salt and about 2 ozs. of grated cheese. Pile the mixture into the potato cases, sprinkle the tops with a little more grated cheese and return to the oven to brown.

2. Mix the scooped-out potato with about 4 ozs. of cooked meat or fish, finely chopped. Season with salt and pepper, pile into the cases, sprinkle with chopped parsley and reheat in the oven.

3. Mix the scooped-out potato with any left-over cooked vegetables and serve as above.

Potato Pastry

There's no end to the things you can make out of potato. Try this recipe some time. You'll need :—

4 ozs. sieved, cooked potatoes, ½ teaspoonful salt, 8 ozs. plain flour, 3 ozs. cooking fat, 2 teaspoonfuls baking powder.

Sieve the flour with the baking powder and salt. Rub the fat into the flour, add the potato and rub in lightly. Mix to a very dry dough with a small quantity of cold water. Knead well with the fingers and roll out. This is delicious with either sweet or savoury dishes.

Cautionary Tale !

Those who have the will to win
Cook potatoes in their skin,
Knowing that the sight of peelings
Deeply hurts Lord Woolton's feelings

Remember to turn on the wireless at 8.15 every morning to hear useful hints and recipes.

THE MINISTRY OF FOOD, LONDON, S.W.1

Off the ration sweets !

This is how to make delicious Turkish Delight

2 oz. SPA GELATINE
¾ pint HOT WATER
5 oz. SUGAR
Juice of 1 FRESH LEMON

COCHINEAL
RASPBERRY ESSENCE
1 oz. chopped ALMONDS
1 oz. chopped SULTANAS
CORNFLOUR

Mix SPA, sugar, 1 teaspoon cornflour and hot water in saucepan. Heat gently until sugar is dissolved. Boil for 15 minutes. Add few drops of cochineal, raspberry essence and lemon juice. Pour into greased tin. When cool but not set, stir in nuts and fruit gently. Leave until firm. Cut in squares and roll in cornflour. There are 20 other attractive gelatine ideas in the Spa Recipe Book—price 2d from grocers and stores or post free from address below.
SPA Gelatine—2/3d per ½ lb ; 4/- per 1 lb. tin.

"spa" gelatine

B. YOUNG & CO. LTD., 83 SPA WORKS, GRANGE ROAD, S.E.1

BISCUITS KEEP YOU GOING

Issued by the Cake and Biscuit Manufacturers War Time Alliance to remind you that although biscuits are still scarce, they remain the most compact energy food.

SUGAR FOR JAM

DEAR EDITOR,—The Minister of Food has announced we are to have a double jam ration in October without the alternative choice of 1 lb. sugar. This is not much help to the real countrywoman who would much rather have the sugar to make her own fruit into jam, especially blackberries. We are told the ration is to be in plum; most of us will have made our plum jam in August.

Yours sincerely,
N. BAGSHAWE
County Secretary
Brecon County Federation of Women's Institutes.

CHERRY PLUM JAM

DEAR EDITOR,—The pectin content of the Cherry Plum (*Prunus cerasifera*) varies greatly from season to season and even from place to place. The sample which I tested this year would not have made a well-set jam. Yet Mrs. Gilman and another reader report invariable success. It all goes to show that this jam should only be attempted by an expert.

Yours faithfully,
PHILIP HARBEN

" THE HIGH SPOT OF THE JOURNAL "

DEAR EDITOR,—The recipe given by Mr. Philip Harben in HOME AND COUNTRY for a strong concentrated jam is excellent. I have used it recently in more than one combination. I wonder if he would be kind enough to give some biscuit recipes (using a limited amount of fat) including one suitable for glazing with such jam.

I should like to say thank you for all the very useful recipes he has given us during the war and since—for me they are the high spot of the journal.

Yours faithfully,
C. ALEXANDER
Rowlands Gill W.I., Co. Durham.

THE DOMESTIC PIG KEEPER

The Minister of Food is urging country dwellers to supplement their rations by keeping a pig. W.I. members who have facilities and are sure they can feed a pig adequately are advised to write to F. Russell, Secretary, Small Pig Keepers Council, 64 Bell Street, Henley-on-Thames, asking for form NPC 67/2, and for the address of the nearest pig club.

General Regulations. 1. Two pigs only may be killed in any one year for home consumption. If more are kept instructions as to disposal must be obtained from the Food Office or the Regional Officer of S.P.K.C.

2. Pigs must be kept on the owner's premises or on premises rented by him.

3. Licence to slaughter must be obtained from the Food Office on the prescribed form not less than 14 days before the proposed slaughter. Note—This form is *not* the licence.

4. The licence must be handed to the slaughterer before the pig is killed.

Regulations affecting members of pig clubs. 1. A monthly ration of seventy pounds meal is obtainable through the club secretary and must be applied for at least 3 weeks before beginning of the month in question.

2. A member may keep not more than four pigs during the year.

3. Pigs must be looked after by the owner or a member of his household.

4. All movement of pigs must be notified to the club secretary.

Regulations affecting domestic pig keepers who are not members of pig clubs. 1. A monthly ration of fifty-six pounds meal is obtainable from the County Agricultural Executive Committee.

2. The owner is not restricted as to number of pigs kept.

General Advice. 1. The novice should ask an expert to buy his pig. The price today for a three-months-old pig will be about £6.

2. Members are strongly advised to join a pig club, to insure their pig through the club, and obtain particulars of veterinary assistance available.

3. In case of accident or other reason for immediate slaughter, a veterinary surgeon or police officer should be sent for.

4. Breeds vary in popularity according to district but many think the Wessex Saddleback crossed with a Large White boar gives the best results for bacon. If two pigs have been kept together they should be disposed of at the same time.

5. The meal ration must be supplemented, e.g. by *boiled* swill, cooked potatoes and certain non-rationed foods. Expert advice should be obtained on the value of these before purchase.

6. Recommended: S.P.K.C. Bulletin, 2d. monthly; *Feeding the Pig*, S.P.K.C. Free Leaflet, No. 3, and *Pig Keeping* by A. Brett, 1s. 6d.

D.S.T.

Spud-Bashing

TWO weeks spent at an Agricultural Camp last year has, of course, made me an expert in the ungentle art of potato-lifting. This year I'll spend my holiday at the same job—I like it ! I tried other varieties of the hard labour open to one who has nervously offered to lend a hand on the land, but potatoes remain my real love, for in spite of the initial suffering, it is quite remarkable how the operation takes hold of one.

Spud-bashers, as we call ourselves, are a brotherhood apart. We evolve our own language (we talk of little else but potatoes) and our own varying techniques. All other differences—of age, sex, race, class—are forgotten in the absorbing discussion of how to beat the tractor driver to it.

Bus loads of spud-bashers, decked out in their oldest clothes, arrive in the morning from their camp, and wander on to a vast field of potatoes. Grabbing a partner (with the prayer that he or she will prove strong, tireless and co-operative) the amateur agricultural labourer is allotted his pitch on the outer perimeter of the field. A horrid chugging noise is then heard—the tractor is warming up.

When potatoes are lifted early in the season, it is necessary first of all to pull the green tops off. So the first operation is for each partner to stand astride the furrow at opposite ends and work inwards, pulling furiously and flinging the tops as far away as possible, usually in the teeth of a gale. The veteran who knows the ropes rushes on to the field as soon as he arrives, and tries to pull several rows of tops before the tractor starts its rounds. He is then in a strong position, having so many rows in hand, and can work at a decreasing rate all day.

THE TRACTOR SETS THE PACE

The tractor then starts its inexorable round. A plough attached behind it churns up the potatoes, and the devotees, some bent double, some squirming along on their stomachs, scramble in its wake with baskets, which when full are emptied into sacks. When the last potato has been picked up, the labourers rush to pull another row of tops. The dreaded sound is then heard—the tractor is on them again.

The tractor driver, being paid 2d. per sack bonus, keeps on grinding round the field. Sabotage is, of course, widely cultivated. The couple at the end, where he has to turn and sometimes re-fuel, have the greatest scope for this. They offer him cigarettes, they admire his dog, they ask him technicalities about his tractor—anything to slow him up so that the weak couple half-way along may have a chance to catch up.

Character soon shines forth from each spud-basher. There is the conscientious, painstaking type, scuffling about in the soil to make sure not one potato has been left, shaking the earth off each one. And there is the man of enormous physique, thrashing his way through the tops like a beast through the jungle, then gathering up the potatoes at tremendous speed, losing about half. He is often to be found at full length resting, wondering why the others can't keep up. There is the inevitable funny man, the statistician, and the factory girl who thought she was coming to a holiday camp, and considers that loud-speakers blaring " Music While You Work " might have been fixed up. And there is the logical foreigner, who can't imagine why all farmers don't pay on piece-work. How can they expect good results if they pay so much per hour whether one works well or ill ?

At the end of the first day the back will ache as it has never ached before, but at the end of the week all pain will have worn off, and everyone feels and looks as fit as a fiddle —glowing too, with gratification at the thought of a worth-while job well done.

Yes, I shall most certainly go back to the spuds again this year.

ROSALIE THOMAS

ON THE KITCHEN FRONT

How to eat wisely in wartime . .

So much of our food comes from overseas, using valuable shipping space, that care and skill in its choice and preparation is now an urgent national necessity.

TO eat wisely in wartime we should vary our meals as much as possible. There may be a shortage of some of the foods we usually buy but there will always be others to take their place. To keep fit and well we should choose something from each of the four groups below, every day.

THE FOUR FOOD GROUPS

(1) BODY BUILDING FOODS :

Milk, cheese, eggs, meat, fish.

(2) ENERGY FOODS : *Bacon and ham, bread, butter or margarine, cheese, dried fruit, dripping or suet or lard, honey, oatmeal, potatoes, rice or sago, sugar.*

(3) PROTECTIVE FOODS

(Group 1) : *Milk, butter or margarine, cheese, eggs, liver, herrings or salmon (canned or fresh).*

(4) PROTECTIVE FOODS

(Group 2) : *Potatoes, carrots, fruit (fresh or canned but not dried), green vegetables or salads, tomatoes, wholemeal bread.*

ISSUED BY THE MINISTRY OF FOOD

(53 D)

Why Not Keep a Goat?

WE ALL NOWADAYS want to make the best use we can of our holdings and to be more self-supporting. A good way to do both is to keep two or three goats, thus assuring ourselves of an ample milk supply. An average pedigree goat, weighing 130 to 140 lbs. will, if properly cared for, yield in milk in a fortnight the equivalent of her weight, and in a year 2,000 to 3,000 lbs., equalling 200 to 300 gallons.

Two goats are recommended for a start, because they are companionable animals and one, by herself, does not do well. On the other hand, do not keep too many. Goats readily respond to individual care, and can be made or marred by their management. Therefore begin cautiously and give time and thought to the enterprise, remembering that it is kindness and intelligence on the part of the owner that puts special " bloom " on the goat's appearance and an extra pint or two of milk into the bucket.

To get an immediate return, it is necessary to buy one goat that has borne a kid, but her companion may be either a kid or a goatling (a maiden goat, between one and two years old). They should be hornless and registered in the British Goat Society's Herd Book so that you may know that they come of " milky " stock. Beyond this, the actual breed does not matter, for there is nothing to choose in milking qualities between black, brown, and white. Pedigree goats need not be bred from every year, for a good milker will give a profitable yield for 20 months after kidding, so, by keeping two that are well bred, and breeding from them in alternate years, a useful milk supply can be maintained.

Before buying the goats, light airy and weatherproof accommodation must be provided for them. Possibly an existing shed can be converted; otherwise a new wooden stable must be erected. If space is scarce, adult goats can be tied in stalls, but loose boxes must be provided for kidding times and young kids. There must also be storage space for a few foodstuffs and a little bedding material.

For feeding, ample supplies of greens of all sorts are invaluable. Almost anything from the kitchen garden will be relished, if it is tied up and is fresh and clean. Profitable use can thus be made of pea and runner bean haulm, outside leaves and stems of cabbages, cauliflower, broccoli and brussels sprouts, overgrown spinach, also carrots, beetroots and artichokes. Lucerne and kale may also be grown, if space allows.

The amount of corn required for maintenance and production depends largely on the yield of the goat, the season of the year, and the amount of green food that is available. Normally, a gallon milker will want 3 lbs. of corn a day, made up to a dairy ration. She should also have plenty of hay—preferably clover or seeds—which helps to stimulate cudding.*

Grazing is not necessary for goats. If provided, it should be of the rough type, for they are browsers rather than grazers, and do not flourish on luscious dairy pastures. **They should never be tethered.** Anyone having goats and a limited acreage will get the best results from stall-feeding and providing a paved yard, preferably adjoining the stable, for daily exercise.

The milk is rich, wholesome, and easily digested. Goats are healthy animals and practically immune from tuberculosis. The milk, besides being excellent to drink, makes creamy milk puddings, butter, clotted cream, and cheese, while many a country wiseacre has declared with conviction, " I did not know what a good cup of tea was, till I kept my goats."

E. M. GRESLEY HALL.

---

* The British Goat Society publishes some excellent leaflets on small scale goat keeping (obtainable from the Secretary, The Cottage, Roydon, Diss, Norfolk), and beginners would be well advised to study the detailed information they give.

In the Kitchen

Hot Cakes for Cold Days

If you have a girdle, the first two recipes will interest you.

GIRDLE-SCONES. *1 lb. plain flour, ¼ teaspoon salt, 1 teaspoon syrup, if liked, 1 teaspoon bicarbonate of soda, 1¼ teaspoon cream of tartar, milk or buttermilk to mix.*

Method: Sieve flour, mix dry ingredients and make into a soft dough with milk. Turn on to a floured board and knead lightly. Handle as little as possible, pat or roll out to ¼ inch thick. Cut in four or in rounds, put on a hot dry girdle or plate, cook to a pale brown, turn to cook both sides.

PAN CAKES. *2 teacups plain flour, 2 teaspoons sugar, ¼ teaspoon salt, ¾ teaspoon cream of tartar, 1 teaspoon syrup, 1 egg, milk to mix.*

Method: Sieve dry ingredients into a basin, make a well in the centre, drop in egg and syrup, add a little milk, beat well together with a metal spoon, add milk to make mixture into a thick batter, just thick enough to drop from a spoon. Have girdle or hot plate **hot**, grease, and drop on spoonful of mixture. When surface rises in bubbles turn with a knife and brown on the other side.

The writer demonstrates Scotch girdle cookery in the open air.

GINGER SPONGE (this old Scots recipe contains no ginger). *¼ lb. butter or margarine, 1 cup sugar, 2 eggs, ½ teacup syrup, about 6 level tablespoons plain flour, 1 teaspoon spice and a little nutmeg if liked, ½ teaspoon bicarbonate of soda, ½ cup of milk.*

Method: Beat butter or margarine and sugar to a cream. To this add the beaten eggs, syrup, flour, and spice. Dissolve the bicarbonate of soda in the milk and use the milk to mix the ingredients, adding more milk if the mixture is too stiff. It should be like thick cream. Pour the mixture into 2 greased sandwich tins and bake 20 to 30 minutes in a moderate oven. When cold spread with butter icing or whipped cream.

– 1946 –

COLDS—WITHOUT LEMONS

I. I. H. ORAM.

During the lemonless, onionless wastes of last winter we knew for the first time how bleak could be the onset of a cold with neither of these comfortable remedies at hand. We shan't lack onions this year: but even onion milk has not the efficacy of the hot - lemon - drink - last - thing-at-night which used to work so magically.

This time I am determined that if the family *must* fall victims to other people's colds it shall not spend its hard-earned shillings on patent medicines.

The common cold is cursed far back in literature, and there was a time when lemons were inaccessible to most people. What, then, did

they do ? Here are some answers: and the country housev with herb garden and hedgerow at hand, is the lucky woman these days.

In *A Worcestershire Book*, produced by the Women's Institutes of that county, the section headed " Recipes and Ancient Remedies " tells of a cure for a cold. Boil a sprig of rosemary (obligingly an evergreen !) in half a pint of cider for fifteen minutes and drink it at bedtime as hot as possible. It is advisable to drink it when in bed as it causes great perspiration.

For colds, inflammation, etc., take a handful of elderflower and one of peppermint, put in a jug and pour over it 1½ pints of boiling water. Let it steep for thirty minutes on the hob. Strain and sweeten with black treacle or honey. Drink hot in bed. The more you drink the sooner will the cure be effected. (N.B. Four parts fresh herbs—one part dried.)

Coltsfoot Tea for Colds : 2 ozs. dried coltsfoot leaves. Boil in three gills of water for fifteen minutes. Sweeten with candy or honey. A wineglassful to be taken four times a day—half the quantity for children.

From another W.I. book, *Gleanings from Gloucestershire House-wives*, came a recipe needing no herbs.

For a Cold on the Chest : ½ pint best vinegar, ¼ oz. cayenne, ½ oz. saltpetre. Mix together in a bottle. Saturate a piece of flannel and rub on chest.

The chemist at the end of the road is a gentleman. When I showed him these recipes and asked his professional opinion of their merit, he batted never an injured eyelid towards his own neat rows of proprietary cold-chasers. Instead, he told me that the third on the list, the Coltsfoot Tea, was more use for coughs than colds: that the requisite herbs could easily be obtained from herbalists if not from chemists : and he contributed his own favourite, a really good—

Gloucestershire Cold Cure : Into a pint of hot draught cider stir a good teaspoonful of ground ginger. Make a bee-line (if you can) for bed. He also—

crowning courtesy—lent me a most precious book of his own. It is in early eighteenth-century hand-writing and is entitled *Choice Receipts in Phisick & Chymistry Being Experienced Medicines By Several who have Known the Benefit thereof. James Bristow His Hand Anno Domini 1721.*

James Bristow lived in spacious, if not squeamish, times. Alas, what avails in 1941 " a Remedy for a Cold ", which begins, " Take a Quart of Brandy of 1 shilling a quart " —or, for that matter, a recipe, irrelevant here, " For the humour in the Eyes: Recd. from a travailing woman," to cure which ailment unmentionable things must first be done to " a Quantity of House Snaills " !

Two at least of the recipes are fairly practicable—would we could have seen Mr. Bristow sampling the second !

Good for a Cold, and against ye flegm: Take Treacle, Sallad oyl, Brandy, & mix together: & take a little, well shaken together.

A Recipe for a Cough & Cold: Take half a peny worth of Rock allum in powder: and the same quantity of liquorish powder: viz half a peny worth & half a peny worth of Elecampane powder & mix it in a Little honey and take a Little on the top of a knife mornings and evenings.

(Modern equivalents—approximately ¼ oz. alum, ½ oz. each of liquorice and elecampane; honey up to ½ lb., as it can be spared.)

And now I can face that sinister first-tickle with equanimity. . . .

I shall rout it with rosemary.

Festive Meal Without Rations

THIS meal is really a stunt or *tour-de-force*. It was done originally to win a bet. But in the course of doing it I was able to prove to myself and to my challenger (who lost a cigar) the quite useful fact that it is actually possible to produce a slap-up meal, good enough to offer guests at Christmas or any other festive occasion, without touching any rationed food whatsoever. Not that one really needs to do this in practice ; but there is a type of over-punctilious guest who can be a positive " skeleton at the feast " with such remarks as " I'm eating all your precious rations "—and will even deprive you of the pleasures of a host by declining your invitation on those grounds. Here, then, is a meal which can be produced for as large a company as you like; and of which you can assure your guests that, though it cost you time and trouble (what worth-while piece of work does not ?) does not contain one single scrap of your, or anybody else's, rations.

THE MENU.
Gratin of Sea-Food and Mushrooms

Braised Goose, Spanish Style
Peas   Fried Onions   Fondant Potatoes
Port Wine Sauce

Apple Turnovers, Flaky Pastry

Ingredients required (for 8 people): Assorted sea-food as available; such things as mussels, prawns, escallops, soft roe, crab, etc., and a little plain white fish—to a total weight of about 1 lb. A few spoonfuls of white wine or cooking sherry (optional). Bread crumbs. A quart of olive oil (of which only an ounce or two will be used). ½ lb. fresh mushrooms. 1 goose—as fat as possible. Flour. A jar of olives. 1 large packet of frozen peas (if unprocurable substitute another vegetable and alter the menu). 2 lb. onions. 3 lb. potatoes. A little cooking port (optional). 2 lb. apples (Cox's Orange Pippins for choice). ¼ lb. jam. Herbs and seasoning. A little meat extract. 1 large carrot.

GRATIN OF SEA-FOOD AND MUSHROOMS. Cut large pieces into small, cook the assorted sea-food in a pint of fish stock or water containing (optional) a little white wine or sherry, adding a bay leaf and a pinch or two of mixed herbs. Put 2 oz. of olive oil in a saucepan and blend in 2 oz. of flour. Add the liquid the sea-food was cooked in, up to one pint, and boil to thicken. Range the sea-food in a fire-proof dish, cover with a layer of mushrooms thinly sliced (not peeled, merely washed) mask with the thick sauce, cover with fine bread crumbs and brown off in a hot oven.

BRAISED GOOSE, SPANISH STYLE. Cook the goose the day before, not in the oven but in liquid—water or stock. Geese, especially old and fat ones such as we need for this meal, are often tough; so give the bird long, slow cooking; 4 hours at least with the liquid below boiling point. Next day, when the liquid is cold, you will find set on top a good quantity (I have known a goose to yield as much as 3 lb.) of the most excellent fat, which is perfect for pastry making.

Next day take two quarts of the liquid the goose was cooked in and reduce it to one quart by rapid boiling in an open pan, cooking in it a large carrot and a few onions. Enrich the flavour with a little " meat " extract. With this make a quart of thick sauce, using 4 oz. of goose fat and 4 oz. flour for the roux. Flavour with port wine (optional), season, and add stoned olives. Carve the goose and re-heat in this sauce.

FROZEN PEAS. *On no account* follow the instructions on the packet, but thaw in a warm place and then bring to the boil in very little water—conservative method.

FRIED ONIONS. Slice thinly in rings, coat lightly with flour and deep fry in smoking oil.

FONDANT POTATOES. Cook in the oven, just like roast potatoes, but instead of using fat half cover them with goose stock containing an ounce or two of goose fat.

APPLE TURNOVERS, FLAKY PASTRY. *To make flaky pastry:* rub 1½oz. goose fat into 8 oz. flour, moisten with water, roll out into oblong 3 times as long as it is wide. Cover two-thirds with another 1½ oz. goose fat in dabs, fold in three, turn, roll out to oblong again; repeat twice more, thus using 6 oz. goose fat altogether. Roll out very thin. Cut into 6 in. rounds. Fill with layers of sliced apple, jam between the layers. Fold over, seal and bake.

You will probably have a fair amount of goose fat over, in which case you can, if you like, use it in place of the olive oil in the recipes.

PHILIP HARBEN

– 1949 –

Let's talk about XMAS FOOD

There won't be turkey on many tables this year ; but the Christmas atmosphere will be there and the children's eyes will sparkle at simple treats, served gaily. From what we know of you, you'll make your Christmas catering a grand success in spite of difficulties, and we're out to help you all we can. Here are a few suggestions of general interest from letters we have sent to correspondents. A Happy Christmas to you !

I'd like a recipe for Christmas pudding without eggs.

Mix together 1 cupful of flour, 1 cupful of breadcrumbs, 1 cupful of sugar, half a cupful of suet, 1 cupful of mixed dried fruit, and, if you like, 1 teaspoonful of mixed sweet spice. Then add 1 cupful of grated potato, 1 cupful of grated raw carrot and finally 1 level teaspoonful of bicarbonate of soda dissolved in 2 tablespoonfuls of hot milk. Mix all together (no further moisture is necessary), turn into a well-greased pudding basin. Boil or steam for 4 hours.

SOME HINTS FOR CHILDREN'S PARTY FOOD, PLEASE ?

Chocolate squares are popular. Melt 3 oz. margarine with two tablespoonfuls of syrup in a saucepan, mix in ½ lb. rolled oats and a pinch of salt. Blend well, and put in a greased, shallow baking tin, flattening the mixture smoothly. Bake for half an hour to 40 minutes in a moderate oven. Take out, and whilst still hot, grate over it a tablet of chocolate. The chocolate will melt with the heat, and can be spread evenly with a knife. Cut into squares and lift out.

Amusing little figures, cut from short-crust or biscuit dough, go down well. Roll the dough about ¼-inch thick. "People" can be made by cutting small rounds for heads, larger for bodies, strips for arms and legs; pinch  the various pieces of dough firmly together. Prick out eyes, noses, mouths, with currants. If you can draw a little or have a friend who can, make thin cardboard "patterns" of animals, lay them on the dough and cut round with a small sharp knife.

Chocolate coating for your Christmas cake. Mix together 3 tablespoonfuls of sugar with 2 tablespoonfuls of cocoa and 2 tablespoonfuls of milk. Stir, in a stout saucepan, over low heat until the mixture is thick and bubbly like toffee ; then, while hot, pour it over your cake.

A Christmassy sparkle is easy to give to sprigs of holly or evergreen for use on puddings and cakes. Dip your greenery in a strong solution of Epsom salts. When dry it will be beautifully frosted.

I'll miss my gay bowl of fruit on the Christmas table. Not if you have a bowl of salad in its place. Vegetables have such jolly colours — the cheerful glow of carrot, the rich crimson of beetroot, the emerald of parsley. And for health's sake you should have a winter salad with, or for, one meal a day. Here is a suggestion; it looks as delightful as it tastes.

Salad slices. Cut a thick round of wheatmeal bread for each person and spread with margarine. Arrange a slice of tomato in the centre of each slice and, if liked, put a sardine on top. Surround with circles of chopped celery, grated raw carrot, finely chopped parsley or spinach and grated raw beetroot on the edge. Sprinkle with a little grated cheese.

Let's talk about FOOD

*F*IRST *a word about the new National Wheatmeal Bread. It is nice and it is nourishing and it costs no more than white bread. Wheatmeal Bread is invaluable in times like these, when it is not always easy to get in other foods the vital nutrients and other elements essential to health, and which Wheatmeal Bread plentifully supplies.*

QUESTIONS YOU ASKED

I find difficulty in providing hot meals for my evacuee foster-children, who are at school all day, taking packed dinners, while my family return for their chief meal at midday.

A good way is to start supper with soup, varying the flavour to suit the children's fancy. A hearty vegetable soup, chock-a-block with carrots, potatoes, and other vegetables in season, thickened with oatmeal, is a good meal in itself. Make it in quantity when convenient and heat up as necessary. Slightly brown the vegetables in a little fat, then add stock or water and seasoning, and cook gently.

Can you give me some advice on foods for the expectant mother?

A *most* important food, for your own health and the development of the coming child, is milk. Although there is some restriction on ordinary household supplies of milk, there is no cut in the quantities allowed under the National Milk Scheme for expectant and nursing mothers and children under 5 years of age. Ask your local food office for particulars. Other foods you should have are butter or margarine (equal in health protection), oatmeal, wheatmeal bread, carrots, potatoes, greens, raw salads. Fish is good too ; especially herring and sardines, if they agree with you. Your meat ration is ample as long as you have plenty of milk.

★ ★ ★

FOOD FACTS

In the newspapers and Kitchen Front Wireless Talks every weekday morning at 8.15, contain many seasonable hints and recipes which you will find both interesting and helpful.

*Pat-a-loaf, pat-a-loaf
Baker's Man,
Bake me some Wheatmeal
As fast as you can :
It builds up my health
And its taste is so good,
I find that I like
Eating just what I should.*

Issued by The Ministry of Food.   (S.11)

PRESERVES FROM THE GARDEN

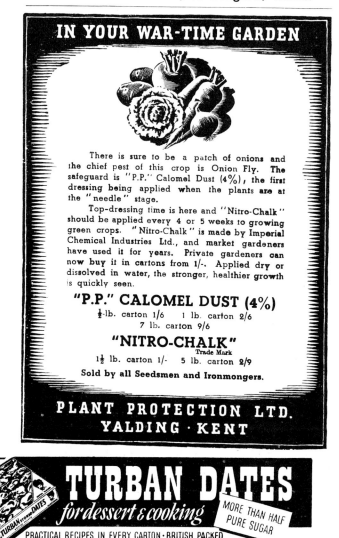

THE PENTECON
as illustrated complies with the Ministries' requirements

"Sterilizing should only be done in a pressure cooker fitted with a pressure gauge, otherwise correct temperatures are not assured."

—*Extract from Grow-more Bulletin No. 3, issued by the Ministry of Food and Ministry of Agriculture and Fisheries.*

SEND FOR PARTICULARS AND PRICES

PENTECON LIMITED

Hindle Street Works, Accrington, Lancs.

WORLD FOOD CRISIS AND THE W.I.s

No-one today can fail to be aware of the crisis which has developed in the world's supply of food, and particularly of wheat. From the daily stream of statistics and appeals two facts stand out. Owing to loss of crops through drought, floods and the devastation of war, the importing countries—chiefly Europe, India and China—are making bigger demands than ever on the producing countries—Canada, U.S.A., Argentine and Australia. Even by drawing upon their large carry-over stocks, the producing countries cannot hope to meet this demand in full.

If famine on a vast scale is to be averted every possible ton of wheat or rice has to be collected and shipped without delay to the needy countries. This means that the big wheat growing countries must become more economical in their use of this most important of all foods and must restrict the amount used for feeding to animals. Even so, the purely physical difficulties of transporting grain in such quantities from the inland agricultural areas of the United States and Canada to the seaboard are creating a major problem. The lives of many millions of people in the " hungry " countries depend upon the extent to which farmers in America can be persuaded to sell their wheat stocks now and move them quickly to the coast.

The problem for the "hungry" countries is how to make the most of whatever wheat reaches them—and it must be remembered that in point of fact we are one of the " hungry " countries—although not so unhappy as most others in Europe. This is where the Women's Institutes can do valuable work:

1. By not talking about or criticizing the darker loaf, but accepting this wholesome food without comment.
2. By seeing that all vegetable gardens and allotments are fully cultivated, especially with a view to winter supplies of fresh vegetables.

Students of the recent Produce Guild Leaders' School at Moulton examine a bunch of promising calves.

3. By seeing that no food is wasted.

This last point will bear elaboration. It is not enough merely to see that any uneaten scraps of food are fed to pigs and poultry. **There should be no uneaten scraps.** Housewives must so apportion their families' food that all is eaten up. Their success will depend on good planning and good cooking, and all the training of W.I. members during the war years will stand them in good stead. Let us all work together to win the last battle, against want.

THE BATTLE FOR BREAD

The good loaves that we see in the shops did not arrive there without a battle. The seed was selected and sown and the corn was grown with care and many an anxious hour for its well-being. It was reaped and treated and ground into flour, made into dough and baked. Then you came along and bought the loaf, and no doubt, together with the burden of other shopping, carried it home. Do not waste any part of the precious loaf, the least crust of which would be considered a great gift if it were put into the hands of anyone of many millions of our fellow human beings.

Frozen Food Locker Plants for England?

FROZEN Food Locker Plants in Canada and America started from scratch back in 1935 and now there are 6,000 plants in the United States and about 1,000 in Canada, serving from 8 to 10 million people and freezing approximately 700 million pounds of fruits and vegetables a year. In addition to fruits and vegetables, 90 million pounds of eviscerated poultry and the same amount of sea foods are quick frozen. Meat is also another large item which is quick frozen.

WHAT IS A LOCKER PLANT?

A Locker Plant with approximately 300 Lockers, and all necessary rooms, will occupy a space of about 2,000 sq. ft., and consists of (1) a Chill Room with a temperature of about 35 degrees Fahr. (Generally all meats, fruits and vegetables are chilled before processing.) (2) An Ageing Room, which is kept at a temperature of 50 to 60 degrees Fahr., with a relative humidity of 85 to 90 degrees Fahr. Beef is aged in this room under Sterilamps from three to seven days. With the use of the Sterilamp the room can be kept at a higher temperature. The Sterilamp prevents mould and bacterial growth, thus avoiding loss in trim after ageing. (3) A Processing Room where quarters or sides of beef are cut into normal size roasts and steaks for each individual family or locker patron. The fruits and vegetables are processed and wrapped in a special wax proof paper prior to freezing. (By processing we mean cleaning, cutting, blanching, cooling, packaging, and quick freezing.) (4) A Freezer Room. All meats, fruits and vegetables must be quick frozen and usually at 20 degrees Fahr. Freezing foods quickly gives a much better product. When food is frozen slowly the ice crystals are large and pierce or rupture the cells and tissues of the product frozen, which results in the leakage of juices (drip) when thawed. Do not confuse the ordinary cold storage or frozen foods with quick frozen foods. (5) A Locker Room. The Locker Room consists of an ordinary sized room, well insulated and kept at zero degrees Fahr. Each locker is numbered and has a separate lock and key, which is rented by the patron for a

U.S.A. housewife visits her Food Locker.

period of twelve months at two to five pounds a year, depending on the size of the locker. These Lockers have a capacity of about 6 cu. ft. and will hold from 300 to 350 pounds of frozen food.

One of the reasons why quick frozen fruit and vegetables are better than the fresh variety sold at markets and retail stores is that fruit and vegetables for retail and market sale usually take from 24 to 60 hours, and sometimes longer, before the housewife has purchased them. During that time the food is handled from five to seven times. With the additional handling, plus the length of time before the housewife gets the food into her kitchen, the products have lost a considerable amount of flavour, colour and vitamins, plus wastage of the outer leaves of vegetables, such as cabbage, spinach, brussels sprouts, etc.

In order to have a better variety during the winter months, the housewife could pick or order several extra pounds of fruits and vegetables when in season and when the products are cheapest and best, quick-freeze them and then enjoy strawberries, cherries, peas and asparagus from four to eight months later.

Locker Plants serve not only the urban areas in U.S.A. and Canada but the rural as well. The farmer is able to harvest a portion of the crop in the morning and take it to the locker plant for processing and quick freezing in the afternoon. The portion he does not freeze can be sold fresh at the local market. The part of the crop quick frozen can be sold from four to eight months later, and the quality will be just as good as the fresh product sold at the market.

When harvest time arrives for any fruit or vegetables, there is all too often a glut, resulting in some of the food not being sold and finally wasted. The farmer could take his home-grown fruits, vegetables, chickens, etc., to the Locker Plant for necessary processing and store in his Locker for future use. It is possible that W.I. Markets might be able to make use of Locker Plants in order to even out their supplies of produce.　　　　　　　　　　H. E. CLASS

HOMELY WARTIME DISHES

The recent arrival of tinned foods from America has placed in the housewife's hands materials of good value which can be converted into many appetizing homely dishes for the mid-day dinner, for supper and breakfast. Here is a form of **Cornish Pie**, baked on a tin or an enamel plate, which is a satisfying dish for a family when served with gravy and vegetables.

Allow half a pound of the tinned pork shoulder meat, one onion, a pound of potatoes, pepper and salt, 7 ozs. of flour, 3 ozs. of fine oatmeal, 4 ozs. of cooking fat, a saltspoonful of baking powder, and water for mixing. Make a piece of pastry with the flour, oatmeal, baking powder, cooking fat and cold water to form a smooth, rather stiff paste. Roll out and cut it in halves. With one half line an enamel plate or a sandwich tin. Fill in with the pork cut into small pieces, the potatoes peeled and cut into dice and the grated or chopped onion. Sprinkle this with salt and pepper and a spoonful of water and cover with the remaining piece of pastry. Bake for about an hour in a moderate oven.

Mince Dumplings. These are excellent for supper served hot and, being equally good eaten cold, any that remain pack well in the lunch basket of the war worker. First of all make a piece of plain short crust pastry: roll it out and cut into rounds. For the filling take a cupful of any kind of cold meat—preferably with a little fat—chopped finely, a cupful of bread pieces that have soaked until soft in cold water, then squeezed dry and beaten free from lumps, two cupfuls of mashed potatoes and carrots—or other mixture of cooked vegetables available—salt, pepper, half a teaspoonful of mixed herbs and sauce for binding these ingredients, made by cooking a dessertspoonful of cornflour in three tablespoonfuls of milk until thick.

Mix all the ingredients, moistening them with the sauce and make into dumplings, using a little flour to prevent sticking. Place a dumpling on each round of pastry: secure the edges, as with apple dumplings, and bake in a brisk oven for about twenty-five minutes.

Cheese Squares. These help considerably in making the cheese ration go as far as possible. With 10 ozs. of flour mix a teaspoonful of baking powder and a little salt and pepper. Rub in from 2 to 3 ozs. of fat and add 2 ozs. of grated cheese. Dry pieces and rinds grate well for this. Moisten with just enough cold water to make a stiff firm paste. Roll out and cut in halves. On the one half spread about one teaspoonful of meat or savoury vegetable extract and sprinkle with another two tablespoonfuls of grated cheese. Cover with the second half of pastry and press together in sandwich form. Bake for about twenty-five minutes and when cold cut into squares.

Bread Economy. Though modern science has worked wonders since the outbreak of war in discovering substitutes for many things, no substitute has been found for bread which is the very foundation of energy and vitality. It cannot be urged too strongly that not a scrap of bread should be wasted and although stale pieces will accumulate, however careful may be the housekeeper, these are valuable material for making many nourishing dishes.

A Good Carrot Pudding. Here is one way in which 4 ozs. of stale bread may be used to help in making a delicious pudding. Break the bread into small pieces—or make it into crumbs—and over it pour a quarter pint of boiling milk. Add a tablespoonful each of sugar and magarine: cover the basin and let them soak. Meanwhile wash, scrape and grate two carrots of medium size. Beat the breadcrumb mixture until fine and then add the grated carrots, and sprinkle in a tablespoonful of flour with which has been mixed a teaspoonful each of ground ginger and baking powder. Another spoonful or two of milk may be needed in the mixing and then pour the mixture into a greased pie-dish. Bake in a moderate oven until firm and nicely browned.

Savoury Bread Pancake. Cut a good slice of stale bread into small cubes. The crusts can be removed and used for drying and breadcrumbs. Fry the cubes for a few minutes in a very little fat, moisten with a little gravy or meat extract and simmer until the bread has absorbed all the gravy. Then add pepper and salt and mash the bread finely with a fork. Then mix a heaping dessertspoonful of egg substitute with eleven dessertspoonfuls of water: beat this into the mashed bread, etc., pour into a well-greased pan and fry or bake in a good oven.   JESSIE J. WILLIAMS, M.C.A.

WHALEMEAT

IT was a pity that whalemeat, such a good answer to the butcher's meat shortage, made so poor a start in this country. To begin with it was sold, in rather uninviting dark slabs, by fishmongers. Therefore many people decided that it tasted of fish. (Perhaps it sometimes did.) The quality was variable, for the suppliers little understood their fine product, and whether one got a piece as tender as fillet steak with excellent flavour, or a tough and stringy piece with no flavour at all, was largely a matter of chance.

Now there is no reason on earth, or in the sea for that matter, why whalemeat (unless handled by fishy hands) should taste fishy. The whale is not a fish; it is a *mammal*, like the ox or the sheep. It does not even live on fish; it is a vegetarian, like the ox or the sheep. In fact, both in texture, appearance and flavour it more nearly resembles good beef than anything else. But it seems to be a gastronomic law that very large things are sometimes dull things, and this appears to be as true of the whale as of the vegetable marrow. Thus, far from there being anything to complain of in the flavour of whalemeat, my only complaint is that it does not taste enough, and calls for a certain amount of flavour assistance in the cooking.

But slab whalemeat is, I think, on the way out and its place is being taken by *canned* whalemeat. Originally this was processed on shore from whalemeat frozen on the depot ship. But now they have carried the thing a stage further and the new arrivals of canned meat were processed actually on the depot ship in the Antarctic, from fresh whalemeat *unfrozen*, with a resulting improvement in flavour. I bought a case of this " Antarctic Pack " and as far as I am concerned the meat shortage is now over. Points free and in unlimited supply, it is a very much better proposition than the flavourless, scarce and very high-pointed canned Stewed Beef Steak. It costs about 2s. 6d. a pound tin, and being already cooked and so " pre-shrunk " as it were, it works out no dearer than equivalent butcher's meat and is, for a large range of purposes, as good or better.

Meat Shape—Continental Style. 1 tin Whale Steak, ¼ lb. onion, ¼ lb. carrots, gelatine, ½ teaspoonful mixed herbs, ½ teaspoonful powdered sage, ¼ oz. salt, 2 good pinches pepper or 8 grinds, 2 good pinches mixed spice, a piece of garlic about the size of a pea, breadcrumbs or mashed potato powder, 1 oz. fat. Chop the onion and carrot fairly small and cook in the minimum of water (conservative method) till well done. Aim to have little or no water left when cooking is finished. Strain the liquid from the can of Whale Steak, heat it, and in it dissolve ½ oz. gelatine. (If using a low-melting point gelatine, e.g. " Spa ", use double this quantity.) Add to the liquid the herbs, seasoning and spice; and the fat, beating it well in. Mince together the whalemeat, vegetables, and garlic finely chopped. Mix up well in a basin, add the liquid and again mix very thoroughly. Add dry breadcrumbs or mashed potato powder until the mixture is of a fairly dry, plastic consistency. Pack into a basin and bake uncovered for one hour in a low oven (say 300° F., gas 2 or C.). Cool under the heaviest weight you can arrange.

Deep-Fried Savoury Meat Pasties. Mince the whalemeat and mix it up with the same quantity of herbs and seasoning (but not spice) as in the recipe above. Add onions fried brown, mix well. Make some ordinary short paste, not too rich, say 2 oz. fat to 8 oz. flour, roll it out ⅛th inch thick and cut into rounds with a 3½ in. cutter. Place a good blob of the whalemeat mixture on the disc of pastry, moisten round the edge, fold over and seal well. If any meat oozes out the pasty is too full—empty and do it again. Deep-fry 5-10 minutes in hot olive oil. Crisp and rustling, with their savoury filling, these pasties can be kept hot (unlike chips) and are extremely tasty and filling; one tin of whale meat would yield enough for eight quite hungry people.

Needless to say canned Whale Steak also makes the basis for a first class curry.

PHILIP HARBEN

STRETCHING THE BUTTER RATION

DEAR EDITOR,—I believe that my butter stretch is even stretchier. Half as many ounces of butter as margarine and one tablespoon milk (top milk if possible) for each ounce of margarine. Cut up butter and " marge ", put it in a basin with the milk. Put basin where contents can warm to softness without oiling. Then beat and stir and cream till all the milk is absorbed. Sometimes if I have been heavy handed with the milk, I add a little milk powder. This mixture keeps good in a cool place, even in summer, for a week. My daughter calls it " Marbut ".

Yours sincerely,

1 Fore Street, Winsham, Somerset.   H. M. EVANS

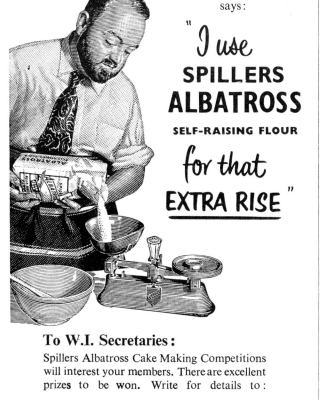

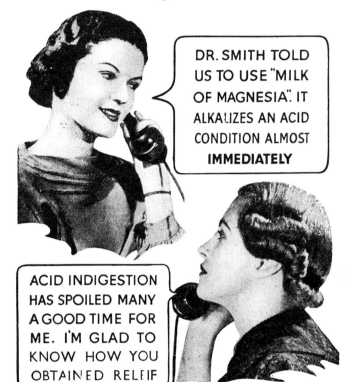
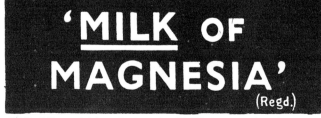
The Feeding and Management of Your Pig

THE domestic pig meal ration is 70 lb. monthly for one fattening pig if obtained from County Agricultural Executive Committees, or 84 lb. if drawn through a registered pig club. A club member is also entitled to this ration for one further pig if two or more pigs are kept. No allowance for breeding is normally made to new domestic pig keepers and only those members of pig clubs who were breeding before 1941 may obtain the special farrowing ration for one breeding sow. The meal ration is supplementary to collected waste and home-grown foodstuffs. Apart from household waste, potatoes, followed by artichokes, are the pig keeper's chief standby. When the potato crop is good, there may be a surplus available for stock-keepers, but it is much better to grow one's own, if possible. Their feeding value lies chiefly in the starch which they contain; they can, therefore, replace starchy foods such as cereal meals. They should be fed along with foods which are rich in protein, such as beans, peas, clover, meat-meal, blood-meal, fish-meal, etc. It is also preferable to use them with something of a fibrous nature, such as bran or middlings. In the absence of these, some green food should be given with the potatoes. Potatoes contain 0·1 per cent. of oil and are useful in making a firm carcass.

While it is possible to feed potatoes raw, this sometimes causes irritation of the digestive tract, and boiling is recommended, as the bitter principle, which is responsible for the irritation and, in severe cases, poisoning, is thereby removed from the skin. For this reason, it is better to throw away the water in which the potatoes have been boiled. If, however, a normal sample of potatoes is boiled together with other ingredients, as for example edible waste, no harm will be done. It is advisable to clean the potatoes as far as possible before boiling because, although a little soil will not harm pigs, it does tend to accumulate in the boiler, which leads to waste of fuel. "Greened" potatoes should always be well boiled before use. All sprouts and shoots should be taken off potatoes before boiling.

The following crops are also valuable. BEANS are most nutritious, especially if grubbed out before drying-up and with a few remains of the crop still attached; DRUMHEAD CABBAGE, planted from January to April in well-limed and manured soil with plenty of water; MANGOLDS have a nourishing sugar content and should be fed chopped and not frozen. Tops may also be fed. Sugar mangolds are best. Feed pulped and mixed with the meal and not before Christmas. They should not be given in excess, or scouring will result; SWEDES AND TURNIPS, but boil turnips before feeding and split swedes to encourage the pigs to eat them; RAPE, if planted in the spring, provides a valuable food until late autumn. Cut when 8 to 10 in. high and do not feed when it is old and weedy; KALE is also relished by pigs; SUGAR BEET yields a very high quantity of pig food. Introduce gradually into the ration after 80 lb. liveweight, one or two tops daily. Feeding these

various kinds of vegetables provides the pig with the minerals which are so necessary to its effective growth and not obtainable in sufficient quantities in kitchen waste and meal alone.

The actual feeding of the pig is quite a simple matter. Give regular meals (preferably three times a day) and no more food than it can clear up in about 20 minutes. If food is left in the trough it is a sign

Collecting Kitchen Waste

Most kitchen scraps are valuable for pig food and are best collected in a special bowl, covered bucket or colander. Never throw in tea leaves, coffee grounds, citrus fruit skins, salt or rhubarb and yew leaves. Egg shells, however, are welcome

CHAPTER FIVE
Home Skills

HINTS ON EMBROIDERY.

JOAN DREW.

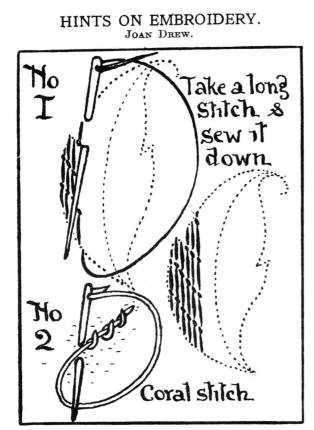

HERE are two stitches which you will find useful : Laid Oriental, and Coral stitch. No. 1 gives a flat appliqué effect. A long stitch is taken and then couched down ; it may curve with the shape of leaf, or lie straight with the threads of the material ; it needs an outline as a finish. No. 2 can be used in several ways, when a more varied or thicker line is needed than stem-stitch gives. I want you to remember, however, that you can do beautiful work without a very wide knowledge of stitches, *provided those you do use are well executed.* Seek in every way possible that your work shall show charm of design, beauty of colour, and careful, fine workmanship. This can be done as well with few stitches as with many.

We have now come to the end of our four articles on embroidery, and I should like to point out some general considerations that we should bear in mind. W.I. members who have children should take pride in seeing that their frocks have that little touch of beauty and individuality that embroidery and hand work can alone give. Next we should welcome the fact that we can put this same individuality into our own garments, and give pleasure to our friends as well as to ourselves. In our sitting-rooms, too, we can have one or two pieces of embroidery on *washing* material that have not been factory produced. Many of us now aim at giving to our sitting-rooms a look of happy use. Such a sitting-room I know, where low seats with cushions have been contrived in the corners by the fire, where " one more " can always be tucked away when there is a sing-song or a happy evening together. Embroidery that needs tissue paper over it all the week would be out of place here, but there is plenty of room for that which will stand fair wear and tear.

Next, looking outside our homes, let us think about our village room. Has *it* got something pleasant or beautiful in the way of Banners or hangings ? If not, why not ? " Ah," you say, " but that is quite impossible for us."

Why impossible ? Try thinking about it. It is quite wonderful what thinking about a thing will produce. It may offer us an opportunity for *Co-operative* working.

Such co-operative working was undertaken by the Ewhurst Institute in the making of a very interesting counterpane (see illustration). The design was carefully planned out, crochet workers made the insertions, and needle workers embroidered the squares. Initials, dates and other symbols were introduced, and the whole work carried out in blue cottons on a white ground.

When a wedding present is needed, or a presentation to an honoured member, might not other Institutes do something of the kind ? In our Embroidery there is *happiness* in skill of hand, *happiness* in creating, and further *happiness* awaits us when we can give. Let us therefore Seek Beauty, Make Beauty, Hand on Beauty

A transfer, price 1s , suitable for the centre of a cushion, in which the stitches given above can be used, can be obtained from Miss J. Drew, Blatchfold, Chilworth, nr. Guildford.

HOW TO IMPROVE THE CIRCULATION OF " HOME AND COUNTRY."

JOAN RAXWORTHY,
Member Hambledon (Surrey) W.I.

THE circulation of " HOME AND COUNTRY " could be largely increased if a prize of something really useful to any W.I. were offered for the greatest number of coupons collected by any Institute during a certain time, say four months. The coupons could be put on the back cover of the paper, so that by cutting them out one would not destroy any of the reading matter, and if any Institute did not wish to enter for the prize, it could be allowed to give its coupons to one which was doing so.

I would suggest a large tea-urn as a prize, as I know several Institutes where an urn would be most welcome for the tea problem is often a difficult one.

This means to increase circulation is at the moment employed by the Editor of the " Guide," a weekly paper for Girl Guides, although in this case, the prize is to be a trek-cart.

Of course, it should be made clear that non-members of the Institute may help by giving coupons. In this way the paper would find its way into houses where it had not been even heard of before, and I am sure that once a person takes in the paper for a month or two, they feel they cannot be without it.

In order to ensure the success of this scheme, it would be a good plan to make a special appeal to all Presidents and Secretaries, for their help in the matter, so much would depend on local interest in the competition.

FIRST PRIZE ESSAY.

AN INTERVIEW WITH A THATCHER.

Mrs. A. Belcher (Headley W.I.).

Passing a certain rick yard this morning I noticed "Old Jarvey," our local thatcher, preparing to thatch a corn stack against the elements of the coming winter. Thinking that this was my opportunity I accosted him and as he was about to begin his work, I was able to watch the whole process and to gain information from him at the same time. It needed a great deal of coaxing to get the reasons for certain processes, but by dint of careful questions and of praise for what had been done, I was able to arrive at the knowledge of the "why's and wherefore's."

First he took a heap of wheat-straw, which he told me "was the best for the purpose, though some people use rye-straw, rushes, or even heath." He shook the straw lightly out and sprinkled it with water to soften it. He let this "soak for a while," as he said while

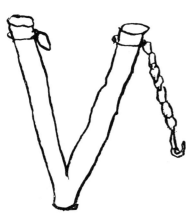

he prepared his rods for future use. Then, pulling the straw straight with his hands, he worked it up on his knees into a flat mass about three inches thick and fifteen or sixteen inches wide. These masses he called "Yellums." Next he took a forked stick of hazel, like a large letter "V," which he called a "Dog." This had a short chain fixed to one point with a swivel and having a hook at the end. The other point had a link into which to fasten the hook. The part with the chain attached was placed against a hurdle. If no hurdle had been near he would have used a gate for the purpose. He placed about a dozen "Yellums" into the "Dog," one at a time, keeping them quite flat. Then drawing the two points together, he fixed the hook of the chain into the link on the other point, which held the "Yellums" in place. This he then carried up a ladder, which he had placed on the side of a stack near to the right end. The "Dog" was fastened to the top of the ladder by the chain being hooked over on the left hand side. He then proceeded to work on the right of the ladder. The "Yellums" were taken out of the "Dog" one by one and placed on the stack, beginning at the bottom of the roof and letting each "Yellum" overlap a little until the peak was

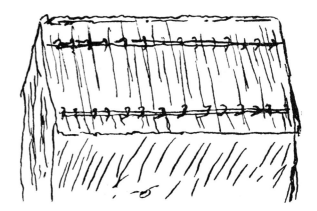

reached. The last "Yellum" stood up a little above the peak, forming what he called a "Comb." The ladder was then moved to the left and the process repeated until the whole stack was covered in. Every

course was raked down with a Thatcher's Rake which had iron teeth before the ladder was moved.

Two lines of hazel rods were placed across the "Yellums" about a foot from the bottom of the roof and a foot from the "Comb." The rods were fixed with other pieces of split hazel. The hazel is pointed

at both ends, twisted to stop it from breaking and bent like a hairpin. The "Comb" at the top was trimmed evenly with shears and the bottom of the thatch was

allowed to extend five or six inches beyond the stack, as "Old Jarvey" said "to shoot the water off." He told me that "sometimes bands of twisted straw were used to fix the 'Yellums' instead of rods." These were pegged down in the same way as the rods. At other times tarred string was used, which would be

pegged down with straight pegs like hooked sticks used for blackberrying, only smaller.

A CRADLE SONG.*

By kind permission of W. B. Yeats.

The Angels are stooping
  Above your bed ;
They're weary of trooping
  With the whimpering dead.

God's laughing in heaven
  To see you so good ;
The shining seven
  Are gay with His mood.

I kiss you and kiss you
  My pigeon, my own ;
Ah, how I shall miss you
  When you have grown.

* From Poems by W. B. Yeats. (Fisher Unwin, Ltd., Adelphi Terrace, London. 10s. 6d.)

CRADLES AND COTS.*

A GOOD cot can be made from an orange or egg box, or from a banana or onion crate. A banana crate is the best and a greengrocer will often sell one for a few pence.

The two ends and at least eight of the cross bars should be whole, that is strong and not much split.

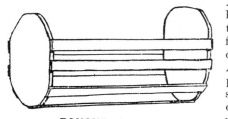

BANANA CRATE.

All the cross bars should be taken off carefully by pulling out the nails. Any rough places must be smoothed with coarse sandpaper, and the cot will look nicer if all the wood is sandpapered. The bars should be nailed on to the end pieces about 2½ inches from each other, to form the bottom and sides of the cot.

It takes three yards of unbleached calico to line the cot. Tack it over each top bar to form a hammock nearly touching the bottom of the cot. There will be enough calico left over to line the head and foot of the cradle.

The filling for mattress and pillow should be of chaff or bran. A good filling is made of three parts of chaff and one of bran, well mixed. The mattress and pillow should be lightly sewn at one end so that

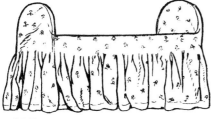

COT MADE FROM THE BANANA CRATE.

they can be easily unpicked, washed, and the stuffing thrown away and replaced with fresh.

The bed clothes should be warm and light, and the mattress protected either by a sheet of brown paper, a piece of American cloth, or of waterproofed paper.

* Extract from " To Wives and Mothers," 5d. post free. A pamphlet compiled by the Association of Infant Welfare and Maternity Centres and published by the National League for Health, Maternity and Child Welfare, 117 Piccadilly, London, W.1. This is a little book which can be highly recommended. It is full of practical hints for the management of the health of the mother and child.

– 1923 –

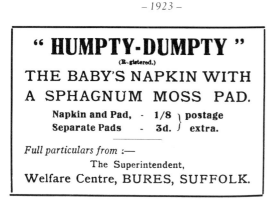
The Easy Cot

HERE ARE DIRECTIONS for making a baby's cot, designed by Mrs. Hodges of Long Marston, Gloucestershire, for use in emergencies. It is easy to make, erect, move, wash, and iron, and is suitable for a baby up to about six months old. It hangs on the backs of two chairs, placed with seats facing each other, swings clear of the seats, and when strongly made is perfectly safe

ANY STRONG MATERIAL can be used—a washed sack or bag, calico, cretonne, linen, or silk. It can be lined if not strong enough, or if two colours are required, and is most useful when made in good washing or boiling material.

Material cut to the dimensions shown on the diagram below will make a cot large enough to slip over the backs of two ordinary bedroom chairs. Two yards of 50 inch material, or two and a half yards of 30 inch material are required. If mattress and pillow are made, an extra half or three quarters of a yard will be needed.

Hem or bind the two 20 inch ends, and fold as marked. Material can be joined at any of the dotted lines. At the corners, the three raw edges are joined together on the right side and made neat by binding with a narrow piece of material; this makes the pockets to slip over the chair backs. If liked, the binding can be put around the top edge.

If required, the cot can be strengthened with four rods cut the length of the two sides and two ends, and slipped into slots made with narrow strips of material machined to the bottom. For extra security, tapes can also be sewn at the corners and tied to the back legs of the chairs.

An ideal filling for a baby's mattress is oat flights: that is, the husks of oats, obtained when the corn is threshed; they are best collected straight from the threshing machine. Oat flights cost very little in the country, and can be renewed as often as necessary. An ordinary pillow can be used in place of a mattress.

The cot pillow should be made of white down-proof sateen and should be filled with stripped feathers, not with down.

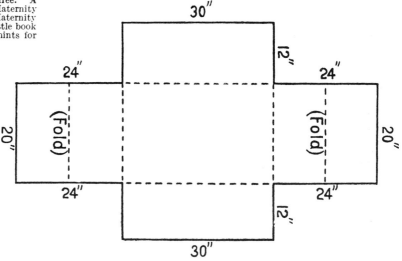

Diagram showing how to cut material to make the Easy Cot

– 1939 –

HOME AND COUNTRY ARTS.

VI. Village Arts and Crafts.

W. R. LETHABY.

HERE I want to consider three things and I hope you will think them over with me : (1) I want to determine what seems to be the natural and proper place of craft-work in a reasonable form of country life, more or less supplementary to farming ; (2) I want to put on record some testimony as to the

present position of such crafts ; (3) I want to speak of the possibility of still carrying on some of the old industries as secondary and alternative employments.

As an introduction to what I want to say I will begin by condensing a passage from an article on traditional country crafts by my friend, Mr. Alfred Powell, in a little volume called " Handicrafts and Reconstruction " (Pitman, price 12s. 6d.). This chapter indeed will be largely quotation, for several interesting replies have been sent to me in answer to enquiries as to what craft work is being done in country districts.

" Agriculture and building have suffered from our neglecting to make full use of the traditional knowledge and work of which the villages are still the great repository. . . . We should remember that the effort necessary to provide intelligently food, shelter and clothing, leads along so many interesting ways, that a nation quietly trained to hand craft is an educated nation. . . . A long list might be made of essential occupations still being carried on. Of the works connected with agriculture, not including the art of cultivating the ground, we find the following still being done by hand : waggon- and cart-building, the wheelwright's work, the making of all such farm implements as harrows, ploughs, rakes, prongs,

hurdles, fencing, gates, sheep-cots, cribs, troughs. And of works dependent upon building, stone-quarrying and the preparation of it at the quarry ; brick and tile-making ; felling and squaring of timber ; carpenter's work, mainly with axe and saw ; local forms of walling—as cob and timber framing, weather-boarded barns etc. ; thatching with straw, reed and heather ; carving stone and wood which has almost entirely disappeared. There are still at work tin-smiths, copper-smiths, saddlers, whipsters, cabinet-makers, clock-makers, potters, basket-makers, mat-makers, shoe-makers, spinners and weavers. And in the farmhouses brewing, baking and dairy work. If all these works were in a flourishing condition it would give to our country that look noticeable in Holland or Denmark, of full, flushed life. . . . One or two good thatchers to each county would probably be an overestimate, and of those who know how to stake and lay a hedge properly the number is far too small. . . . This month of May, when the undergrowth of hazel has been cut, there are men making wattled or ' flake ' hurdles. These are precisely the work used by the ancient British for building the walls of their houses, the knowledge of seasons, of the nature of the copse woods, the quality of the hurdle and of how to make it, is one of those inherited wisdoms that are being neglected out of existence. . . . The blacksmith's, too, was a marvellous art. Until quite recently there have been scattered all over England little potteries supplying local needs. One after another they have shut down and the flood of machine goods inundates us."

This passage suggests much to think over ; as, for instance, the traditional development of the old arts all of which came down to our time from remote antiquity ; the idea that these things embodied much that seems essential to human development, that they are in fact "inherited wisdoms" and made the workers " an educated nation " ; and finally the general picture of life on the land—a sense of things being done and something going on, " a look of full flushed life."

HAYRICKS at Blatherwyck (Northants), "thacker," Mr. Sturgess.

The craft which best maintains its traditions is probably that of the waggon-builder, but even this seems to be rapidly changing under modern conditions of making up machine-made parts. A characteristic of these naturally exercised crafts is the skill the "artists" have for foreseeing the completed work and going ahead without bungling. I remember talking to a Devonshire waggon-builder whom I passed working in a jolly open shop by the wayside. "Do you make a drawing of a cart before you begin it?" "No, we know what we are going to do and match the shafts and things in pairs." Their ornaments of notches and chamfers are perfect for their kind of work—a natural embroidery with the tools they use. The skill of framing and fitting is amazing—all has to hold together without nails and glue. Then the cart painters have a wonderful instinct, lost by the rest of the world, for using the brightest colours harmoniously—gay red for the wheels, bright yellow or blue for the body, and their power of hand in striking long lines of paint is astonishing. A Royal Academician painter could no more do it than fly without a machine. In some places flourishes of curves are skilfully painted,

which are the most living painted decoration done in England.

A Government report on farming in Berkshire in 1794 remarks that " the Berkshire waggon has long been noticed for its peculiar lightness and elegance." Yes, indeed, it is one of the most *elegant* things still made. I remember that William Morris calling something handsome, added " not the handsomeness of a fashionable dress, but of a farm-waggon " ; and that reminds me that handsome must properly mean a thing well made by hand.

Blacksmiths, too, still hold on here and there. I take a note from my diary, of a walk one July day in 1918, within thirty miles of London in uninjured country : " Passing a blacksmith's shop and attracted by the ringing strokes and glowing sparks, I looked in. 'How tidy and jolly you look ; what a nice place a workshop is.' 'Yes, I like to keep it tidy.' Then, noticing his tools and things—'What pretty fire irons !' 'Do you think so ? I made them myself

when I was a boy.' ' They are splendid, such a good handle to grip—the second piece is welded on, isn't it ? ' ' Yes ; it's been a good deal worn with use.' ' Did you think of it yourself ? ' ' Well, I saw some of the sort and thought I'd make mine something like.' "

Harness-making and saddlery was an extensive and beautiful craft up to " my time." One of my early memories of beauty is of the pretty and intricate patterns which were stitched on ladies' side-saddles. Somehow even to this day horses seem to object to vulgarity and to like old-fashioned things ! In Kent, I am told, that the brass trappings (how pretty they are !) and the red fringed cloth worn by cart horses are called " housings " and this, I believe, is a good old-fashioned word. Of a Northumberland village a correspondent says that local saddlery disappeared with the corn laws, after which much more land was turned to pasture.

Even shoemaking seems to be " going out." The most interesting piece of current everyday leatherwork I have seen is a pair of " hedging cuffs " or gloves, which has been sent to me from Burford, in Oxfordshire. They are made of thick horsehide, with marvellous skill—that skill which is so simple when you can do it ! " The right hand glove is more supple in order that the bill-hook may be properly grasped. The left hand glove has to be thick in order that it may be pushed into the hedge. At the same time one ought to be able to grasp a branch with the thumb. This pattern has been made in the same place in Burford for over 100 years and is characteristic of the neighbourhood." I was not told the maker's name, but from a label it appears to be Mr. Hudson. Each glove is made of two principal pieces of ∩ shape and a small extra piece attached to the palm to complete the thumb. I say complete the thumb, for half of it is made in the most ingenious way, out of the palm piece itself, by cutting in at an angle and turning up the flap. It is impossible to explain in words, the geometry is too difficult and all is done to avoid waste of material. The sewing is by a thick hide thong and where the stuff has to be

" gathered up " to make room it falls into a series of rolls each bound over by the thong in a way delightful to see. We have taken these things for granted, but they embody centuries of tradition with high skill and the thing is perfect of its kind—a work of art. Two hundred years ago I find Burford described as famous for saddles and horses. Such cuffs have doubtless been made there for hundreds of years.

Mrs. Huddart mentions the making of trug baskets in Sussex and adds " There used to be Rope walks, Tan yards and local coopers, which I remember, but they have disappeared. The one-man industry cannot cope with machinery." These trug baskets seem to have been invented nearly a century ago by Thomas Smith of Hurstmonceaux, where they are still made.

Of Essex Miss Christy writes: " Just a few old people remain in this county who can plait straw for hat-making and until lately one of the old 'dummy' heads for fitting the hats on was in existence. An attempt was made during the war to revive this industry but it was found it would be hopeless to compete with machine-made straw hats. The old men in Essex are still able to make straw bee-hives or ' skeps.' In the same way they twist straw into round flat mats, about two inches thick, used at a garden or greenhouse door to wipe feet on and not too good to be thrown away when dirty and sodden."

Mat-making as a domestic occupation is done in several counties. Miss Ruth Anderson, of Saxmundham, has been good enough to show me two, one ingeniously made of long rows of twine in a spiral (like a steel spring) on a base of strong sail-cloth. " This type was made long ago and has recently been revived." The other is " a plaited rag mat " of a very pretty colour, compact and with both sides alike. This, too, must be of old fashion, for I am told that " rag mats " are made in America.

Miss Bosanquet says of Cambo, Northumberland, " In this district ' stobbit mats ' are made of old cloth cut into fragments, each pushed, ' that is stobbit' through a piece of sacking. ' Sometimes the workers make their own designs for arranging the

several colours or else they get them from each other. The men sometimes draw them out and help with the work. The farmers take their wool to be woven into blankets, rugs and tweed at the old mills at Otterburn and Netherwitten. Beautiful tweeds and rugs are produced which are famous in the north. Much of the wool comes back to the farms as blankets and tweed. The last of the old cottage weavers died in the year 1860 (?). He wove beautiful house linen supplementing it with other work.

In the old days the people used to sit round the fire making besoms (brooms), wooden bowls, spoons, and ' swills ' (large open baskets) to be sent afterwards to the Newcastle firms which took them. The children sat round listening to the stories the old people told. The men used to carve knitting sheaths for their wives or sweethearts; the sheaths often took the form of a chain carved out of a single piece of wood, with a pocket-knife. The sheath was made to hook on to the skirt band and one needle was fixed in it as the woman knitted. Date, initials and designs were carved on the sheaths or a chain would be carved with tiny loose balls, one inside each link. Wooden spoons and all sorts of useful contrivances in wood or metal are still made by handy men for their homes.

The people at Cambo have told me of three men who used to make violins—none of them living now. Three of the violins have been shown to me—two signed with the maker's name. The maker had another trade and only made the violins in the evenings, so it took more than a winter to make one. They are of beautifully grained wood, well finished and have a good tone. I was listening three weeks ago to the playing of Northumberland pipes, bag-pipes, worked by a wind bag under the arm. Another piper said his pipes had been made by his father—a piper before him—and he mentioned half a dozen people for whom he and his father had made pipes. Kid-skin is used and ivory is shaped to the forms required. The piper is also a shoe-maker."

That surely is being alive and being an " educated " man, with a knowledge of science and art !

Mend silk stockings
with Clark's Filosheen

Here's just the very thread you've been looking for—offers **a** remarkable range of colours from which practically any stocking can be matched exactly, does not fade, does not wash harsh. Is firm but soft, never tears tiny holes in the fabric of your stocking, yet gives darns that last. Ask to-day for Clark's "Anchor" Filosheen wound on cards specially for your convenience.

Remember, always, that whatever your needlework requirements, you make sure of getting the best possible article, the newest shades, the fastest colours, if you look for the famous names of Clark and Coats.

Clark's
Threads, Embroideries & Cottons

CLARK & CO. LTD. AND J. & P. COATS LTD. PAISLEY   C104a

W.I. FURNITURE.

THIS CHAIR was made for the Warwickshire W.I. Exhibition, by a W.I. Member, from an apple barrel bought for 1s. The second picture shows the handles which lift up the seat, disclosing a lined receptacle for hats, or needlework etc. The photographs were taken by the owner of the chair.

"I love it—I love it, and who shall dare
To chide me for loving that old arm-chair!"
The Old Arm-Chair.

"No pent-up Utica contracts your powers,
But the whole boundless continent is yours."
Epilogue to Cato.

TWISTED SEAGRASS

ANN MACBETH

To twist seagrass, bent or small rushes, is extraordinarily easy and can be done quite successfully even by children or blind people. The rushes, if they are used, must be quite small, just the common little wild rush which grows in damp fields or bogs. The seagrass can be either the flat leaved Bent, Marram or Starr grass, by which names it is known in various parts of the country, or the round Bent, a harder round leafed variety (round when cut sectionally, that is). The curing of all these is the same. They should be gathered in July when they are full grown but not hardened by wind and weather. Then they should be made up into bundles

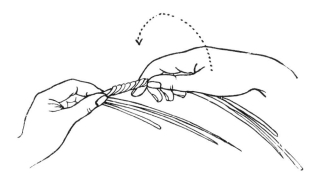

about ten inches in circumference with the thin ends all caught together and tied firmly. The bundles should be hung up in a dry place out of the sun and out of the rain.

To make the twist the grass should first be soaked for a few minutes in water. Then, sitting with your bundle of rush or bent between your knees, pick out three or four stems and put the thin ends of two to the thick ends of another pair, seeing, however, that their various ends do not all come too near together. Now double your strand of four stems in the middle and catch the doubled bend between left thumb and forefinger. You will now have two separate strands standing out towards the right hand from the point at which they are held. With the right hand, now take hold of the upper strand (Diagram A)

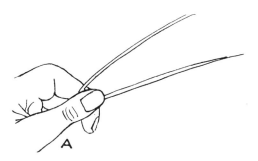

and with a firm movement upwards and away from you put a tight twist or spin on to the strand for about one inch between the two hands. Holding the twisted portion still firmly, carry it towards you

and (Diagram B) bend it firmly and closely downward over the other strand of stems and move the left thumb and forefinger forwards in order to grip the twisted strand, while the right hand picks up the other loose strand and repeats the movement. The whole making of the cord consists in the alternate twisting away from you of the single strands and folding it over the other strand in the opposite direction towards you.

New stems of rush or bent should be laid into the cord as they are required, laying in the thin ends first, and it is very important to keep the twisted cord of an even thickness all the way. Ends of rush or grass which stick out after twisting can be cut off or singed to finish the twist neatly.

Rushes eight to ten inches long are best, do not try to get very thick ones. In Westmorland in many of the villages there are still held every July charming festivals called "Rush bearings." These festivals celebrated the harvest home of the rush workers. The rushes are usually said to have been strewn on the church floors, but to judge from en-

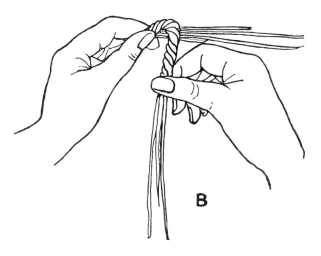

quiries among some of the old people a great many were used for chairseating or for plaited rush mats and rushlights. The little common rush has to be twisted into cord in order to be used for chairseating. The writer has a plaited mat made of the small common rush which has been in use for almost twenty years. When new its sweet scent filled the whole house. It seems a pity to import immense quantities of twisted grass when we could perfectly easily produce the twist ourselves or get our blind or disabled people to make it.

I am much indebted for knowledge of the method of twisting this grass or rush to Mr. William Kirkness of Orkney. His father manufactures a remarkably interesting chair known as the Orkney chair. Its back is made of thick strands of oaten straw sewn together with "twist" made of flat leaved bent or seagrass, "Flossy bent" as it is called in Orkney. The seat is made of the twist made from the harder and less pliable Round bent. Mr. Kirkness tells me that the old folk and the children sit round the fireside making twist, singing and telling tales as they work.

HOW TO NET A HAMMOCK

P. A. Cumming

THE appliances and materials for netting are both clean to use and extraordinarily cheap and, once the knack of making the knots is captured there is no end to the useful and attractive things that can be made, such as hammocks, shopping bags, fishing and

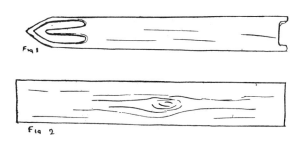

Fig 1

Fig 2

landing nets, tennis, badminton, cricket, rabbit and fruit nets.

There are only two tools required, Fig. 1, the needle, and Fig. 2, the mesh, both of which can be bought at a crafts shop for a few pence or made at home out of smooth soft wood. The mesh is one foot in length, the breadth depending upon the size of the stitches desired : between one and a half and two inches is a suitable breadth for netting a hammock. The length of the needle may be between five and eight inches and the breadth must be half an inch less than that of the mesh employed, otherwise it will not pass easily through the stitches when loaded with string.

Before starting on a hammock it is a good plan to net a trial piece out of cheap string.

Load the needle by winding the string up, round the prong, down the same side, then up the other side and down again until the needle is comfortably full. Wind the string fairly tightly as you wish to carry as much string as possible to avoid constant joining on.

Next make a large loop of spare string and hang it from something firm, such as a hook or window-catch. To this tie a second loop, in such a manner that it will slip easily round. Knot the end of the working string to this loop, then all is ready to cast on the foundation row of loops, about eight of which is a good number for practising.

Hold the mesh lengthways between the left finger and thumb, and close under the knot. With the other hand bring the needle and working string down, over the mesh and up through the back of the second loop, pull tight and secure against mesh with left thumb. Then bring the string round in a circle towards the left shoulder, insert the needle again from the back, this time between the *entire* loop and the circle just made, Fig. 3. Draw tight, releasing string

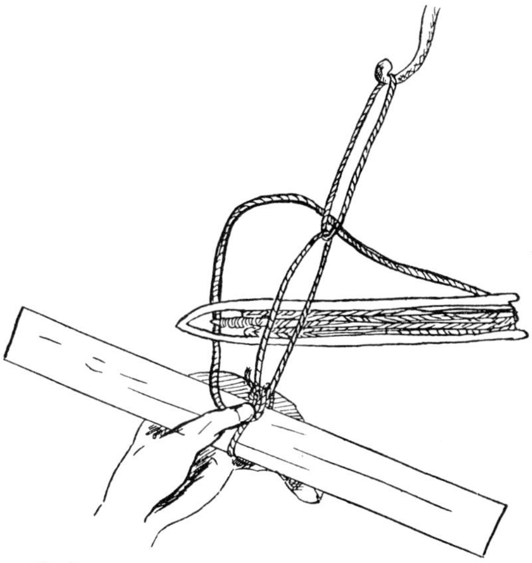

Fig. 3

under thumb and the first knot is completed. Repeat the whole process until the required number of stitches are on the mesh, with a row of knots all along the top.

Slip the mesh out of the stitches, turn the work over and start again from the left, working one knot into

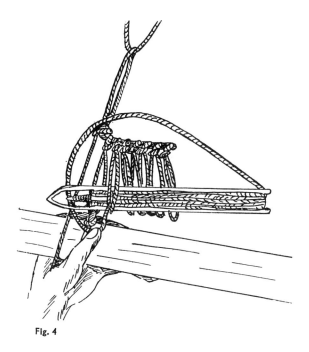

Fig. 4

each of the foundation loops, Fig. 4. Turn the work at the end of every row and after a few rows you will have a piece of netting similar to Fig. 5.

It is very important to pull the knots as tight as possible, as this makes them stronger and neater in appearance.

When the needle is empty, it is necessary to reload it and join on again and the best knot for this purpose is the Weaver's knot, Fig. 6.

The most suitable string from which to net a hammock is a fairly thick softish kind, of which about four balls are needed for the netting. A broomstick cut in two for struts, a couple of iron rings and some lengths of strong rope are all that are required for slinging the hammock.

For a normal sized hammock cast thirty-two stitches on to the mesh, in the way described. If the mesh will not hold them all at once, let some slip off the left end and hang down as you work. Turn the work, net into the loops and turn again until you have netted forty-six rows, remembering that it takes two rows to make a complete diamond. Net one more row with double string, as on this row of loops most of the weight will depend.

Now cut the loop upon which the *first* row hangs, draw out the string and the knots will come undone easily, leaving an ordinary row of loops. Into these net another row with double string, as you did for the last row at the. opposite end.

After that there is nothing to do but to make the hammock up.

Take each of the halves of broomstick in turn and bore a hole through each end, then slip the halves of the broomstick through the end loops of the netting, Fig. 7, so that you have a strut top and bottom.

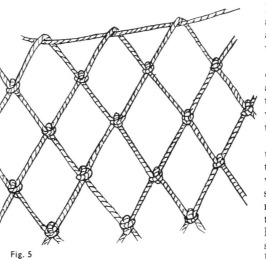

Fig. 5

Cut two lengths of string a little longer than the length of the hammock, thread the ends through the holes in the top strut, fasten with knots, thread all down the sides of the hammock and tie through the holes in the bottom strut. This will prevent the

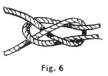

Fig. 6

hammock from going flat when anyone is lying in it, but care should be taken not to get the side lines so short that the weight falls upon them and not on the network.

Finally thread some rope through one of the iron rings and tie to the ends of the top strut in the form of a " V " ; do the same with the other ring to the bottom strut and your hammock will be ready to sling in a shady nook between two trees or posts, Fig. 8.

SADDLE SOAP

J. D. U. WARD

A TIN or cake of saddle soap is a most useful thing to have in the house. Saddle soap preserves and softens leather and gives it a wonderful polish too, if a little elbow grease is used.

Though primarily intended for harness, this soap gives excellent results when used on shoes (brown especially) or leather sandals, kit-bag or portmanteaux, despatch cases or school satchels, gaiters or gloves of the heavy pigskin type now so popular.

Bicycle saddles also will wear and look the better if soaped and polished once or twice a week.

New brown shoes or a new coat of smooth leather should always be well soaped two or three times before wear in the wet, otherwise they are liable to be stained by the rain.

Saddle soap should only be used on perfectly clean leather : the soap gives the best results when applied with a soft sponge that is just damp, no more than slightly damp for the soap lathers easily and lather should be avoided. A soft dry cloth or a chamois leather is the best " polisher."

Saddle soap, which is clean and pleasant to use, is sold in a variety of makes. One of the best and oldest kinds is to be purchased in round tins : a modern product, also very good, is marketed in transparent, brick-like cakes. Prices vary from 6d. to 2s. but 1s. 6d. is the usual price for the popular size of good soaps.

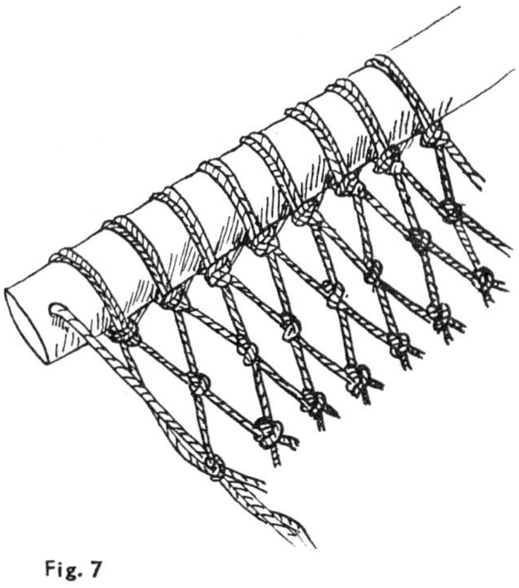

In a former age saddle soap was better appreciated but today few establishments boast a harness room so even in farm and country houses the usefulness of saddle soap is apt to be forgotten. When people dispensed with a harness room, they generally dispensed with the cleaning equipment too.

Fig. 7

A **Gardening Anecdote** sent in by Miss Turney, member of Plumtree and Tollerton, Nottinghamshire.

John, aged six, saw a root of stinging nettles growing in the orchard. His mother told him not to touch as they would sting. A while after he saw a bee fly towards the nettles and he made this enquiry : " Mother, would the bee sting the nettle, or the nettle sting the bee, do you think you could tell me ? " She could not.

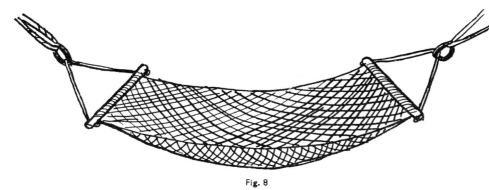

Fig. 8

"REPAIR SQUAD, PLEASE!"

Yesterday ... in the garage ... repairing cars..." a little trouble with the plugs, sir ? Soon get that fixed !" Today a soldier— Right in the thick of it ... shells bursting . . . snipers taking a crack at him. But he does it! And repairs another tank—ready for action ! Salute his toughness —his endurance ! Salute the Soldier — with more savings ! Let us all vow to-day to mobilize our money—by cutting spending and increasing lending. Let us lend to our country—and so lend practical help " to the boys out there!"

SALUTE THE SOLDIER

OVERHEARD AT THE BENCH

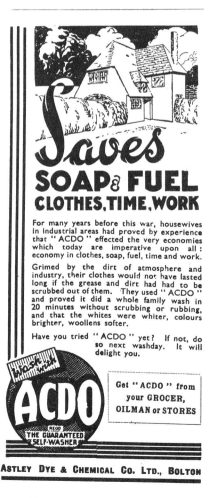

New ways with the new SALT FISH

Baked Cod with Parsnip Balls and Piquant Sauce

2 *lb. parsnips, salt, pepper, browned crumbs,* 1 *lb. soaked salt cod,* 4 *tablespoons dripping.* SAUCE : ½ *oz. margarine,* 2 *level tablespoons flour,* ½ *pint vegetable stock, salt, pepper, mustard,* 1 *tablespoon vinegar.* QUANTITY : 4 *helpings.*

Cook the parsnips till quite soft. Drain and mash well with seasonings. Form into balls and coat in browned crumbs. Skin and bone fish, place in baking tin and spread with dripping. Bake in a quick oven for 5 minutes, then add parsnip balls and bake together for 20 minutes.

Sauce : Melt margarine, add flour, cook 3 minutes. Add liquid gradually, stirring well, and cook for another 5 minutes. Season and stir in vinegar. Serve with fish in centre of dish, the parsnip balls round and the sauce over the fish.

THE salt fish we get now is proving very popular. Are you serving it often ? You should ; because salt fish is every bit as nourishing as fresh fish—a really first-class body-builder, as good in this respect as a meat meal. Grand for children as well as grown-ups, and what a bargain at only 10d. a pound !

As you know, this fish has to be soaked for at least 24 hours to get the salt out. Ask the fishmonger, and if he hasn't soaked it for long, finish the soaking at home. To do this, put the fish, skin side up, in plenty of cold water. Then cook it the same day.

HOW TO BOIL SALT FISH. Drain off the soaking water and rinse the fish under the cold tap. Cut in convenient pieces; put in a pan with cold water to cover and bring slowly to the boil. Cook until tender, about ten minutes. Drain well, and use as required.

You can use any of your favourite recipes calling for fresh fish. But, to give you something new, here are some special recipes :

COD PANCAKES. ½ *lb. salt cod, cooked and flaked in small pieces,* 1 *level tablespoon chopped parsley, salt and pepper,* 2 *level tablespoons mixed herbs,* 6 *oz. mashed carrots.* Batter: 4 *oz. flour,* 1 *level tablespoon dried egg (dry),* 2 *level teaspoons baking powder, salt,* ½ *pint water.* (*Makes 4 helpings.*)

Make the batter by mixing together all the dry ingredients, adding sufficient water to make a stiff batter. Beat well and add the remainder of the water. Add to the batter the flaked cod, parsley, seasoning, herbs and carrots. Melt some fat in a pan and when smoking hot drop in large spoonfuls of the mixture. Brown the pancakes on one side and then turn over and brown the other.

SALT FISH LYONNAISE. 1 *medium sized onion, sliced, fat for frying,* 3 *medium-sized potatoes, cooked and sliced,* 1 *lb. soaked salt fish, cooked and flaked,* 1 *teaspoon vinegar, pepper, chopped parsley.*

Fry onion in a little fat till tender, add potato and fish and fry until brown. Sprinkle over vinegar, pepper and parsley. If liked, serve with a sauce and salad, or with vegetables coated with sauce and extra potatoes.

TASTY FISH-PASTE SANDWICH FILLING. 3 *oz. finely chopped cooked salt fish,* 3 *oz. well mashed potato,* 1 *tablespoon chopped parsley,* 2 *tablespoons chopped raw onion,* 2 *dessertspoons vinegar,* 1 *teaspoon made mustard, pepper,* ½ *oz. melted margarine.*

Mix all ingredients together very thoroughly to give a smooth paste.

Above: Basketmaking at the Chilham Rally, Kent, 1953

Below: HRH Duchess of York at the 1938 craft exhibition

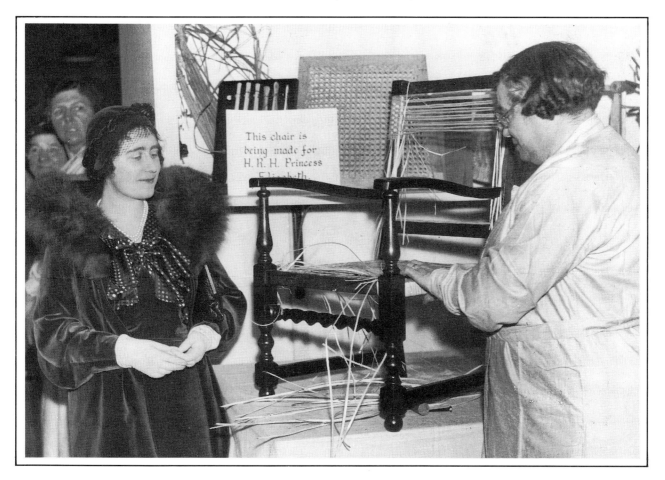

CROCUS
Non shrink

A two-piece bathing suit, consisting of knickers and brassiere, is quite new and quite easy to make. The wool is "Crocus," which makes warm, comfortable suits which do not lose their shape and never shrink or fade. 8 ozs. only is required to knit the suit illustrated. Instructions are given in Booklet No. 3/576, price 3d. post free, with free samples of wool, from Dept. 25, Patons & Baldwins Ltd., Alloa, Scotland, or Halifax, England.

KNITTING WOOL

Φ259

★ THE RUG YOU MADE YOURSELF

It's very bright and welcoming and much admired. What did it cost you? The price of the wool and canvas, and some short and pleasant hours of work.

Rugmaking is the simplest of crafts. It does not require concentration, and can be done whilst talking or listening to the wireless. It does not demand any skill. The method of using the "Turkey" Rug Hook is mastered in a few moments. Rugmaking saves your pocket and increases your pleasure. There are 100 shades of "Turkey" Rug Wool, and a big selection of rug patterns to choose from. Send for the latest edition of "RUGCRAFT," an instructive book containing six coloured charts, price 6d. post free, together with free samples of wool, to Dept. 25, Patons & Baldwins Ltd., Alloa, Scotland, or Halifax, England.

TURKEY RUG WOOL

BEST AND GOES FURTHEST Φ101

GRAFTING ON STOCKINGS.

DEAR EDITOR, In reply to the letter of E. A. Hindes in September "HOME AND COUNTRY" may I say that every diplomée or properly qualified teacher of plain needlework can teach stocking mending and grafting? I myself often teach re-footing stockings by machine to Institutes, but I should not teach grafting unless I were asked as the work is somewhat complicated. The subject could be clearly taught with the help of large diagrams and I should be glad to do so if required.

"A Member" should ask her Hon. Secretary to tell the demonstrator or lecturer clearly when writing the time allowed for the lecture. This would be most welcome to the teacher and avoid overtiring the audience.

I am, yours faithfully (MRS.) VIOLET BRAND,
Diplomée National Training School of Cookery, London.
5 Upper Hamilton Terrace, Hampstead, N.W.8.

DEAR EDITOR, I note the enquiry from E. A. Hindes regarding the "grafting" of stockings. In my book, "Educational Needlecraft" (Longmans), I give a diagram showing a darn as it was taught to me by a Silesian lady

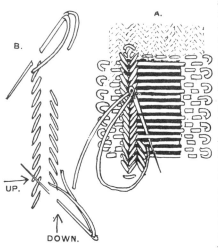

and I find this a most practical and simple way to graft and the only way by which one can imitate the ribbed effect of stockings.

The diagram shows how the work is done.

First after trimming away loose edges round the hole, darn in the usual way *across* the knitting from side to side on the outside of the stocking till the hole is covered with horizontal stitches, each spaced, as far as possible, on each successive row of the knitted stitches. Then begin working vertically up this ladder-like surface of stitches with a row of so-called "outline" stitches. picking up each successive step of the ladder in turn and passing over *two* steps each time. Keep the tension very regular and make vertical lines as like the knitting as possible. Bring your thread out each time on the same side of the needle. At the end of the ladder run your needle a certain distance beyond the hole and turn down again. Next work, another row *down* the darn alongside and close against the first row of "outline" stitches. but slope these stitches in the opposite direction to those of the first row. This produces the herring bone or chain stitched effect of the knitted stitches.

If you are darning a ribbed stocking the effect of the ribbing can be perfectly worked by turning your darn wrong side out and working the same way on the wrong side for as many rows as there are stitches between the ribs.

Yours faithfully, ANN MACBETH,
Chief Instructress of the Glasgow School of Art.

H.H.H. !

To clean an enamel bath. If in the last stages, the bath should be scraped clean and then enamelled with a good bath enamel, like Ripolin. If the dirt is merely temporary and the enamel is unbroken, a mixture of paraffin and finely ground sand is good, but the bath must be thoroughly rinsed afterwards. Zog for daily use is good.

– 1926 –

RENOVATING CLOTHES

THERE IS NOTHING more depressing than a wardrobe full of shabby and semi-shabby clothes, yet at the present moment it is not wise to get rid of old things and to buy new ones. A very great deal can be done to tone up shabby materials by using the right methods and to renovate old garments by careful stitchery and pressing

HOT BRAN is a first-rate tonic for tweeds and light clothes. When cleaning with it, have two pans of bran, keeping one in the oven or on the stove while the other is in use. Rub the hot bran into the material, and then brush it off.

Ground rice is excellent for cleaning white or very light cloth. It should be applied with a clean piece of white flannel, left on for two or three hours and then well brushed and shaken out.

Powdered magnesia will clean all delicate fabrics such as lace, embroideries, white kid or suède gloves. Place the article to be cleaned on a clean dry towel and sprinkle the magnesia over it liberally. The towel should then be folded over and the whole wrapped up and left for twelve to fourteen hours. After this, the fabric should be well shaken and any magnesia dust gently brushed off with a very soft brush.

A Sovereign Tonic

Oil of eucalyptus is, of course, one of the most valuable of clothes tonics. Jaded silks, faded crêpe de chine as well as serge and cloth will all look rejuvenated after an application of it. Do not be afraid of rubbing it well in, preferably with a piece of the same material as the article that is being cleaned. It will remove grease and dust, and dry out without leaving any mark.

A splendid remedy for cleaning men's overcoats, suits, etc., and making the shabbiest felt hat look like new, is Clensel, using equal quantities of the Clensel and water.

Potato pulp is good for cleaning cloth gaiters, leggings and similar articles. To prepare this, peel and grate two or three potatoes and put them through a mincing machine. Sponge the material thoroughly with this pulp, rubbing it well into any parts especially soiled. Hang the gaiters up to dry and then brush them well.

A Special Old-Time Recipe

Before the days of commercial cleaners, our grandmothers used the following home-made preparation for cleaning treasured silks, and although it may be a little expensive at this time on account of the price of the spirit needed, it is a recipe well worth keeping for future use.

Mix well together three ounces of strained honey, two ounces of castile soap and a half-pint of gin. Lay the garment flat on a clean board or table and rub or brush it on both sides with the preparation. Then rinse it in several lots of tepid water, but do not squeeze it. Hang it in the open air to drip until half dry. Then iron with a cool iron on the wrong side and the fabric will look like new.

The Art of Pressing

A garment that has become "tired-looking" can be successfully revived by pressing. It must be remembered that pressing is not ironing, and that a hot, fairly heavy iron must be used for it. In most cases, pressing should be done on the wrong side, except for heavy cloths and suitings, and a cloth wrung out in cold water must be placed between the garment and the iron. If, however, a shiny place is left after pressing, this can be removed by putting a dry cloth over it and a damp cloth over the dry one and passing a hot iron lightly across several times.

The Care of Men's Clothes

If a man's clothes are to be well preserved, it is specially necessary to hang them up after the day's wear in such a manner that any creases can disappear. It is more hygienic to hang them for a time where the air can reach them than to put them straight into a wardrobe. Mudstains are very ugly, but never attempt to deal with them until they are quite dry.

Frocks with Varied Accessories

NOW THAT we can look forward to spring, some of our readers will be thinking of making new frocks. Here are two useful afternoon dresses, on which the accessories could be changed; different collars could be used with one, and the other, if in a dark material, could have, say, two brightly coloured sashes.

No. 145643, for the younger member, takes 4 yards of 36 inch material in bust size 36. No. 136353, which can have either long or bracelet length sleeves, takes 6¼ yards of 36 inch material with long sleeves or 6 yards with short sleeves in bust size 42 inches.

The patterns cost 1s. 3d. each, post free (including Purchase Tax).

ORDERS, stating the number of pattern and bust size required, should be addressed to the Paper Pattern Department, HOME AND COUNTRY, Puddephat's Farm, Markyate, Herts.

No. 145643
In bust sizes 32-40 inches.
(*Price 1s. 3d.*)

No. 136353
In bust sizes, 32-48 inches.
(*Price 1s. 3d.*)

CHAPTER SIX
Issues and Ironies

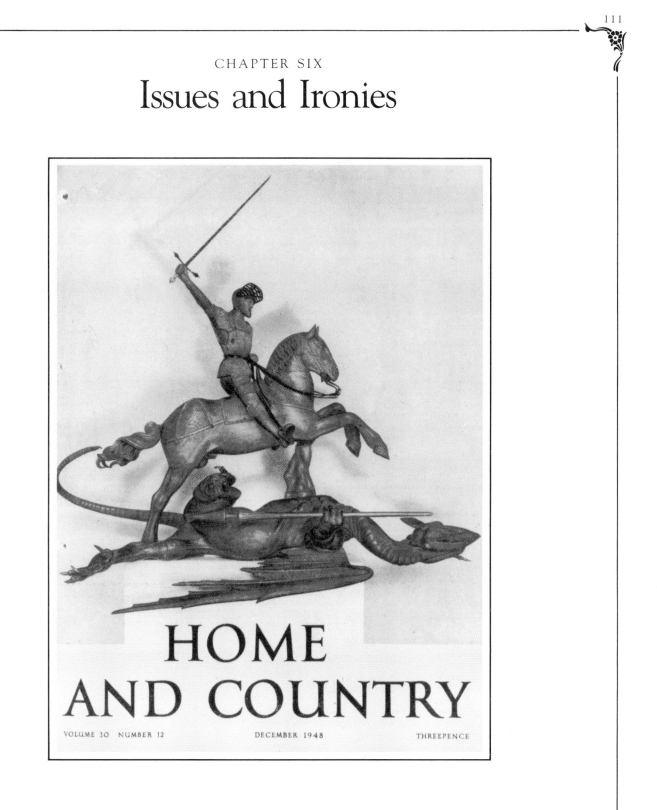

HOME
AND COUNTRY

VOLUME 30   NUMBER 12   DECEMBER 1948   THREEPENCE

CORRESPONDENCE

STEEL TRAPS.   – 1928 –

DEAR EDITOR,   As a member of a Women's Institute, I should like to add a personal experience to the letter on the above subject which appeared in the May number of "HOME AND COUNTRY."

Motoring to town one day, with my cook, we saw on the road an unfortunate cat with a steel-toothed trap fastened to its paw.   Whilst I pulled up as quickly as possible, my cook, who is a great lover of animals, jumped out and secured the cat just as it was attempting to escape through the hedge.   Between us we managed to undo the trap and release the cat.   Fortunately its leg was not broken.   Needless to say after this revolting and cruel experience, I was delighted to see the letter in "HOME AND COUNTRY" and at once wrote off for some petition forms.

I trust this letter may be the means of spurring on other Women's Institute members to do the same.

Yours sincerely, MAUD HALL,
President, Burstwick.

PIT PONIES AND THE MINES   – 1945 –

DEAR EDITOR,   We are in a position to assure your readers that many thousands of pit ponies are shamefully overworked in the mines.   This was also true long before the war—as records from our investigations and files can prove.   We believe that the time is ripe when all coal mines should be completely mechanized.   Mechanical haulage is long overdue and this would at once withdraw all ponies from the mines.   In many pits conditions are bad despite assurances given to the contrary.   Adequate inspection of the ponies is an impossibility, and present inspection by Government officials totally inadequate.   The only remedy is the total withdrawal of the ponies and such is practicable.

To this end we are organizing a petition to Parliament and will be grateful to every W.I. member who will write to us for petitions and literature.   Every form filled with signatures will help.

Yours faithfully, ALFRED BRISCO
Organizing Secretary, The National Equine
Blackwell, Carlisle.   *(and smaller Animals) Defence League.*

HUMANE PIG KILLING   – 1947 –

DEAR EDITOR,   Noticing the letter signed "Violet E. Oates" in February HOME AND COUNTRY, I was elated to find somebody else championing the cause of the poor pig, that wretched animal which has so often and so unnecessarily to endure a death of indescribable agony.

May I give an example of what may be achieved, by personal effort, towards ridding the country of this barbarity?

Three years ago, as a member of the Humane Slaughter Association, I started a vigorous campaign in the local press upon the subject of this cruelty.   In co-operation with the H.S.A., I was able to offer licensed slaughtermen free gifts of the humane killer if they would use it.   Since starting, I think we have so far supplied between 30 and 40, and as each man would kill on an average 100 pigs a season, it can be seen that many thousands have thus received a painless death which otherwise would have suffered the other.   Lincolnshire was notoriously bad, according to statistics of the H.S.A., but I am happy to say that no pig is ever *heard* dying in this village or in many localities far around.   Therefore, if other W.I. members in other counties would start similar campaigns, the number of pigs dying unmercifully would drop to a minimum.

All slaughtermen I have known prefer to use the humane killer, and charge no more, and I have never yet heard a complaint about the meat consequent upon its use.   In cases where it is still not used, the reason is always ignorance or prejudice.

Yours faithfully,
Carlton-le-Moorland W.I., Lincoln.   SYBIL LARKIN

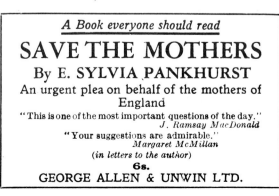

FINE FEATHERS MAKE EMPTY NESTS.

WHEN the readers of HOME AND COUNTRY turn up the advertisement pages of their daily newspaper and read that fashion has decreed a feather year, that "ospreys" (which are the marriage plumes of the egret and white heron) now cost large sums of money, that so-and-so was seen at a ball with nine Birds of Paradise plumes as a head-dress; when again they visit the London shops and see the windows filled with many-coloured wings and quills; when they see thousands of London women walking Oxford Street bedecked with feathers like savages—do these readers need ask themselves what this means?   I do not know, but all the same I am now going to tell them.

Except for ostrich feathers and poultry and imitations which can be distinguished at a glance from the real thing, these wings and quills and plumes belong to wild birds which have been shot at their nests to provide them.   For every single wing, quill or plume that you see in a woman's hat, it has been calculated by our greatest naturalist that ten birds had suffered death.   For some of the birds are wounded and cannot be found, while their young, after their parents have been killed, die of starvation in the nests.   But why, you will ask, are the birds killed in the bridal season?   This is the reason.   Every year there comes a season of gladness, love and renewal, and as trees put forth their buds and the earth its flowers, so the plumage of wild birds acquires a new gloss and brightness or grows new ornaments which disappear when the young are fledged.   This is the time when plumes and wings fetch the best prices, and so out go the hired ruffians of the East End plume-trader, and, taking full advantage of the ease with which they can approach the birds, occupied with rearing their young, they slay these birds in millions, in order that our brides and our mothers may look as smart as their victims.

Few, if any, of the readers of HOME AND COUNTRY can have any idea of the immense slaughter that goes on year after year all over the world to supply the London feather market.   The annual import of bird skins before the war was £35,000,000; of that great and noble bird, the white albatross, 300,000 was slain in one raid, and great numbers (as reported by the United States Government) had their wings cut off and were left to bleed to death; of one species alone (the blue and chestnut Smyrnian kingfisher) 162,750 skins were sold at a single sale; 40,000 condors (the highest flying bird) were sold at *one* sale by *one* firm only, and 152,000 "ospreys" at two sales in 1912 and 1913. And so on, myriads of these loveliest, most harmless and necessary creatures massacred year after year under conditions of sickening cruelty to swell the profits of a few alien traders (largely of German, Austrian and Italian origin) and to feed the vanity of fashion.   I cannot tell you a fiftieth part of the appalling truth about this wickedness, but I can that the figures have been proved over and over again by Government enquiries and the evidence of the most distinguished scientists and personal eye-witnesses of the slaughter.

Now this must be stopped for three reasons—(*a*) because it is a shameful thing to permit such savagery when we can end it; (*b*) because the race of foreign birds is being killed right out of the world; and (*c*) because vast numbers of these birds are insect-eaters and their death is already bringing famine and disease upon the world.   The Government has promised to introduce a Plumage Bill, but it will keep on delaying matters unless public opinion forces it to stand by its promise.   So I should like to see the Women's Institutes all over the country pass resolutions at once demanding the Bill, and send them up to Sir Auckland Geddes, Board of Trade, Whitehall, S.W.1.

H. J. MASSINGHAM,

Founder of the "Plumage Bill Group."
22, Westmoreland Road, Barnes,
London, S.W.13.

– 1920 –

HENS IN CAGES

WE have recently published two articles dealing with do's and dont's for the amateur poultrywoman. This month a correspondent gives an account of a new professional system of intensive egg-production

THE barnyard fowls of our pre-war childhood, often the products of a few dozen nondescript eggs (perhaps Irish) which lived a carefree life about the farmyard to produce a few eggs for the house and a very little " pin-money " for the farmer's wife, have been old-fashioned now for about a quarter of a century. Barnyard fowls have given place to well-managed poultry departments on a large number of farms, and they are run on the lines of the large specialist poultry farms which have more than doubled the pre-war poultry population of England and Wales since 1921, for the pre-war figure was about 30,000,000 and today we have nearly 70,000.000.

Not only are there something more than twice the number of fowls in the country ; they produce about five times as many eggs. That looks like progress with a capital " P." But progress has a bill to present and it has presented it in several ways in recent years.

The old barnyard fowls lived under conditions not so very far removed from the natural conditions of the jungle fowl—the ancestor of the domestic fowl—with plenty of hard grit and hard food, scratching to do, a hard life to weed out the weaklings, and laying few, if any, more eggs, than the jungle fowl, which lays a couple of clutches a year. Today upwards of 200 eggs a year are expected, and laying must begin a month or two earlier. The incubator and the brooder provided a cheaper and much more convenient method of rearing than the broody hens, at the same time making it possible to respond to the vigorous demand for stock in the immediate post-war years.

The departure from relatively natural conditions has gone on as the inevitable result of these new ideas. It has all been necessary to cheapen production and meet the lower egg prices as more and more home-produced eggs came into the market. But it has taken its toll. The strain of heavy egg production, the departure from hard and relatively natural conditions, and the difficulty of keeping ground free from parasites under enclosed conditions on small areas, have all contributed to a general loss of stamina and the spread of hereditary and other diseases.

These facts suggest, perhaps, that we had better go back to the old barnyard ways. But the barnyard method is economic only when there are no management charges and nothing more than a little " pin-money " is expected. The immense market for home-produced eggs that has been developed could not be supplied on such lines, and the specialist poultry farmer could not exist, for if his hens were kept under something more nearly approaching natural conditions, land, housing, and labour costs would leap up.

A way out seems to be offered by the laying battery system. The principle of rearing chickens in batteries of small cages naturally followed the mass production methods of the giant incubators, which hatch chicks in thousands at a time, and its adaptation to fattening birds was only a short step. A little experience with fattening birds led to cages for laying birds, and it is possible that about 10 per cent. of the 40,000,000 birds over six months in England and Wales are now in batteries.

Each bird has a cage just large enough for it to eat from the hopper of dry mash in front of it continually and to drink from the running water. A set of 24 cages in three storeys measures roughly 12 ft. by 7 ft. by 2 ft. 6 ins., and about 500 birds can be housed in a building of about 60 ft. by 20 ft. On such a system one person can attend to about 2,000 birds comfortably, and the general report is that the birds lay better than on other systems, assuming proper feeding. The cost per egg is less than on other systems and what is more, although the birds are kept on far less land than ever before, they are never on ground infected by other birds, which establishes a fairly rigid control over most diseases.

EIGHT complete changes of air an hour are arranged for the buildings which house the batteries of cages and the climate is therefore always under control. (Oilskins and rubber boots do not enter into the attendant's life any more.) Birds of doubtful stamina or birds which have been backward and bullied thrive remarkably under their protected conditions, and it is clear that the laying battery has come to stay, for, wisely used, it solves a grave problem for the specialized egg producer, as distinct from the general farmer, who can do better by " folding " his poultry in movable houses over his land.

But there is no getting away from the fact that it turns the laying hen into nothing more nor less than a living egg machine. Those rows of heads sticking out of cages give one a feeling that "It ain't accordin' to Natur'," as the old farm labourer said.

True. " It ain't." No more is it according to Nature to confine pigs to a sty and to fasten up cows in the shippons for several months in the year (in some cases throughout the year). That the birds do well argues that there is neither mental nor physical suffering. The system is kinder to the weakly and the bullied than Nature, and for that reason laying battery stock should never come to be used for breeding. Beyond that I will not go. Sentimentally I dislike the laying batteries; but my reason on all the evidence I have, cannot support my sentiments. I leave it to you.

F. A. RUSH

Matron is in charge of the Mothercraft Training Society, organized in London by Dr. Truby King, the Director of Health of Women and Children in New Zealand, which has the lowest infant mortality in the world.

A NOTABLE MOTHERCRAFT SERVICE

Does Baby eat too little or too much? Are habits irregular? Is weight unsatisfactory? Is there a tendency towards constipation? Is Baby's skin irritated? Is the food formula right? If there is anything about which you are in doubt, Matron will give you the benefit of her wide experience. This Motherhood service in "Woman's Pictorial" is the finest thing ever organized by any paper in this country, and every Mother should take advantage of it. Questions will be answered free by post if desired. For full particulars see

WOMAN'S PICTORIAL

Of all Newsagents.

Every Wednesday, 3d.

THE BOY VAGRANT

Mary Higgs

In social life, when a new situation imperceptibly arises, it is some time before society grasps its significance. Remedies lag behind diseases. Thus, for instance, in the era that forced on the formation of the English Poor Law, the host of "broken men" compelled the creation of "the casual ward" in order to enable men to reach "their place of settlement" where the workhouse provided work. The harsh laws which compelled "vagrants" not to wander, also took count of the boy by apprenticing and "binding" him to some master.

In the great upheaval of society which we call "the industrial revolution" this idea of apprenticeship expanded, under the need of the cotton spinner, to what are called in the North "the chitty children" and their wrongs found voice in Mrs. Barrett Browning's "Cry of the Children."

When this new wrong produced the swarms of ragged children, ragged schools arose and eventually from these evolved a system of national education.

But all the time children had *homes* of some sort, even if supported by Poor Law, and such children as had not homes were supported by charity or the State "until they became wage-earning."

Today the new phenomenon is the juvenile unemployed wage-earner and, as a consequence, the increasing stream of "boy vagrants."

Now even if we could regard the casual ward as a fitting place for the man who has "spent his life in tramping," it is evidently quite unsuitable for a boy setting out on the uncharted sea of life, even if the "reformed casual ward" locks him up in a solitary cell for hours of darkness or semi-darkness, without even a Bible (as in a prison cell). Still more unsuitable if he haps upon it, is the unreformed casual ward as it still exists.

Picture to yourself a low building, more like a shed than a room, a place reported to be frequented by vermin, rats and mice (and hence known on the road as "the Rat Hole"), with six wooden beds, so close as to touch and on the end of each of five of the beds because there is no other seat or room to move, a man sitting, waiting for "supper" : and on the sixth bed a respectably dressed lad ! There, in those close quarters, he would undress and roll up in three blankets and incur any contamination of mind and body that happened in the dark hours of night. *Well*, if, instead of this man-invented hell, he were in some other ward, shut up, locked up, with an unknown man "of the tramp class" can mothers imagine what schooling he might get in vice and crime, even in unnatural crime ?

"What's the harm : its human nature," said one contaminated boy emerging from such schooling.

But how comes the boy to be there ? What happens to the motherless unemployed adolescent ? What to the fatherless, or to the lad with stepfather or stepmother ? "Kicked out of home" is the expression that has been used to me, as part of such a life history. "I've brothers and sisters, but don't know where they are."

What I want to emphasise is that this appearance of the boy in the vagrant ward is a new phenomenon. Is it the sign of a break-up of society ? For "the boy is father to the man." Of what sort will be the fathers of the future if they are unemployed wanderers ? Nature's urge and sex satisfaction does not stop : rather when all other pleasures are cut off the sex urge becomes an unnatural hunger : sex crimes become more common.

It is time that society realised its new peril. No adolescent boy should roam the country, half-starved, ill-clothed and above all, workless, "thrown like rubbish to the road." For the future depends on the new generation, if this rots, where are we ? No adolescent should be unoccupied.

In the cotton famine those who were workless were either "found work" or "schooled."

As the failure of our staple trades is producing "adolescent unemployment," we must face the situation or, to our national peril, the fringe of the untrained will be pushed off into "the abyss" to recruit the ranks of crime or to sink into "the wastrel." Our potential wealth is boy life, "the rising generation." What else is it on which England depends ? Every boy is an asset or a debit. For him at least a Help Centre should exist, that, if he drops into the stream, he may be salved before he "goes under."

THE SAME STARS

Living in basements
With dingy casements,
They watch the stars
Through the iron bars
Of poverty ;
But all men see
The self-same stars.

The planet Mars
Is no more bright
On a winter's night
To emperors
Than to stevedores
Watching through casements
In dirty basements.

IVY O. EASTWICK

FURNISHING THE WORKER'S HOME

by Jennie Lee

THE Government recently published a report on the furnishing of the working class home. Miss Jennie Lee, daughter of a Scottish miner and formerly M.P. for North Lanark, writes about it as one who both understands actual possibilities and has worked for slum clearance

MUCH interest has been roused by the recent report on *The Working Class Home : Its Furnishing and Equipment.** It is a sign of the times that an officially sponsored document should even consider such a subject. And everyone interested in housing questions is bound to study its findings with scrupulous care.

One piece of painful knowledge has been impressed on all who know the slums of Great Britain and have tried to abolish them : to transfer a family from a slum to a new house is little use if it takes with it household goods that are vermin ridden, ugly, and falling to pieces. If there is to be happiness in the new surroundings, the contents of the home as well as its external structure must be radically changed.

That immediately raises the question of furnishing costs, of how much a family can afford to spend, and of the type of goods available at reasonable prices.

The committee that undertook to investigate those problems was set up by the Council for Art and Industry, and included a representative of the Board of Trade. The Government, however, as is customary with such committees, is not in any way bound to act upon its suggestions. Nor will any experienced housewife find herself agreeing with all it has to say, for home-making is an infinitely individual art.

Nevertheless, the adventures of this distinguished committee in territory seldom officially explored has a wide general interest, and the published report is bound to become an authoritative reference book, particularly for those engaged in local government work.

AS a first step, the committee examined current market prices and concluded that a minimum standard to enable a family to live in reasonable comfort could not be laid down for less than about £50 ; that an additional outlay of £16 or £17 was

* *The Working Class Home : Its Furnishing and Equipment* (H.M. Stationery Office, 1s.).

highly desirable ; and that an ultimate expenditure of £100 ought to be aimed at wherever possible.

Estimates for the minimum standard worked out as follows :

				£	s.	d.
Living room	..	..	..	15	12	3
Parents' bedroom		..	..	15	8	10
Children's bedroom		..	..	12	0	9
Kitchen, scullery and bathroom			..	2	2	3
Equipment :						
General hardware		..	..	1	6	1
Cooking utensils		..	..		14	6
Pottery	..	..	..	1	10	0
Cutlery	..	..	..	1	6	9
Linen	..	..	..	1	3	11
Glass	..	..	..		3	0
Total	..	..	..	£51	8	4

Just what can be done for this expenditure can be seen at the Building Centre, Bond Street, London, where a set of rooms has been furnished and equipped to illustrate the report. The exhibition is open to the public, free of charge. I wonder if I should say it is worth visiting ? Frankly, I am in doubt. The furniture and equipment displayed, although they would be very Heaven to families imprisoned in dismal slums, are admittedly beyond their means.

The committee had no illusions on this point. It clearly states that it based its calculations on the needs of a family consisting of husband and wife and two young children, and enjoying a regular income of £3 per week.

That is a sobering consideration. It means that in the view of Housing, Health, and Industrial

WARDROBE (£10 12s. 6d.) AND CHEST OF DRAWERS (£4 17s. 6d.)

The first illustration in the report : furniture that is certainly "of good proportions and simple construction," but that would run away with an impossibly large part of the £50 suggested as the minimum sum required to furnish a home for a man, wife, and two children decently experts, even a satisfactory minimum standard of comfort and convenience is above the purchasing power of whole sections of working people : for instance, the agricultural labourer, the miner, the unemployed.

On the other hand, no one who knows the work-ing class homes of Great Britain would dream of saying that only those with incomes of at least £3 per week and with no more than two children have an atmosphere of well being.

THE truth is that what the experts found beyond their powers, thousands of housewives accom-plish. Most homes are assembled by bits and pieces added from time to time, some new, some second-hand, some home-made. Like Topsy, they often cannot tell where they come from. They just grow. And in this way a snug hearth is evolved for the family to shelter around.

But the missing element is—convenience. A bright fireside for an hour or two in the evening purchased at the cost of unceasing drudgery during the rest of the day.

I looked carefully around the exhibition to see what labour-saving hints it had to offer to the working-class home, both those above and those below the £3 a week income level.

Furniture selected was of simple design, drawers moved in and out easily, space was used to the best advantage, colour schemes and patterns of walls, floors and curtains avoided the astounding clashes in which Victorian taste delighted, fireside chairs combined reasonable comfort with trimness. But an inevitable bleakness marred this mechanical assembling of a household.

Successful simplicity is not so easy as it may sound. In furnishing, as in clothing, only the well-to-do can really achieve it. Cheap imitations are apt to be merely drab.

WHICH brings me back to my first approach to this report. Its value to an intelligent housewife whose family consists of two children, and who has a regular income of £3 per week is slight. Both its furnishing hints and labour-saving devices are probably already known to her. These things are part of the modern mood. The younger generation, where the cost is not pro-hibitive, have already adopted them. Older folks, on the furnishing side at least, are not likely to change radically. There is a spirit that goes to the making of a home as well as its material equipment. They would not feel happy in the alien atmosphere of "model" housing equipment, however hygienic and praiseworthy it might be.

But the derelict slum dwelling is another question. In relation to it, the report and the exhibition displaying its findings, are of immense value. We now have established for the guidance of local government authorities just how much it costs at current market prices to bring sweetness and light into the darkest corners of our com-munity.   **JENNIE LEE**

(above) BEFORE CONVERSION   *(below)* AFTER CONVERSION

NEW HOMES
by Conversion

BUILD YOUR OWN ideal home from an old house or building! The secrets of conversion, and practical examples of how it can be done, are contained in the JULY issue of IDEAL HOME Magazine.

See, for instance, the Mayfair flat fashioned from a hayloft; a converted West Country cattle shed; the transformation of a small suburban semi-detached house; and a contemporary home that was a Victorian house.

OTHER SPECIAL CONTENTS INCLUDE

1. Using new furniture with the old; 2. Space-saving bed-room furniture; 3. IDEAL HOME gardener remakes an old garden to save labour; 4. Versatile, easy-growing suc-culents; 5. Producing your own electricity by petrol, wind and water. 6. Modern solid-fuel cookers; 7. Best of the baby cars — all under £600. 8. The latest equipment for comfortable picnics.

Order your copy NOW — IDEAL HOME Magazine sells out so quickly

IDEAL HOME
MAGAZINE – JULY ISSUE
OUT FRIDAY, 24th JUNE—2/-

OUR HUSBANDS AND SONS

THE Women's Institute Movement has many keen members in the mining villages of England and Wales. Here is a glimpse into the life of their menfolk written by Mr. Aneurin Bevan, the miner M.P. for Ebbw Vale, who brings his own experiences into relation with two recent Government reports.*

I SHALL never forget the first day that I went down the pit. I was thirteen years of age. My mother begged me not to go. She wanted me to stay at school in order to become a school teacher. But I longed to join my companions in the pits, wear long trousers, earn wages and have pocket money to spend at the week-end.

My mother was no exception to the general run of mothers in the mining areas. Few of them want their boys to become miners. Some people imagine that sons of miners become miners as a matter of course. That is true only in the sense that there is hardly any other occupation available in the colliery districts. The morning when the boy puts on his pit clothes for the first time is a proud one for the lad but one of dread and anxiety for the mother. His small wage is an acceptable addition to the meagre family income, and this is usually the sole reason that reconciles her to the necessity.

If she were in the habit of reading the annual reports of the Chief Inspector of Mines her reluctance would be reinforced. For in these she would find in full the story which the incidents of her daily experience teach her piecemeal.

---

* *The Sixteenth Annual Report of the Chief Inspector of Mines* (4s.) and *The Fifteenth Annual Report of the Miners' Welfare Fund* (1s. 6d.), both obtainable from H.M. Stationery Office.

The Report tells us that there were seven hundred and seventy-one thousand men, boys and women connected with coal mining in 1936, as compared with one million, two hundred and fourteen thousand in 1924. Those figures in themselves tell the story of the tragic unemployment which has afflicted the mining industry in the last decade.

There are, therefore, between three and four million persons directly or indirectly involved in the mining industry. The welfare of so large a community is an important concern for the whole nation.

The accident rate is frightening. Of the 137,163 men and boys killed or injured in the coal mines of this country in 1936, 784 were killed. The following figures will reveal the basis for the fears of the mothers of coal miners : 17,572 boys under twenty years of age were killed or injured ; 5,797 were between eighteen and twenty, 7,079 were between sixteen and eighteen, and 4,736 were between fourteen and sixteen years of age.

It is customary to think that the miners themselves are responsible for many of the accidents which occur. It is true that they might be more careful, but the circumstances of their work is their excuse. In most occupations the greatest number of accidents occur in the morning before the worker has freshened up and towards the end of the shift when he is fatigued. These two periods are also the times of the lowest output. The opposite is the case with the miner. Most accidents occur in mining in the middle of the shift. In other work the act of production is at the same time the act of safety precaution. The miner on the other hand has to stop production in order to attend to safety, like putting up props, etc. It is when the miner is most absorbed in production that he is exposed to the

BELOW GROUND —AND ABOVE
The Report of the Miners' Welfare Fund states that ninety-two per cent. of miners use pit-head baths wherever they are available

greatest risk. Here is an urgent field of inquiry for the Chief Inspector of Mines.

The report of the Mining Industry Welfare fund for the year 1936 is an interesting document. The Welfare Fund was established in 1920 out of the proceeds of a penny per ton per annum imposed on all coal raised in Great Britain. As its name signifies the purpose of the Fund is to provide money for social amenities for the miners and their families.

At a penny per ton the levy produced a million pounds a year. Splendid work has been done, and much more would have been accomplished if in 1932 the levy had not been reduced to a halfpenny per ton—a change that reduced the annual sum available to five hundred thousand.

Recreation grounds have been made, halls and institutes erected, and a hundred and one other worthy objects assisted, in particular the provision of convalescent homes for the miners and their wives. If one criticism may be made of the administration it is that too little attention has been given to the provision of facilities for the womenfolk.

NO single amenity means more to the miner and certainly to his wife than pithead baths. Considerable progress has been made in recent years, but even so many pits are still not equipped. The Report shows that when they are available 92 per cent. of the miners use them, and we are told that the demand far exceeds the supply. This is a complete answer to those who said that the miner was too conservative in his habits to want the baths. It is to be hoped that the women in the mining districts where they do not yet exist will bring pressure to bear on the authorities to speed up their installation.

ANEURIN BEVAN

*   *   *

"SNOW-PICTURE"

WHO goes down to the lake
   When Winter has frozen it over ?
Who steals out of the grass
Forsaking its chilly cover ?
Who calls loud from a tree,
A naked tree in the meadow ?
Who slinks out of the light
   Into the shadow ?

The heron goes down to the lake
When Winter has frozen it over ;
The rabbit sniffs at the air
And forsakes its chilly cover ;
The rook, like an old black hag,
Croaks from a tree in the meadow ;
And the fox slinks out of the light
   Into the shadow.

IVY O. EASTWICK

BACK TO BARBARISM?

THROUGHOUT HISTORY, persecution of helpless racial and religious minorities has been an ugly recurrent symptom. It is with us again today, and fills us with peculiar horror because Western Europe seemed to have risen above such barbarism. Professor H. Levy here shows how persecution has always occurred against a similar background

A COLONY OF BIRDS, if it is invaded by a strange specimen, will attack the intruder and ultimately destroy him. Birds live in flocks; they have a life of their own, customs of their own, and a stranger with his strange habits arouses their antagonism.

Is this why the Jew is persecuted? Is he so different from his neighbours that instinctively they rise against him? Is that why throughout the last two thousand years he has moved from country to country seeking a resting place?

For ourselves it is important to understand this problem. After all, it may not so much be the case that the Jew is a strange animal as that his neighbours have themselves been changing in some peculiar, some subtle way; so that like the person who ill-treats a child, they find all sorts of fantastic reasons to justify their cruelty.

Today we can look across the North Sea and watch with horror the persecution of the Jews in Germany, the enslavement of the men in concentration camps and the terrorization and starvation of the women and children. And we over here wonder to ourselves how civilized human-beings can behave like that. Does this mean that we are unlikely to do the same thing?

A generation ago the Germans were very like ourselves. They would have scorned to justify the things they consider right today. Can we suppose that such a fundamental change can take place in them while we remain unchanged? What is the cause of all this?

FOR TWO THOUSAND YEARS the Jews have moved about the face of the earth, a nomadic wandering people without a settled land long after other peoples have built their homes on soil they call their own, and become transformed into nations. Because the Jews have been strangers in strange lands they are foreigners everywhere; there has always been a resistance to absorbing them. Thus they in their turn have developed a strong community feeling among themselves, and the combination of these two tendencies has intensified the feeling of separation. Very rarely have they been able to remain long enough in any one environment for true assimilation to take place—that requires many generations of residence, and no nationality has so far been able to maintain its moral outlook unimpaired sufficiently long on the question of persecution of minorities to see the Jews actually assimilated.

When we look at it from this angle we begin to see that the problem is as much one concerning the changes that come over us as of the nature of Jews themselves.

Why are minorities periodically persecuted? What happens to us that at intervals we should get into the state of mind that believes beating to be a good thing, to serve a good purpose?

We can answer these questions and so obtain an understanding of ourselves if we look at the history of this particular people that has been so consistently ill-used in this way.

For the Jews certain periods of persecution stand out very sharply: the Crusades, that is about A.D. 1000; the persecutions in Spain at the end of the fifteenth century during the time of the Spanish Inquisition; at the end of the nineteenth century with its attacks on the Jews in Eastern Europe and particularly in Tsarist Russia; and finally today on a grand scale in Central Europe in Germany, Poland, Hungary, Rumania, Italy—in all the totalitarian states.

THE IMPORTANT POINT in this is that all these periods corresponded to widespread misery and want and to internal struggles in the countries within which they occurred. These struggles and this misery were not necessarily in any way connected with the Jews. One can see parallel cases in relation to so-called religious strife, struggles between Mohammedans and Hindus, between Catholics and Protestants. Now it is remarkable that these outbursts never occur among the well-to-do; it is always in the most depressed areas and among the most poverty-stricken sections of the population. There, naturally, the stress is greatest; the sense of irritation is at its peak and the tendency most natural to turn round and blame something, if not for the general poverty, at least for holding a different set of beliefs, for being a strange animal, for existing at all.

The Crusades occurred at a period of great poverty in Europe, when towns which had been thriving on the trade of the East had begun to decay. The occupation of the Holy Land by the Turks was preventing the flow of merchandise, spices, etc., to Europe. Bands of wandering children left their poverty-stricken homes, many seeking to join in the Crusades. (We note in passing the similarity to the situation today with its masses of refugee women and children from Germany, Spain, China.) The Crusades that sought to clear the Turk from Palestine were also the occasion of violent slaughter and pillage of Jewish communities. It is stated that 300 Jews were put to the sword in York prior to such a pilgrimage.

At the end of the fifteenth century, Spain, acutely affected by the competition of the Genoese, Venetian, and Greek merchants who had monopolized trade throughout the Eastern Mediterranean, was in deep depression. Money was required for the searching out of an alternative route to India. It is significant that in the year 1492, when the Jews were expelled from Spain and despoiled of their property, Columbus sailed for America—a journey towards the financing of which Ferdinand and Isabella had pawned their Crown Jewels so desperate was the situation.

THE ATTACK on the Jews in Tsarist Russia had precisely the same setting—poverty-stricken peasantry ground down under an absolute autocracy. It was out of that struggle towards the end of the nineteenth century that the new Liberal movement for emancipation developed in Russia. To divert the attention of the peasants from the real cause of their misery, it was vital that the poverty-stricken Jews themselves should be the scapegoats. In the history of Tsardom the encouragement of pogroms was a matter of high imperial policy during times of stress.

The situation in Europe today can be understood only in this setting. In those countries where poverty and misery is growing apace, there also are the most excessive brutalities of anti-Semitism. We are inclined to think that we in this country could not sink to such depths of moral debasement; but to ensure that this may remain true we must see to it that distress among our people is not allowed to reach such acuteness that these bestialities become possible; for history assures us that we also have sunk to the level of the beast, in periods of unbearable economic stress. **H. LEVY**

OLD BUILDINGS AND THE LAND

W. R. LETHABY

IT was a great pleasure to me recently to read that Lady Worsley-Taylor's motion at the last Annual General Meeting, urging the Institutes to assist in the preservation of old buildings in their several localities, was fully approved.

The care of our ancient buildings is a very important part of the preservation of the beauty of England. So much has been written about beauty that there is a danger that we may think of it as something exceptional and strange, what people go to Switzerland and Italy to see. This is quite a mistaken view, mistaken because hurtful. We have to appreciate and preserve our own neighbourhood beauties : we must find and see them everywhere. The typical beauty of England is not immensity and grandeur, but homeliness and friendliness : it is a land of hedge-bordered fields, full-foliaged trees and hay-ricks : a land of cows and sheep. The kind of building which we unconsciously think of as representative is not a great castle on a crag, but a cottage with its well-kept flowering front garden. Our country more than almost any other has been man-made by the labour of thousands of years. The old buildings which the land bears are almost inseparable from the tilled soil and the enclosed fields. These buildings are extended works of nature bearing long histories and carrying forward very deep and ancient traditions.

Some idea of the beauties of England might be gained by looking over past numbers of "HOME AND COUNTRY." It seems easier sometimes to recognise beauty in a picture than directly with our eyes. In many of these pictures it will appear how intimate with the scene are the old buildings, even the very humblest. One characteristic of these old buildings is that they were done by custom. Like Topsy, "they just growed." They are examples of folk-art. How can that be ? we may question : but farming operations, the binding of sheaves and building of ricks are still (or were recently), carried on in that same way. The repair and preservation of even the humblest old

building like a cart-shed at the next corner of the road, are important for that particular scene. A smart new bungalow or an old cow-house which has had the mossy tiled roof replaced by corrugated iron, may spoil a whole landscape. No one could paint or photograph it now, the unity and poetry are gone and it will not appear as a picture in "HOME AND COUNTRY" !

Serious questions of cost in the repair and conservation of these old buildings arise and they are coming to weigh more and more heavily on individual owners. One man has to pay for substantial repairs and a good roof, while everyone who sees the result of such care will profit by it. All I can see in regard to this big question at present is that the man who repairs a dear old building is really a public benefactor and we must find ways of recognising his well doing.

The best defence against injury and loss in every district would be a generally diffused concern for the maintenance of local beauties and the prevention of neglect and vulgarisation

1
Falling into ruin : Almshouses on Longridge Fell.

with a ready appreciation of good will (and works) in preservation. Well informed public opinion is what we need. We are all part of what we live in and we all have to share what we see. We say : my house and garden, my neighbourhood, my county and country : they are possessed by us, they are our property.

I always feel that horrible advertising hoardings, and untidy motor stations are a form of violent assault, although they may be on private land and I am only passing along the road. Private they may call themselves, but in making themselves public they have no right to smack my face, and I resent it. The fact is, we have such claims in regard to anything which we are compelled to see that the land and public roads should not be used in such ways. It may be a trespass for me to go on private land, but it is also a trespass for the owner to annoy me on the road, so there !

On the other hand tidily kept farm buildings and cottages are public courtesies and generous gifts, for which we should be duly grateful and, if possible, we must find out ways to show our appreciation. The only suggestions I have to make are very small but they might help. We ourselves have to develop "taking notice" of such things and we must talk about them more. Stop in the lane, take a long breath and look at it all more consciously than you have ever done before. Then mention to the next friend you see how nicely Mrs. A. has thatched her house and how well Mr. B. has repaired his farm gates, if they have! Occasionally let the subject at Institute meetings be on local beauties and their preservation. Then possibly a vote of thanks might be offered for some thoughtful care, or a protest made in regard to proposed injury or destruction. This really might have considerable influence, for our people are well meaning and often act in misapprehension. The most terrible doings have been introduced in the past under the name of "improvements." More and more it seems to me that we shall have to depend on Women's Institutes for things that matter and I should be proud if I could induce them to take up another burden and pleasure. Perhaps some day the local authorities may find out a way of recognising parish patriotism.

In School education too—and much of it, as interpreted by devoted teachers, is now very good— I should like to have some suggestive talks, followed by little essays on seeing poetry and beauty in common things, on opening our eyes to the neighbourhood, and love of the land.

Several societies are now working for the preservation of English country character and old buildings. The S.P.A.B. (Society for the Protection of Ancient Buildings) is more than fifty years old. This society has not only urged preservation but has developed a science of repairing ancient buildings. Lady Worsley-Taylor is on the committee which has recently prepared a special leaflet which may be obtained by Institutes (address : 20 Buckingham Street, W.C.2). An important National Trust for the acquisition of sites of special interest and old buildings has also existed for many years. Old cottages have been acquired by the Trust and repaired according to the advice of the S.P.A.B. and thus made sound and fit for habitation. More recently the Society of Arts has started a fund specially for the preservation of old cottages. An appeal says : " Many of the most beautiful old cottages in England have been demolished to make room for ' improvements ' and many more are in danger of disappearing." Again more recently an influential Council for the Preservation of Rural England (C.P.R.E.) has been formed, on the executive committee of which Lady Trevelyan sits as representing the National Federation of Women's Institutes.

An excellent Society exists for controlling the abuses of Public Advertising (S.C.A.P.A.) : and there are others like the commendable Surrey Society for preventing litter and general untidiness in country places, and the Commons and Footpaths Association. As Mr. Hugh Walpole has recently said of these societies, " Our common ground is the preservation of the beauty of England. Our general alarm is the same."

Save the Countryside. As a memorial to Richard Cadbury and George Cadbury, who created Bournville fifty years ago, the firm of Cadbury Bros. Ltd. has presented Frankley Beeches, near Birmingham, to the National Trust to be preserved free from buildings. Frankley Beeches is a prominent viewpoint eight hundred feet above sea level, and can be seen well from Bournville and many other parts on the South side of Birmingham.

2
Falling into ruin : Cottages in Somerset.
(Reproduced by permission of the Society for the Protection of Ancient Buildings.)

Fire on a Bird Island. Careless picnickers, who have been responsible for many a heath fire, nearly succeeded at Whitsuntide in burning out an entire island and destroying the only considerable English colony of Gannets, the most remarkable of English sea-birds, at a time when they were engaged in incubating and brooding their young. Thousands would have been burned alive in their nests, but for the efforts of the representatives of the Royal Society for the Protection of Birds, and of others on neighbouring island and mainland. The whole story is told in the Summer Number of " Bird Notes and News " (82 Victoria Street, London, S.W.1)—the alarm, the smoke clouds, the deep-burning peat, the spread of the fire, and the trenching of the entire area by the combined efforts for several days of naval ratings, coastguard and volunteers. Some of the nesting gulls could not be reached in time, but all the Gannets were saved.

It will be said of this generation that it found England a land of beauty and left it a land of beauty spots. MR. C. E. M. JOAD.

THE LOOK OF THE LAND

MR. IVOR BROWN, the well-known novelist, essayist, and dramatic critic, levels caustic comment both at the aesthetic lover of picturesque but insanitary cottages —for others—and " those insatiable rodents, the rats of development "

THE significant feature of our epoch is the destruction of distance. No place can now call itself remote : every place can therefore be economically and speedily invaded. I can think of nothing which more differentiates my boyhood from my middle-age than this matter of milage. When I was a boy to go eight miles in a dog-cart was a terrific outing, an adventure, a mystery. When I was at Oxford to go into the Cotswolds was a day's journey. One had made some effort and entered new country. Now an undergraduate makes no effort beyond getting a lift in a car and he is there in a few minutes. He has no sense of strangeness.

The abolition of distance has not only abolished the awe and excitement of travel and the delicious sense of going a journey. By scattering towns and, in the London area and along the coast, by multiplying the week-end cottagers, caravanners, hut-builders, and shack-spreaders of all kinds, it has attacked, mutilated, and frequently destroyed the beauty of the country too. Efforts at planning have been made in a despairing kind of way, but the motor-car has outdistanced them with a derisive tootle of its horn.

The Government of this country, as Mr. Keynes points out in a vigorous contribution to *Britain and the Beast,** considers that the preservation of Beauty and the control of the Building Beast, riding the all-powerful Machine, is uneconomic and so essentially an unpolitical matter. Even a statesman like Mr. Baldwin, constantly featured as the Worcestershire pippin of Parliament, as English as his own pipe, and often nobly rhetorical about the glories of our landscape, never made the slightest use of his power as Prime Minister, while commanding a huge majority, to take public action for the defence of our vanishing amenities.

The policy has been to leave it all to private bodies and to shuffle responsibility on to the National Trust and kindred organizations. These organizations may not conflict but they certainly overlap, and they are all undernourished as far as finance goes. There is a very good account of them in a privately printed pamphlet, *Vanishing England*, by Mr. G. K. Menzies. There is also a very good case stated for comprehensive action by the Government : " By the time that public

* *Britain and the Beast.* Edited by Clough Williams Ellis. (Dent. 10s. 6d.)

opinion is ripe for a Ministry of Amenities, the last of our amenities may have vanished."

There is a constant flood of books, pamphlets, articles, and speeches on this matter. There is a vast amount of isolated keenness to stop further spoliation. But nothing effective is done, beyond a little scheduling of ancient monuments and occasional salvation of " a beauty spot " by purchase for public benefit before those insatiable rodents, the rats of development, get to work. All that does, however, is to make the countryside into the likeness of a museum. We want something better than that.

In a volume like *Britain and the Beast* to which all the Amenity Experts contribute, there is plenty of suggestion for improvement. But we must not let the Aesthetes have it all their own way. After all, housing is the essence of the matter, and housing is a subject on which the feminine opinion should be heard. Only two women out of twenty-six authors contribute to this book, and some of the men are so much concerned with defending the old that they would keep the evil along with the good. Mr. Scott-Moncrieff, for example, actually writes : " The value of a W.C. is vastly overrated when it is set above that of the aesthetic. An ugly house with a bath is less of an asset than a beautiful house without one."

THAT sort of talk is easily made an excuse for leaving the rustic poor in " picturesque " cottages which are no better than rural slums, small, dark, damp, undrained hovels whose pleasant aspect delights a certain type, i.e. those lovers of beauty whose love of humanity stops short at enquiring how their fellow-humans live. I am revolted when I think how many cottagers' wives have to drudge at carrying water and similar needless and slavish tasks in an age so boastful of its labour-saving tasks. I know, too, of a so-called " good landlord " in one of the Home Counties who will not sell sites to cheap bungalow-builders and insists, where houses are built, that there should be considerable expenditure and some show of style. So he keeps a beautiful village beautiful and is much praised. Also he keeps the local workers on land and in garden abominably cramped and confined in the damp, insanitary cottages which look so charming to those who walk or motor past. If he would build some decent cottages with proper plumbing and use of the light and water which pass by, I would deem him a better landlord, even if the new cottages did alter the aspect of his village.

Things have to change. It is no use playing the ostrich. But they can be made to change far better than they have done. We must combine respect for human need with respect for natural beauty. For those who want to be reminded both of England's beauty and of the possible ways to protect it, I recommend both this magnificently illustrated book and the pamphlet mentioned above.

IVOR BROWN

The Case Against American-type Comics

Illustrations typical of those seen by children—sex and murder (note the bullet holes in the man's neck); nightmare horror

JUST THINK, JOHNNY! YOU'RE GOING TO WALK THE OCEAN FLOOR WITH THE MAN YOU MURDERED!

NO...NO....

JOHNNY'S SCREAM GURGLES IN HIS THROAT. HE CLUTCHES EMPTY AIR...

THE Resolution on Children's Papers and Magazines, which was passed by a large majority at this year's A.G.M., has shown the great concern which W.I. members feel at the circulation in this country of certain types of " comics ". Their interest will be further stimulated by the personal opinions expressed in this provocative article which PETER MAUGER has written for the Public Questions Sub-committee space this month. Mr. Mauger, who has made a special study of this subject, is experienced in (to quote our Resolution) " the upbringing and education of the young ", since he is a W.I. husband with two young children, and is in charge of Social Studies at a Boys' Secondary School.

*   *   *   *   *   *

THE " Comics " that are arousing so much indignation among those concerned with the upbringing of children and young people are very different from those we knew in our youth. On the whole, ours were—and are—innocuous enough. True, they are sometimes guilty of vulgarity, the standards of taste they set are often poor, and other criticisms may be made on educational grounds. But if they don't do children much good, they certainly don't do them a lot of harm.

The American-type comic is in a category so different that the only point in common with the home-grown variety is the name. And the name itself is misleading, since it is very certain that there is nothing comic about them. For the overwhelming majority deal with one subject—violence. Some are devoted to crime, some to the strong-arm exploits of supermen and super-women, others portray struggles against the inhabitants of distant planets. Two newer subjects are War, with every kind of killing pictures in terrifying realism, and Horror, where the innocent as well as the guilty are pursued and done to death by monstrous creatures or rotting bodies imbued with an obscene life-in-death.

Their sole raison d'être is the vivid portrayal of cruel and sadistic acts, of murder and torture. They rely for their sales on the administration of a series of exciting shocks to the imagination, and the plots are constructed as vehicles to carry the maximum number of brutal actions. Consequently the degree of violence must increase with each issue, or sales will be lost to a rival publisher who has found a new way of showing violent death.

Effect On Children

Are these comics meant for children ? Probably not in the first instance. It is more likely that they were produced for " adults " who were unable to read books. A rule for a successful film scenario is that it should be written for those with a mental age of not more than 14, and these comics are in essence films without the projector—and free from the censorship that would delete so many of their episodes. Many adults read them in the country of their origin.

But just because their format is so simple, a series of pictures with a few sub-titles or bits of dialogue, they can be understood with ease by children barely able to read. In fact, it is precisely the educationally backward child who is the most avid reader of this type of comic.

Now it is bad enough to think of adults whose main reading is crime comics; but it is still more serious where children are concerned. Most people identify themselves with the central figures of the books they read, children especially so. Their minds are impressionable, they are intensely imitative, and a steady diet of these comics can have a disastrous effect on the way their characters are formed. From them they will learn, by endless repetition (that is to say, in the most effective way) that mankind is evil, living in a world dominated by hate, fear, greed and lust, and that for success—indeed for very existence—brute force is the attribute most necessary to cultivate. They will learn that foreigners and coloured peoples are their natural enemies, to be exterminated by any method, since the blond hero is unquestionably right.

They will grow up, too, with the most degraded ideas about women. There are no normal women in American comics. Drawn in skin-tight costumes, the portrayal of their bodies amounts to visual pornography, and their prurient appeal to the adolescent is obvious. Worse is their characterization. In one typical comic, suggestively-drawn girls are shown cheating, robbing and murdering—21 deaths by shooting, and one by the knife, in 36 pages. In another a gangster kills a husband to make the widow his mistress, kicking his former gun-moll out of his apartment to make room for the new one.

The treatment of women emphasizes the essential and important fact about these comics—that in them life is shown as being grotesquely abnormal. It is this abnormality and preoccupation with evil that constitutes the real and urgent danger to young minds. There is plenty of evidence from the United States that a steady diet of them provides a ready-made pattern of crime for adolescents who are already unbalanced and anti-social. Equally important is the effect they must have on normal children. For they teach the exact reverse of the principles that we as parents and teachers try to instil into our children. If it is obvious that these powerful pictorial stories have an effect,

A distorted approach to science; many of the illustrations in this category depict supernatural horrors, cruelty and violence.

can it be doubted that that effect will be to give a grossly-distorted idea of the world, and a " tough " cynicism towards decent moral values, humanity, fairmindedness and tolerance ? And the effect on the sensitive child surely needs no comment.

Sales Are Increasing

There is unfortunately no doubt as to their fascination for the young. The bright, gaudy colours, the similarity of the characters to the films they see all too often, the thrilling shocks on every page— all comprise a combination that immature minds find irresistibly tempting. And the temptation is easily satisfied. Though imports from other countries have now been prohibited, the matrices are sent over by the American publishers when they have finished with them, to printers in England who apparently have no difficulty in obtaining paper. Being in book form and durable, they pass from hand to hand and have a life far longer than the ordinary children's paper. Anyone who conducts an investigation into any primary or secondary school will be appalled at the number of children who read them regularly.

What Can Be Done ?

In spite of their debased and debasing contents, they cannot be banned by existing legislation, and it is not surprising that there has been such a demand for Government action to remove them from the market. But the Home Office view is that though they agree that some of these comics are " of a most objectionable character . . . verge on the obscene ", legislation is virtually impossible. The Under-Secretary of the Home Office has said, ". . . responsibility for the moral welfare of a child must primarily rest with its parents and teachers. There is a limit, and a proper limit, to what the law or a Government can do in this field . . . I believe it lies within the power of parents and teachers to see that this undoubtedly unpleasant form of literature does little or no harm to our children." (House of Commons, 31.7.52.)

I know that this view was the one that prevailed at your A.G.M.; but after three years study of the problem I am firmly convinced that it can only be satisfactorily solved by legislation. Many parents and teachers are doing what they can to persuade children to read healthier literature. But it is no use shutting our eyes to the fact that as long as these comics are on sale they will be read—and re-read. The children who buy them most often are those who pay least attention to their teachers' advice, and whose parents have no understanding of the serious effect of these mental drugs. It is these children who introduce the comics to others.

No, it seems to me that the sales are much too large, and their contents too poisonous, for it to be merely a matter of exhortation

to children by parents and teachers. It is hard to believe that if the will is there, a form of legislation cannot be devised to stop their sale. This has been done in a number of countries, notably in Sweden, where the banning of these publications was incorporated in an Act guaranteeing the general freedom of the press, which has proved in practice to be completely successful. I am not suggesting of course, that the action agreed on by the N.F.W.I. is ineffectual. Far from it; but I do not see how it can be fully implemented while the comics remain on display in the shops and on the bookstalls, with all the attraction of forbidden fruit. Nor do I think that legislation *alone* will do the trick. It was precisely the pressure by parents and teachers on Parliament to do something to *help* them fight the evil that resulted in the matter being raised in the House. Mrs. Neville-Smith hit the nail firmly on the head when she said at your A.G.M.:

> " If we do think this is a fight worth entering into, and a good many of us do, we have to realize that it is going to be a difficult one. A hundred years ago men and women who were fighting against the vested interest which drove children up the chimneys and down the mines, found it a very long and hard struggle, and even laws and prohibitions were no use at all until they were supported by an all too slowly awakening public opinion which decided that the exploitation of children was an evil thing."

It is up to all of us to awaken public opinion in every way possible to the need for action, and action now, before these perverted magazines become firmly entrenched financially. If every Women's Institute gets a batch of these books and studies them, I am convinced that their natural love of young people and their concern for the preservation and extension of our humanist tradition in literature will suggest many ways in which to act. No self-respecting family would permit them in their house, and we can have little respect for ourselves or for our nation if we continue to allow this degenerate literature to get into the hands of our children.

Letters to the Editor

AMERICAN-TYPE COMICS

DEAR EDITOR,—I was interested in the views expressed by Peter Mauger in his article in the October issue. Perhaps my experiences in this field would be of interest.

My husband, who until recently was teaching English at a large Secondary Modern school in Kent, conducted an investigation in his class of 14 year-old boys. While he found that almost every boy in the class of 35 handled and read these comics, he was also confronted with the far more disquieting information that just under half of their parents read them too.

Last Christmas I spent two weeks in a maternity hospital in Kent, where I shared a small ward with a number of other women whose ages ranged from 18 to 33 years. I was able to observe their reading habits, as there were only six of us. Two of them regularly bought English children's comics which were shared by two others. The rest of their reading was confined to a daily picture paper and the cheapest type of woman's magazine. One of them perused nothing but comics and newspaper strip cartoons.

From the foregoing, you will appreciate that I am in agreement with Mr. Mauger that legislation must be introduced to restrict the sale of American-type comics, for although my fellow patients did not read them it probably was because they weren't available in the hospital.

Yours sincerely,
(MRS.) K. WOODWARD
School House, Wilstone, Tring, Herts.

DEAR EDITOR,—I feel I must give expression to the disgust and indignation aroused in me—and doubtless in many other W.I. members —by the article in your October issue on the so-called " Comics " and particularly by the revolting and debasing illustrations ! Surely such an influential body as the N.F.W.I. can make its weight felt sufficiently to ban the production of such things in this country. We should not tolerate the poisoning of our children's bodies by any money-making concern and why should we tamely acquiesce in the poisoning of their, infinitely more precious, minds and souls ?

Yours faithfully,
(MRS.) ELIZABETH M. AITKEN
Larchwood, Boar's Hill, Oxford.

At last—

A message from Enid Blyton—

"In publishing this magazine I had three definite objects:

1 *It should be a part answer to the prevalent 'American-style comics' whose picture strips take the place of proper reading.*

2 *It should contain stories which would impel backward readers to master the initial difficulties of reading and encourage good readers to turn to books.*

3 *It should not only stimulate the imagination, but should uphold steadfastly the decent values of life and point the way to worth-while activities.*

" As a mother who has the welfare of all children at heart, I am glad to have an opportunity to use my influence in a magazine of this kind."

> ENID BLYTON'S MAGAZINE
> IS PUBLISHED FORTNIGHTLY
> PRICE 4d. PER COPY, AND IS
> WRITTEN ENTIRELY BY
> THE CHILDREN'S FAVOURITE
> AUTHOR.
> IT CONTAINS A SERIAL
> AND SHORT STORIES,
> NATURE NOTES, PUZZLES,
> THINGS TO MAKE AND DO
> AND PICTURES.

Best stories for all children—order NOW from your newsagent

THE ONLY MAGAZINE WRITTEN *Entirely* BY ENID BLYTON

QUEER PEOPLE

by ONE OF THEM

Illustrations by BIM

"THEY'RE even queerer than we are", said one member of the Natural History Society to another. They were taking part in a joint excursion with a visiting naturalists' society. Now that we are about to embark upon our field meetings for another season, I wonder once again what makes us so queer. Our activities certainly perplex others. There was the time when we went to a very remote place where one of our members lived. As she led us through the village, all eyes were upon us. Never had so many people been seen there before. Next day she was besieged by questioners. But one old man asked no questions—he knew. "I see'd 'ee yesterday wi' yer gurl guides", said he.

Ornithologists seldom join in our excursions because the voices of other naturalists scare the birds away. Only a visit to a Wild Fowl Trust property or an island full of nesting gulls will attract them in numbers. Geologists have no objection to company, but they are uncommon nowadays. Fossil hunting was fashionable in the nineteenth century, but its popularity among amateurs has declined. Possibly the Latin names of fossils may account for this. The majority of us who regularly attend field meetings are botanists. We are naturally more gregarious than entomologists, for our quarry is stationary, and we are always anxious to glean information from our fellows on the whereabouts of rare flowers.

What mad creatures we must appear to other visitors when we meet at a seaside resort! We kneel on the ground, with heads bowed and bottoms up, searching for minute wild flowers in the short turf. Occasionally we are rewarded by finding one that has never before been recorded in our county. Those who seek insects usually have to catch them as they fly, and I believe some have been known to chase a rare moth across a boundary to establish a county record. The entomologists in our society are all men, and they usually disappear to sweep the herbage with their nets, in single-minded pursuit of uncommon beetles or rare bees. Sometimes they show us their finds, and we gaze at tiny flies in test tubes or listen to a lecture on the life story of some strange insect. The "bug hunters" know far more about plants than the botanists do about bugs. Amateur botanists, on the whole, show a complete disregard for beasts and birds. Soil has some interest for them, but geology none. I once invited a botanist to come and look at a quarry. "What grows in it?" she asked. "Only rocks", I replied, and her scorn was obvious.

WHERE shall we go for our outings this year? Those suggestions made at the general meeting must be considered, but all of them are places that should be visited in June, and we can't have all our meetings in one month. Shall we try new places or revisit the old ones? Who knows this district well enough to act as leader? Shall we have all our excursions on Saturdays? Will the tide be out far enough for us to search the foreshore on that particular afternoon? Will there be enough members to fill a coach? These questions will be resolved somehow and, in time, the programme will be printed. Then the honorary secretary will receive letters saying "Why wasn't my suggestion included?" and "I can't find the meeting place on my map".

As usual we shall visit woods in spring, downs and dunes, moors and marshes, in summer. ("Carry tea and gumboots", the programme says.) The autumn meeting will be a fungus foray—we still use the term which is surely a Victorian survival. The dictionary gives "incursion, raid, onset" as synonyms for "foray". In fact, our depredations are not heavy unless we find edible species. Even then most of the members are too timid to try anything but field mushrooms. What a lot they miss! Sauce flavoured with chanterelle is delicious; so is the taste of parasol mushrooms. Blewits can be dried and used in stews through the winter, and giant puffballs, cut in slices and fried with bacon, make a supper dish not easily surpassed.

The honorary secretary must be prepared for every contingency. She must help the less able-bodied across streams and over stiles, answer the question "What's this?" a hundred times in an afternoon, organize search parties for the member who has been lost, collect and note information from experts, and finally write a report for the local newspaper. This last is important—it brings in new members. Sometimes they confess that, for months, they have gone to the places described in the reports to look for what we found there. Having had little success by themselves, they decide to join the society.

WHAT, I ask again, is so queer about naturalists? The paraphernalia of vasculum or butterfly net, of field glasses or geological hammer, is not the whole answer; for, I must admit, we still look queer when we meet for lectures in the winter. Perhaps the root of it is that we have eyes for things whose existence is unimagined by our fellow men. Perhaps, because we are always looking for such things, we are less aware of human problems. At any rate we are stamped for life if we let our interest in Natural History get a real hold on us.

W.I.

Save the Countryside.

A littered landscape is a shame to England.

Orange peel and papers, bury them or take
them home.

Bottles and tins, remove them; left about they
are a danger to man and beast.

Clear up before you leave.

Others will thank you.

(Harting Anti-litter Card.)

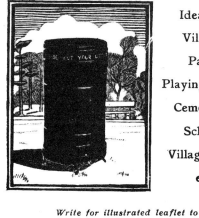
A SUSSEX LAMENT

WIVELSFIELD

Now the day is over,
  Night is drawing nigh,
Traces of the Tripper
  All around us lie.

Shouting, singing, screaming,
  As they drive away,
Leaving tracks behind them
  Of an ill-spent day.

Dirty, greasy paper,
  Broken glass and tins,
Orange peel and bottles
  And banana skins.

How long must we suffer
  From this horrid pest,
Dirty litter scattered
  North, South, East and West ?

Up and down the country
  Sounds the sad refrain :
" Summer's come to Sussex ;
  The Tripper's here again."

ANSWER FROM AN
OXFORDSHIRE WOMEN'S INSTITUTE
TO A SUSSEX LAMENT

Sussex : " Now the day is over,
    Night is drawing nigh,
    Traces of the tripper
    All around us lie.

  How long must we suffer
    From the horrid pest,
    Dirty litter scattered
    N. S. E. and West ? "

Oxon : " Hark ! the tale I'm telling,
    Startling 'tis but true.
    'Twas our very President
    Working in the dew.

  Spearing up the papers
    All along the road,
    Nail on end of walking stick,
    Most efficient goad.

  Say ! O worthy President,
    Why this dirty work
    ' What I urge on other folk
    Who am I—to shirk ? '

  Trippers, too, are human,
    Treat them as a guest.
    Very soon, I'm certain,
    They will learn the rest.

  Now the day is over,
    Night is drawing nigh,
    On one moonlit highway,
    Litter does *not* lie."

GREEN—BUT NOT PLEASANT

ALL sensible people, I am told, read Letters to the Editor before anything else in HOME AND COUNTRY. I hope they do ; I hope they will read from end to end the letter from a member of East Sussex Federation Committee on the subject of tidying the countryside. It is reasonable, practical and heartfelt, and it ends, as all letters should, with a good story. It only expresses a widespread feeling, that a real effort should be made by Women's Institutes this Coronation spring so that the expected thousands of visitors should see our unique and pretty island at its best. A traveller who had just returned from a tour of ten or eleven thousand miles sat staring out of the boat-train window, saying that he had seen nothing anywhere like the summer countryside of Kent. Forests, prairies, glaciers, peaks, cities and coral islands in plenty, but nothing in the world like the deep fields, the snowy hedges, the beech trees with their bluebell carpets, the little woods and lanes of England.

East Sussex begs us not to be priggish about litter. No reformer, of course, ever got anything done who was not prepared to bore his best friends relentlessly on the subject. But let us be frank : nearly everyone enjoys making a mess, and everyone without exception hates clearing it up. There is a noble care-free sensation about hurling away the banana skins. OUR OWN banana skins, that is. But what about other people's ?

All my life I wanted to see Land's End. The name, I suppose, and that photograph on the Great Western Railway. Land's End when seen answered every expectation—but one. It is wild and romantic ; England narrows alluringly upon you ; you even begin to believe your geography book which said that a peninsula is a piece of land nearly surrounded by water. But oh, dear me, the litter ! Those sea ledges were red, not with heather, but with chocolate wrappings, and silver paper, not seagulls, flashed in the summer sun.

Well, can anything be done about it ? Warwickshire and East Sussex say Yes. Get together ; organize clearing up days after public holidays. (We all know high-minded Institute members who prowl nightly on commons with pointed sticks, but there is strength, as well as sociability, in numbers.) Pull in the Scouts and the Guides, who are knowledgeable, athletic and not at all afraid of smells. The New Forest people two summers ago arranged concerted drives of rubbish

collecting, culminating at an appointed place in a general, mighty and well-advertised bonfire.

What a thing it would be if, when we light our festive fires on Coronation night, we could pour the débris of the countryside inside them, saluting the new age on the ashes of the old. How grand, how sanitary, and how symbolic !

The Scapa Society, which with the Council for the Preservation of Rural England has fought a ten years' battle to save the face of the countryside, says—above all, know your own powers. Many people are unaware that litter is a legal offence. County and Borough Councils have power to pass Anti-Litter By-laws forbidding the deposit of rubbish in public places, and any Council which has not so enacted should be industriously badgered by all the societies within reach.

"IT is necessary," says Scapa's excellent handbook,* "for the public to be far more vocal over their annoyance than they usually are."

Quite so. Women's Institutes are well aware that you must know the law in order to make a row intelligently when it is broken. Any member of the public can, if he can identify an actual offender (with a witness) lodge a complaint by simply filling up a form at a police station. And if (like the writer) you hesitate at accosting an outsize motorist in goggles and a fur coat, or a hearty and vociferous picnic party, you can always consult the Scapa Society.†

All men and women are beauty lovers at heart, and beauty has always demanded a great deal of dirty work. Public opinion, says East Sussex, is a heavy sleeper. But *when* it wakes in England, as we have shown more than once lately in world affairs, it can bark to some purpose.

* "Rural Refuse and its Disposal," price 1s., post free 1s. 2d.
† 71 Eccleston Square, London, S.W.1.

AND IN LONDON THEY ARE NO BETTER !

The Strand, outside the Law Courts, after the Jubilee Procession to St. Paul's had passed

Chemical Sprays in the Countryside

*On behalf of the N.F.W.I. Agriculture Sub-Committee, PHYLLIS
CARTER writes about a matter which is arousing a good deal of
concern amongst many country-dwellers*

IF our Annual General Meeting had been held last year, we should
have heard more of the Spraying of Roadside Verges, which is a
subject very much bound up with the use of sprays in agriculture.
The Working Party set up by the Ministry of Agriculture to investigate the risks attached to the use of poisonous chemicals in agriculture
have now published their third Report,* this time about animals, birds
and plants.

They realize that the public are concerned, and rightly so, as they
themselves admit that their enquiries have shown unfortunate gaps in
the knowledge of the effects which
these chemicals may have on life
and crop cultivation, and add that
there is a pressing need for further
evidence and research.

When some major change occurs,
such as that caused by the spread
of myxomatosis or the increased
use of chemical sprays, everyone
starts to talk about the balance
of Nature being upset, but man is
constantly transforming the face of
the earth and changing this so-
called balance. It is quite impossible
to stand still in any sphere of life,
but, as country women, concerned
with the development and improvement of the countryside, 'we need
to be assured that any change
will bring more beneficial than
harmful results.

Selective weedkillers are of immense value if they are properly
used for increasing food production, a vital necessity to our nation
in peace or war. The danger lies in
indiscriminate use by those with
insufficient knowledge of the
effects. It has been stated that
crops one mile away from a hor-
mone-treated area have been
affected by the chemical.

Many chemicals used on crops
are poisonous to man and beast;
and when certain species of insects
are destroyed, it is obvious that
some birds and animals may die
of starvation. Risks to wild life are
always great, and it is hard to
maintain a fair outlook on the proportion that can be attributed to
chemical sprays.

"The wild flowers of the countryside are an essential part of the landscape in which we live" *(from the Report)*

Effect on Livestock

Losses of sheep, cattle and crops that were reported have been almost
entirely due to negligence, either by spraying when the wind was
wrong, by spilling the liquid, or by not maintaining fences or closing
gates, though it is interesting to note that the natural curiosity of farm
animals seems to be a contributory cause! Hormone weedkillers are
not dangerous in themselves, but they make some poisonous plants,
such as ragwort, particularly attractive to animals, which leads to
poisoning of farm livestock.

Appeals are issued every year to fruit growers to use as much care as
possible, when spraying, to protect bees, but losses to beekeepers still
continue.

Some weedkillers do not kill insects, but, when they destroy certain
plants which are the sources of pollen and nectar, the fertilizing insects
which feed on those plants are reduced, and possibly eliminated from a
fruit-growing area. It is reported that there is a serious increase in the
fruit-tree red spider mite, following the use of certain sprays and
washes, which have destroyed the beneficial insects and the plant life
in which they hibernated.

Most insects found on annual crops in farms and gardens have wild
host-plants as well. Hedgerows form a natural haven for these, and
until we know more about the effect of sprays on insects, we
should beware of wholesale removal of hedges, which might have
far-reaching effects, particularly near orchards and other perennial
crops.

Effect on Flowers

Spray operators may become
liable for damage to garden crops,
or even their neighbours' laundry,
but little fuss is made should the
spray fall on uncultivated land,
such as commons or downs, which
might easily destroy many of our
wild flowers. The effect on flora is
a subject about which little is
known, and long-term observations
are essential, particularly on roadside verges. Some people say that
road verges are only a small part
of our land, but there are other
points of view. Visitors to the country, whether from our towns or
abroad, see much of Britain from
the main roads; do let us see that
they can enjoy them with their rare
and beautiful flowers.

Some County Councils are now
doing experimental spraying sanc-
tioned by the Ministry of Transport, but they may do more.
They hoped they had found an
economical way of keeping road-
sides tidy and free from weeds;
but results show that, even after
three years' spraying, the worst of
these weeds are not permanently
killed, and the grass still has to be
cut. The saving in cost seems very
questionable, but new and more
effective sprays may change the
position in the future.

It is to be hoped that Highway Authorities will heed the Ministry of
Transport's advice to keep only to small experimental stretches until
full reports of these are received. We are assured that the Nature
Conservancy and other official bodies, as well as the Ministry of
Agriculture, are watching this spraying very closely, but there is
justifiable concern that unauthorized spraying of roadside verges is
still going on, turning them into blackened masses of vegetation every
spring.

The Botanical Society of the British Isles has made a card index of
roads with uncommon flowers, but many of our most beautiful
butterflies and song birds may be affected as well. It seems that the net
result of spraying roadside verges and hedgerows may be the removal
of many harmless and beneficial insects and plants, leaving others that
the road authorities would like to see destroyed.

In the preface to their Report, the Working Party say they believe
that dangers do exist and that even if these cannot be defined
precisely, measures should be taken to minimize the possibility
of the new toxic chemicals used in agriculture spoiling our
countryside. The findings and recommendations presented in this
Report should be studied by all who feel a deep concern in this
matter.

---

* *Toxic Chemicals in Agriculture. Risks to Wild Life.* H.M.S.O. 1s. 6d.

CHAPTER SEVEN

The WI at Work

HOME AND COUNTRY.

THE WOMEN'S INSTITUTES JOURNAL.

PUBLISHED BY THE

NATIONAL FEDERATION OF WOMEN'S INSTITUTES: ESTABLISHED IN CONJUNCTION WITH THE WOMEN'S BRANCH BOARD OF AGRICULTURE AND FISHERIES.

| VOL. I.—No. 1. | MARCH, 1919. | PRICE 2d. |

Chairman—THE LADY DENMAN.   *Vice-Chairman*—MISS GRACE HADOW.

Hon. Treasurer—MISS ALICE WILLIAMS.   *General Secretary* - MRS. KENYON.

All Communications should be addressed to THE EDITOR, "HOME AND COUNTRY," *National Federation of Women's Institutes, 72, Victoria Street, Westminster, S.W.*1.

PHOTO TAKEN AT W.I. EXHIBITION AT CAXTON HALL, OCTOBER, 1918.

FROM LEFT TO RIGHT

MRS. GODMAN, H.M. THE QUEEN, PRINCESS MARY, MISS ALICE WILLIAMS, MRS. ALFRED WATT.

A WOMEN'S INSTITUTE AT SANDRINGHAM.

By Mrs. ALFRED WATT, M.A., M.B.E.

THERE is surely no Canadian girl who has not dreamt of the day she should "go to London to see the Queen," and if her dreams were of glittering courts, of gracious majesty, of beauty and splendour, of the pomp and ceremony of kings, and the girl herself moving with wonderful calm and beautifully apparelled through the greatest court in the world—what else would her vision be? No girl ever dreamed more than I, and the years, thank God, have made no difference. It was still the dream of all dreams, altering with the march of time, but always alluring.

How could one think that the dream would suddenly come true and in so changed a guise?

The command of Her Majesty to speak on Women's Institutes at Sandringham was as unexpected as welcome to the Women's Institute Department, at the Board of Agriculture. But when it was decided I should go, my first thought was regret for the cherished and vanished dream—whatever the experience might be, the glory of pageantry would never now be realized. I knew that at Sandringham there was a Mother-Queen mourning her little son, a quiet village sharing her grief, and that I alas, whatever else I might take there, although perhaps of deeper significance, would be tinged with the sadness of the war years and undertaken with the sense of responsibility very different from that "fine and careless rapture" of the girl with the dreams.

The drive from the gay little station of Wolverton, the King's own, was wonderful, heath and pines, sand stretches and salt breezes and a nip in the air to make even a Canadian sit up and take notice. But even there the war shadow fell as a sad little cortège passed, an ambulance taking a terribly hurt young airman whose machine has crashed within the royal precincts but a few moments before.

My kindly hosts at the Estate House, Mr. and Mrs. Beck, soon heartened me up. They warmed me and fed me with equal enthusiasm and in any other surroundings, I should have become soporific. But it was all too thrilling for that. Within a stone's throw was York Cottage and through the trees I saw the storied spire of old Sandringham Church. I fear I stood shivering, long after I should have been asleep, at my bedroom window, looking out on the beautiful park wondering if the Royal children fished in the slow winding river and scouted in the woods darkly outlined on the night sky, thinking of the famous house parties and of the statesmen from all the chancelleries of Europe, who must have walked along these pleasant footpaths with that wise old King, Edward the Peacemaker, and at last hoping that I might be led to give the right message to the women in the little village beyond, and at the very last, with a sleepy laugh all to myself, at the queer turn of fate which brought a Canadian from a far outpost of Empire to its very heart, to tell a Queen what should be done for the village of her home.

The next morning I was taken over the estate by Mr. Beck, the agent, who spared no pains to shew me everything to best advantage. I had expressed a wish to see the King's famous Southdowns, as my sheep in British Columbia came originally from the Sandringham flock, so we chased these sheep through enclosures and fields and woods, by motor, by trap, and on foot. They were fine, big specimens in good shape for coming shows. All of the pure-bred stock was interesting, especially Queen Alexandra's herd of Jersey cows, but I suppose the majority of people would have found the greatest interest in the beautiful racehorses, and it was certainly a revelation to see their well planned stables and the care bestowed upon them—fortunate beings, they have no housing problems!

The whole morning jaunt was all like a moving picture. There flashed into view stately Sandringham, "The House," as it is affectionately called on the Estate, the huge woodyard with its steam saws, the electric plant, the water supply, buildings of all sorts, trim well kept enclosures, the great iron Norwich gates, dear little cottages with neat gardens, and all with a charming background of wood and heath and parkland.

We went to the dairy, famous not only for its products, but for the family tea-room with its wonderful array of china, and its very long-tailed bird, and then to the beautiful kitchen gardens where one especially admired the pruning of the espalier and wall fruit. I could but guess at the past glory of the greenhouses as evidently only needs of the war had been considered, but I got a glimpse of brilliant scarlet pioncettias with mauve salvias in a riot of colour, and in another house there was still a wonderful arched roof of rich rose begonias reflecting enchantingly through many mirrors, a rare delight on a grey day.

Across the way was the little old grey church with its pure silver altar, the gift of the Philadelphian, Wannamaker, in memory of King Edward, in admiration of his work for the peace of the world, and next it Queen Alexandra's cross in memory of those from Sandringham who had fallen in the great war—what irony of fate!

York Cottage, the simple country house of the First Gentleman of Europe, might have been any house in any county in England, unpretentious, typically English, pleasantly set in a scene of homely beauty, in the foreground smooth lawns bordered with golden osiers and white Canadian birches and vivid red of the dogwood bushes, and moving in and out the gentle dappled deer, a living picture of great charm. Even the policemen stationed at the gates looked as if they were in no way necessary but obliging "supers" in the panorama.

One heard that the King was spending the day shooting as is usual when he is at Sandringham, and that the Queen and Princess Mary were walking, quite unattended, through the woods and heath beyond. Later in the day one of the gentlemen told me that the King, who as the world knows is a wonderful shot, had taken in the few minutes he stood beside him, five most difficult shots.

The meeting was in the village hall, every village on the estate has a similar room, pretty and suitable for many purposes.

We were all to be in place when Her Majesty should arrive, but the saying on our Women's Institute programmes "Punctuality is the politeness of Kings" was never better exemplified. We were ready, but only just. Her Majesty came at once to me and shook hands, saying "We have met at the exhibition. Do you remember?" Did I remember? The Princess Mary also remembered me, and was very kind about my recent illness. Lady Mary Trefusis was in attendance. I was then introduced to the audience, and with what I can only trust, was a satisfactory curtsey began to speak.

(To be concluded next month.)

THE MEMBER'S GARDEN.

" Kind hearts are the garden,
Kind thoughts are the roots,
Kind words are the blossoms,
Kind *deeds* are the fruit."

HOME AND COUNTRY.

THE WOMEN'S INSTITUTES JOURNAL.

PUBLISHED BY THE

NATIONAL FEDERATION OF WOMEN'S INSTITUTES: ESTABLISHED IN CONJUNCTION
WITH THE WOMEN'S BRANCH OF THE BOARD OF AGRICULTURE AND FISHERIES.

Chairman—THE LADY DENMAN.   *Vice-Chairman*—MISS GRACE HADOW.
Hon. Treasurer—MISS ALICE WILLIAMS.   *General Secretary* MRS. KILROY KENYON, M.B.E.

| VOL. I.—No. 4. | JUNE, 1919. | [ANNUAL SUBSCRIPTION 2s.] PRICE 2d. |

MRS. ALFRED WATT, MA., M.B.E.

OUR Institute members owe a debt of gratitude to Mrs. Watt who from over the seas brought the idea of Women's Institutes. She started our first Women's Institute at Llanfair P.G. in September, 1915, and she had the satisfaction of starting a W.I. at Sandringham of which H.M. The Queen is President.

When Mrs. Watt returns to Canada next month she will take a cordial greeting from our Institutes to the Pioneer Women's Institutes of her homeland as well as our heartiest wishes of goodwill for herself. Her name will be inseparably connected with the Women's Institutes in England and Wales.

A WOMEN'S INSTITUTE AT SANDRINGHAM.

By Mrs. ALFRED WATT, M.A., M.B.E.

(Continued from last month's Journal.)

THERE was a general air of suppressed anxiety about the meeting, and I was trying hard to remember things I was not to say or do. But it was a simple, pleasant, little meeting nevertheless. The Queen and Princess Mary were delightfully interested and I was determined that it should all be simple and natural, and exactly like any other village meeting even to my most homely little stories. I am frequently asked what I said in my speech, but it was in no way different from usual, I spoke of the simplicity and democracy and friendliness of our movement, of the independence of our Women's Institutes, each being self governing and self supporting, and of the sense of responsibility of every member to her institute, and of how it has to do with the little things of every day life.

I saw only two faces in the audience. The dear little responsive face of Princess Mary who saw a joke coming and was ready to greet it with the prettiest little laugh, and that of an anxious little woman whose lusty boy baby was entering vigorous protest. What did he care for majesty or the right of a speaker to be heard? Nothing, bless him! And nobody minded but the worried little mother.

Members of Women's Institues will want to know what institutes I talked about. So far as I can remember I read parts of programmes from Malling, Moreton, Epping, Branston, Llanbedr, Scaynes Hill and Balcombe, and extracts from reports of Madron, Minstead, Ipsden, and of Chilliwack and Nelson in British Columbia. As is usual, also I told some absurd little stories against myself which never fail to please, and made some fun of antiquated notions of house-work.

The meeting was a large one and there were people from all the villages on the estate, and every one looked interested. After my address the Queen asked me to come back and talk about the exhibits, and the meeting became quite informal, everyone crowding about the exhibits and discussing them. I had taken with me to the meeting an exhibition of soft toys and needlework from Sussex, and the Queen had sent the articles she purchased at the Women's Institute Exhibition. There were dried marigold petals from Denton, canned fruit from Cooksbridge, bottled gooseberries, potato starch from Mrs. Clowes' recipe, dried vegetables, "Cuthberts" from Burgess Hill, French doll from Lindfield, ducks and kittens from Wivelsfield, rabbit skin mitts from Northaw (which by the way Princess Mary tried on), a basket from Deudraeth W.I., a Canadian rug made from odd bits of wool, and kettle-holder from bits of cloth, and a parson made from a merry thought!

Her Majesty remained for over an hour after her carriage was ordered, then the lady in waiting suggested departure but it was some time again before the Queen and Princess Mary obviously reluctantly, betook themselves away. While they remained they talked and asked questions and I think learned a good deal about our work.

Owing to Her Majesty's interest and the informal way in which she moved about among us all and the many questions she asked me, I was able to make points I thought would particualry appeal to her concerning our movement. The last point I made, which was the impression I thought might remain with her, was that to have a Women's Institute at Sandringham, would make an enormous difference to the institutes of the Empire.

To have the Queen as a Women's Insititute member of an institute in one of her own villiages would strike the imagination of every Women's Institute member near and far. Her Majesty seemed greatly impressed with this aspect of the matter.

Her Majesty told me that she had read "The First Women's Institute School" book through and had liked the spirit of it all. Miss Lloyd and I are pleased and proud,

We were all most grateful to the Queen for coming to our meeting. I can only hope that when there are several institutes at Sandringham she will feel rewarded.

NOTES OF WOMEN'S INSTITUTE WORK.

GOD SAVE THE QUEEN

INSTITUTE members at home and in Greater Britain beyond the Seas will learn with pride that our gracious Queen has acquired a new title. Her Majesty is President of the Sandringham Women's Institute which has just been started. The knowledge that our Queen, who during the anxious years of war showed such unwearied devotion to duty in sharing in our efforts to make the institute movement a living force in the country, will be an incentive for increased effort to every Institute member.

WOMEN'S INSTITUTES SCHOOL AT HAMPSHIRE.

THE school at Winchester was a great success. Mrs. Watt, assisted by Mrs. Clowes and others, carried out a carefully-arranged programme. One day was devoted to a meeting of the Hampshire Federation, which was a revelation of the progress and activity of the work in the county. Miss Kingsmill and Miss Dent were responsible for the excellent local arrangements. The most generous and kindly hospitality afforded by members of neighbouring Institutes gave the students a delightful impression of Hampshire, which is true to traditions.

THORNCOMBE W.I. gave an entertainment in January. The proceeds, £6 10s. 6d., were generously sent to the National Federation Central Fund.

BRADFORD ABBAS W.I. had a very successful village dance. When expenses were paid a sum of £1 13s. remained, which was most kindly forwarded to the National Federation. Such practical acknowledgement of the Central body is very cheering.

OUR CARAVAN.

By One of the Caravaners.

THE East Kent Caravan Exhibition is now an accomplished fact, and there is no doubt that these Travelling Exhibitions will become a potent factor in W.I. work. For there is no sounder way of reaching the village as a mass, particularly those villages remote from train or 'bus which are such a problem in East Kent, and there is no end to the possibilities opened up by the van, both for propaganda and educational work.

A brief description will suffice of the method employed in this experimental tour. The Secretaries of the Institutes having been previously circularised as to the dates of the visits and the arrangements they were asked to make, the Caravan, a real gipsy one like a galleon in full sail, set out from Wye on May 9th, on a seven weeks' tour of the East Kent W.I.s. A night was spent at each Institute, and an Exhibition held of needlework, baskets, gloves, toys, fur-craft and so on to which the village was admitted at 6d. per head. A horse and man were provided by each Institute to take the caravan on to the next village. The expenses of this and the hire of hall were defrayed by the caravan takings, though in many cases the Institutes most generously lent the horses and shared the hire of the hall. Almost without exception, too, hospitality was given to the two ladies in charge. Some Institutes dividing the honours among some half-dozen members in true communal style !

As regards exhibits, we found the needlework was the great attraction, especially the children's clothes on the Educraft principle which appealed by their simplicity in make which meant ease in washing. The Educraft book and Miss Joan Drew's "Embroidery and Design " and the H.Q. sampler of stitchery were eagerly examined, as well as the many samples of artistic needlework, smocking and handweaving gathered from all parts of England. Furcraft was almost equally popular, as almost every village contained a skin-curer who was delighted to learn how to make up pelts into gloves, slippers and other useful articles. Baskets, particularly the more useful makes, ran a good second and these and the wooden toys were eagerly examined by the schoolmasters, disabled soldiers and boys. The Dunchurch gloves, especially the leather gauntlets, were so popular that we had to lay in a stock. Spindle-spinning and a small toy loom attracted great attention, while talks on haybox cookery proved topical.

We found a stall of local products a very useful feature both for the acquisition of new exhibits and ideas, and for comparison with the samples brought round. Here the H.Q. loan collection provided a good standard, always a great difficulty in village industries.

The tour has been a bold experiment—which has been justified. The enthusiasm aroused has been genuine and the interest wide-spread. The Caravan has paid its way, to the great relief of the County Treasurer ! But there must be changes in arrangements for future tours. It was found that seven weeks of daily exhibitions at a stretch were too long for the same workers. Either these must be changed half-way, or there must be a stay of two or three days in each place. Regretfully too we decided that a horse caravan, though undoubtedly an attractive advertisement, is too unwieldy and slow, especially where long distances and hills are concerned. Nor was it possible to give the Institutes sufficient details of the plan of action beforehand, so that most of the arrangements had perforce to wait until the caravan actually arrived, with the result that much of the heavy work fell on the Caravaners and the Exhibition was in several cases kept open for too great a space of time. People dropped in during the afternoon and evening and it was impossible to get them together for demonstrations or talks. On the other hand, where an Institute concert or entertainment had been arranged the Exhibition was apt to get pushed on one side.

Both sides were working at an experiment, and mistakes were naturally made. Yet we shall always be proud to think that East Kent was the pioneer of what must prove a great asset in W.I. work, the triumphant bringing of the mountain to Mahomet.

[Many congratulations to East Kent Federation on the success of this delightful enterprize, the credit of which should be given, so says the Federation Chairman, to the capable workers in charge of the Caravan. But whose was the brilliant idea ?—EDITOR.]

BEE HINTS.

Ventilation.—Be sure to keep your hives well ventilated during this warm weather ; it is a good plan to place an old parasol over the hive ; this helps to keep the sun's rays from beating too fiercely down on it, and at the same time prevents excessive swarming.—From "The Irish Homestead."

SOME NOTES FROM A VISITOR TO THE N.F.W.I. ANNUAL MEETING.

I VENTURE to send some general impressions of this wonderful gathering. The chairmanship was masterly, clarity, brevity and wit ruled the decisions.

Our President.

Unfortunately the chairman's back was turned to me and the determination and energy expressed by that back cannot be pictured by my fountain pen.

The organisation of the meeting was perfect, the audience was the best behaved that it has ever been

A W.I. Secretary.

my lot to view. The General Secretary on whom the chief responsibility of carrying out the work of Headquarters must rest has a very clever head on very youthful shoulders. The shake of her head as she advised the chairman suggested the wisdom of a Socrates. Alas that I was not seated in the front of the house!

Another President.

The speaking was excellent. The agenda reflected the intrepid spirit of the Executive Committee. I mastered with difficulty the alternative schemes for a suggested new constitution drawn up by this Committee and three or four points would have raised nice discussions in which I longed to hear the delegates state divergent opinions. My hopes were disappointed, the ladies burked the fences. Conservative

Worried W.I. Official.

woman ruled no change until a change is inevitable. The speakers interested me. They had studied the subjects on which they spoke, they wasted no words, they obeyed the rules as laid down for speakers. The docility of these women to the rule of other women amazed me. The audience interested me even more than the speakers. Never before had I seen such a collection of

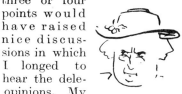

Strong on Procedure.

women, handsome and plain, old and young, fashionable and staid, but all keen members of this great association which it is evident is setting an

Feather-headed Member.

The Jolly Member.

example of good order and progress to other associations less happily constituted. Adam was banished from this new Paradise where the Eves of many shades and conditions are determined to manage their own affairs. We poor men may look over the garden fence and

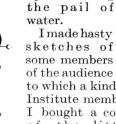

Future M.P.

The Earnest Member.

hope that on a future day, Jill may ask Jack's help in fetching the pail of water.

I made hasty sketches of some members of the audience

The Editor.

A Junior Member.

to which a kind friend, an ardent Institute member, has put titles. I bought a copy of the little magazine with a geographical cover and amused myself by picking out the typical editor. My friend says it is a speaking likeness.

I glanced at the press. One youthful representative appeared almost bored. My prophetic fountain pen pictured him thus in five minutes' time but he wasn't!!

THE PRESS

New Institute Story.

A member's little girl, on being told that Auntie Mary had a new baby said:

"Why, what was the matter with the old one?"

OUR CHAIRMAN, VICE-CHAIRMAN AND OTHER WELL-KNOWN W.I. WORKERS.

– 1922 –

Above: Hyde Heath WI outing to Clacton, 1920

Below: A travelling exhibition of hand industries organised by Oxfordshire Federation, 1921

Above: Northcourt WI choir, 1927

Below: HM Queen Elizabeth and Lady Denman tour a fruit preservation centre during the war

A TEA HOSTESSES' MEETING

EDYTH COLES

THE Strong-minded Member looked at us over her spectacles. "We're all here now," she remarked, "so we had better begin. First of all, let us settle what each one is to do. Who'll do the waiting?" There was silence for a moment, then the Stout Member broke the ice and expressed her willingness to carry a tray around. Everybody looked at her. Really she was very sporty but how on earth did she expect to get between the rows of chairs? Space is limited at our meeting place.

The youngest member.

The Youngest Member whispered to her neighbour, "She ought to take the urn. I don't want to. I've got a duck of a new dress to wear for waiting in. 'Nippy' style you know, and *really* short." The neighbour looked at the dress the Youngest Member had on at the moment and wondered uncomfortably what she considered really short.

After everyone had signified their willingness to "wait," the Strong-minded Member luckily remembered the urn and suggested that she and the Stout Member should take it together, so that little difficulty was solved to everyone's satisfaction. Even the Stout Member herself looked relieved.

"Now what are we going to give them to eat?" asked the Strong-minded Member. "Brown bread and butter of course; everybody eats brown bread nowadays."

"Some of our members still prefer white," said the Oldest Member bravely. "We'd better have a little."

"Let them eat brown for once; they'll get to like it better the oftener they have it," said the Strong-minded Member.

"How about a few sandwiches?" enquired the Youngest Member hopefully. "Cucumber ones are nice. I love them."

"Poison," said the Strong-minded Member decidedly, "and terribly indigestible even to the few people who like them."

The Newest Member paled as she visualised the hapless Institute members dying off like flies during tea. "Egg and cress might be better, perhaps," she suggested hastily.

"Lots of people can't eat eggs I know," said the Strong-minded Member. "We might have plain cress though if you really think it necessary." She made a note of it—reluctantly—in her notebook. "Now cake," she continued. "Sponge cake, that's light and nourishing. What do you think?"

"Yes," said the Oldest Member, "and seed cake, how about that? And some fruit cake?"

"No one ate the seed cake last time it was provided and fruit cake is much too rich. Just a plain tea is all that is needed. There's too much trash eaten these days." The Strong-minded Member looked at her little flock as though challenging them to contradict her. No one did, however, and she made another note in her note-book. Then the hostesses departed.

* * *

The Newest Member and the Oldest walked away together. Said the Newest Member sorrowfully, "How disappointed they'll be. Only brown bread and butter and sponge cake."

The Oldest Member smiled. "Don't worry," she replied. "We've worked with the Strong-minded Member before and we don't take too much notice of her fads. You'll see, there'll be white bread, seed cake, fruit cake *and* cucumber sandwiches."

She was right. There was.

HINTS TO DANCERS.

HE dances.	I dance.
She dances.	You dance.
They dance.	We dance.

Everybody dances!

But do they dance well?

All dancers should bear the following hints in mind. They will increase an evening's enjoyment:—

1. Look happy.
2. Don't talk while dancing.
3. Keep your body as steady as possible, swaying only with the music.
4. Don't wave your partner's arm up and down like a pump handle.
5. Apologise if you have a collision. It is always the other person's fault, but never mind; your partner may realise that, even if other people dont.
6. Don't try too many fancy steps—they are bad form.
7. Never smoke while dancing.

There was never anything by the wit of man so well devised nor so sure established which in continuance of time hath not been corrupted. Book of Common Prayer.

" How did she expect to get between the rows ? "

"LIVING WHIST"

C. A. COOK

Living Whist played by Munsley and District (Herefordshire) at its own garden fête and at the Ledbury Carnival in aid of the local hospital.

LIVING WHIST is very pretty to watch and is most entertaining. It is, of course, really most suitable for an out-of-door entertainment, as plenty of space is needed for the movements of the whole pack of fifty-two cards, moreover, a smooth stretch of grass, a tennis or croquet lawn or a level field has the effect of a green-covered card-table.

What to wear. In the way of costumes, there is the possibility of plenty of variety. The most usual way is to dress the actors, as far as possible, like the court cards of a pack, that is, in Tudor costume, the hearts and diamonds in red-and-white, the spades and clubs in black-and-white. The kings and queens should have long mantles, edged with cotton-wool ermine and covered with the "suit" emblems cut from black or red paper. The knaves should have tabards, like heralds or sandwichmen, a square flat, cardboard-stiffened board, back and front, hung over the shoulders. The queens should carry stiff paper roses in their hands just as on real cards, the kings sceptres and the knaves wands or trumpets, like heralds.

All the rest of the pack wear tabards, like the knaves' of white cardboard, bearing on back and front the number of "pips" of their particular card, either stencilled on or cut from black or red paper and pasted on. Under the tabards should be worn tunics and knickers or short shirts of red or black sateen or of some other cheap material. They may be very simple as they scarcely show. Red or black stockings should be worn and caps to match.

How to proceed. The game itself should begin with a grand march-past. Each suit is led by the court cards, with the knave first as a herald, then the king and queen, with their trains held up by 'twos" and "threes," then the rest of the suit.

The cards then form up along the four sides of a square, leaving an open space in the middle on which to play.

Four "players" now take their seats at an ordinary card-table, with a director beside them.

Before play begins the suit which is trumps is called out by the director, who must be possessed of a strong, clear voice. The four players play out, slowly and deliberately, an ordinary game of whist and, as each card is placed upon the table, the director calls out its name and the living representative steps forward into the middle, bows, if a boy, and curtsies, if a girl, and remains standing there.

When all four cards are played and the trick is taken, the living cards bow or curtsey again and march off, to stand, one behind the other, on one side of the table, led by the winning card.

The playing goes on until all the cards have been played and all the tricks taken.

The procession then marches off to the sound of stirring music, led by the winning hand and, walking this time trick by trick, in the order in which they were taken.

A great deal of variety can be introduced into a game of "living whist."

For instance, when the game has been played out, the pack can remain at the sides of the "table" and some solo dances, or a minuet or gavotte for the court cards, a Morris dance for the jester, knaves and so on can take place.

"I hear your dear wife is to give our Women's Institute a lecture."
"My dear lady, it's no use appealing to me, I can't stop her."

(Reproduced by kind permission from "Punch.")

MESSAGE IN THIS TIME OF NATIONAL CRISIS FROM THE CHAIRMAN OF THE NATIONAL FEDERATION OF WOMEN'S INSTITUTES

How can Institutes help in the National Crisis ? What can we do to help the country during the coming Winter ?

Money must be saved, by the Government and by the individual. What can the Institutes do to add to the national wealth ?

These I know are questions that are being asked by many Women's Institute members.

In the first place much of our work consists in being economical, we learn to make the most of our gardens and of our poultry, we learn good cooking, which means getting the most nourishment out of our food, and we learn about health, which means we are able to some extent to lessen ill health which is one of the most disastrous forms of waste to the Nation. Many of our handicrafts are economical because good and useful things are made out of material which would otherwise be wasted.

So one of the ways in which we can help is to continue our classes, our demonstrations and our educational lectures and to increase rather than to curtail our work.

The Winter will be a hard one for many of our members and for their men folk and a very important way in which we can help is through the friendliness and comradeship of our Institute to make it easier for all of us to bear, cheerfully, the personal sacrifices we shall have to make.

I have had several letters suggesting that Institutes should have a collection and make a direct gift to the Exchequer to help the Nation to make both ends meet. Should an Institute decide that it is wise to take action of this kind the greatest care should be taken to ensure that gifts made by the members are entirely voluntary. Every member will have to shoulder part of the burden through taxation and some members through reduced wages as well. In many cases this will be the utmost that they can manage and Institutes wishing to make an additional gift should be very careful to consider the feelings of members who will want to take part but who may not feel justified in doing so.

We must realise that we can do far more to help the Nation as members of a Women's Institute and of a County Federation and of the National Federation than we can do as individuals, so in our efforts to assist we must not lose members ; nor must we fail to support nor must we in any way weaken our own Organisation.

Institute Committees will want to save their members as much expense as they can and will probably reduce to some extent their money-raising efforts. Many Institutes will, therefore, have a smaller income to spend. To meet this position I can only suggest that socials and outings may possibly be dropped or carried out on a simpler scale. There may be some Institutes which give prizes for competitions which might now try the alternative method of giving marks to the winners and at the end of the year giving a certificate to those who have been most successful. But probably the most useful economy will be for Institutes to appeal to their members, themselves to provide a greater part of the Women's Institute programme than has hitherto been the case and thus save the Institute some proportion of fees and travelling expenses. We have so many experts who are too shy to impart their knowledge, now is their opportunity to come forward and help their fellow members.

I expect every Institute will be able to think out possible economies which will enable them to save expense without cutting down their activities.

Your National Federation has been in receipt of a grant of £800 a year from the Treasury to help in the organisation of handicrafts. Your Executive has decided not to apply for this grant for the coming twelve months as it believes that Women's Institute members would not wish to take this sum in the present crisis. Economies are being considered at Headquarters to meet this reduction of income. As a beginning it has been decided to cancel the October Consultative Council. This will effect a saving of nearly £100 to Headquarters in addition to saving delegates and County Federations some expense. It was possible to take this step, as the National Crisis has so altered conditions, that some of the main subjects for discussion at the Consultative Council would no longer have led to any practical result.

We all have a new and difficult situation to face. We must realise that the Nation will not be safe until our trade has improved. This must, at the best, take many months. We Institute members must follow the course of events and try to understand the National and International difficulties so that we may learn in what direction National safety lies and be ready to do our bit during the difficult times ahead.

G. DENMAN.

OUR VILLAGE WOMEN'S INSTITUTE.

To-night I want to show you a simple and easy way of making a little pull-on hat out of a yard of Petersham ribbon.

First take the size of your head.

Pin the ribbon firmly here.

Now take one end round to the front.

Tuck it in.

Arrange the other end as it suits you best.

And there you have a new hat for three shillings.

And so we had.

A Message from the Minister of Health

THE Women's Institutes, one of the most remarkable developments of the war and post-war years, have been bringing countrywomen together for the common good for more than twenty-one years. I believe they would all agree with me that there is nothing which can be of more vital interest to each and all of them than the health of the individual and of the nation.

In the countryman's home the wife and mother is the chief guardian of the family's health. From the nature of things, medical and nursing aid and advice cannot be so concentrated and close at hand for all in the case of a scattered population living in small villages or isolated cottages as in the large town where there are all sorts of health services within easy walking distance. It is the countryman's wife who has often to cope with sickness or accident as best she can until professional help is available. It is she who has so frequently to bear the brunt of the extra work and anxiety caused by serious illness. To her the family particularly looks to make full use of the health and other services provided for their welfare.

By the time this number of HOME AND COUNTRY appears the Prime Minister will have inaugurated a nation-wide campaign which has as its key words " Use Your Health Services." We want to see a wider use of the maternity and child welfare services, more children drinking cheap milk at school, more schoolchildren getting their eyes or teeth attended to when the school doctor or dentist finds that they need attention, earlier seeking of expert help in diseases such as tuberculosis where there is a good hope of complete cure if only it is treated in time. Last, but not least, we want to see more people making use of all the facilities for open-air exercise and recreation which are becoming daily more extensive.

The health services and the various other facilities making for better health exist for the community ; it is for the community to use them ; and the more they are used, the nearer we shall be to a fitter Britain and the better the individual's prospect of a full and a happy life.

Countrywomen in the villages of England and Wales, I know that our campaign will have your warm support, and I look to you to do your utmost to crown it with success, in the interests of yourselves, your families and the race.

Kingsley Wood

SIR KINGSLEY WOOD IN THE HOPFIELDS

The Minister of Health, who has written the accompanying message specially for HOME AND COUNTRY, paid a visit last month to the Kentish hopfields to inspect the conditions under which the pickers work. He is here seen talking to a very junior picker

At the Village Bazaar.
Gushing Visitor: " And are all these really made by Women Inebriates ? "

WOMEN'S INSTITUTES AND NATIONAL EMERGENCY

A NUMBER of members have been puzzled by the problem of the exact position Women's Institutes may be expected to occupy in the event of a state of National Emergency arising. At the request of the Executive Committee, Miss Hadow, Vice-Chairman of the National Federation since its foundation, has written the following statement

TOWARDS THE END of the World War a Women's Institute President said regretfully: "When the war is over, I suppose Women's Institutes will come to an end ": so entirely, in this country, were they a product of the war and so well were they adapted to war service, that even their own officers did not realize their potentialities in time of peace. Now the pendulum is in danger of swinging the other way. Women's Institutes have become so natural a part of our daily lives, that there are members who feel that should a state of national emergency arise, Institute work must go to the wall.

It is for every individual to decide for herself how best she can serve her country in peace or war, but the fact that Institutes were called into existence in 1915 because such an organization was needed, and that it was a Government Department which fostered their growth at such a time, should make all of us consider whether possibly this work in our own village and our own county, work for which we have been specially trained, may not be that for which we are best fitted and in which we can be of most use.

Here is a great organization ready to be used, but it will cease to be an organization if all its most efficient members are drained away. Between 1915-18 Institutes helped in food production and preservation; they worked for local emergency hospitals and canteens ; they regularly supplied prisoners of war with comforts; they cared for refugees. Certainly all these things will need doing should we ever be involved in war again, and in addition there will, in many counties, be the urgent call for help with both children and adults evacuated from our own big cities.

No one would wish to restrain people from volunteering for National Service, but National Service may lie in simple things, and to help to keep up morale and to prevent life in an emergency from becoming wholly disorganized is in itself work of no mean value.   GRACE E. HADOW

A COUNTRY WOMAN LOOKS ABOUT HER

" THIS WAR'S a proper mix up," said the conductor of the Westshire and District Motor Bus in which I was travelling. "Where it's to end I don't know, I'm sure." He had just unloaded two Austrian refugee maids and a Scotsman. I had come only from across the county boundary, but from the way he looked at me I could see that he thought me a foreigner, too.

I heard lately of a London woman, sent to do war work in the country, who declared it her ambition to "stamp out that county spirit". She will need large boots to flatten the local loyalties from which our greater loyalties grow. But I expect the mix-up, that is stirring our population round like a pudding in a basin, will do us a lot of good.

Wartime factories in rural districts are bringing workpeople from far away. I know one south of England village that has had a little colony of Welsh people attached to it. You should hear how those Welsh voices are improving the village singing ! The parents of evacuee children are learning far more about the country from their own boys and girls than they could find out in a hundred outings, packed into charabancs with their neighbours from the next street. And those sad, frightened outcasts from their own countries, who tremble at a knock at the door, and make such pathetic efforts to learn our ways and language, may, as they settle down among us, give us some of the benefit that came to an older age with the Huguenot refugees from France. But perhaps the biggest change that the mix-up may bring us will come from a decline in the importance of towns.

We all know of big country houses, taken " for the duration " by banks, insurance companies, branches of Government offices, and so on. Habits of years—the nearest teashop for lunch and the 6.15 train home—have been broken. The breaking has hurt in many cases. Smith and Brown have had lunch together for years. But Smith's office has moved to Berkshire, and Brown's to Kent.

THE COUNTRY always seems cold to townspeople ; and this year it *has* been cold. Black coats and thin shoes are not much use in country rain. And there is no tube train to take you from your diggings in Little Muddycombe to Muddycombe House a mile and a half away.

But isn't it possible that some of these wartime migrants may stay in the country ?

Some of the great houses of England, in which no private person will ever again be able to live, might in this way find a new and useful life.   B. St.L.

– 1939 –

BLAKE.
Katherine A. Riches.

Perhaps it would interest the members of the Women's Institutes to hear a little about that wonderful man, William Blake, the author of our " Institute Song." We in Shenley were fortunate in having a lecture from Mr. Wicksteed which explained the meaning of Blake's designs for the "Book of Job," slides of which were shown on the screen during the lecture.

To be able to understand Blake even a little we must begin by realising that he was a mystic, a being in direct communion with the Infinite, his mind and all his soul's energies were concentrated upon the supernatural world whose beings were to him living personalities. All great saints, poets, artists are mystics in their moments of inspiration but Blake, more than most, lived outside our ordinary existence.

Born in London in 1757, the son of a hosier interested in other things besides his shop, William Blake, though he had little actual schooling, heard much interesting conversation especially about the great mystic philosopher, Swedenborg. He began to see visions when he was four years old and at fourteen it is said he refused to be apprenticed to a certain engraver as " the man looked as if he were born to be hanged," a fate which overtook him a few years later. Blake's love for drawing persisted and he was finally placed with an engraver who directed him to make a series of drawings in Westminster Abbey, which was to be afterwards engraved. The quiet months he spent working in the Abbey gave him a passionate love for Gothic architecture and for all Early English art and history. He read much of Shakespeare and Milton and his knowledge of the Bible was far more exact than that of the average, educated Englishman. In his early youth he had an unhappy love affair which so affected him that he was sent into the " country " at Battersea to recover. There he met the girl who was to become his wonderful wife, the best that any man of genius ever had. She was the daughter of the house where he lodged, and she relates that, directly she saw him, " she experienced a peculiar nervous sensation which she could not explain nor describe." That same evening he told her of his unrequited love. " I pity you from my heart," she said. " Do you pity me ? " he replied, " then I love you for that." Like all the story of Blake's life, his love story has a simplicity and an

– 1925 –

element of mysticism. From the time he was married, at twenty-five, until his death at the age of seventy, his wife was, as he said to her on his death-bed, an angel to him. Her health and strength enabled her to be a companion in his thirty or forty mile walks and she was a housekeeper who managed his slender resources so economically that he never actually experienced the worst hardships of poverty. If he felt impelled to write or draw in the night, she would take one of his hands and sit speechless by his side for hours till his work was finished. In those days there were no National Schools and Catherine Blake, like most people of her class, could only put a X in the Church register when she was married. With her husband's help she learned to read and write and even to draw and paint.

Blake's talents were not those of the bread-earning sort. His genius was far higher than the ordinary talent which commands worldly success. He would rather starve than do any work he despised, and wealth never attracted him. There were times when his wife had to place an empty plate before him as a reminder that some commission, however distasteful, must be finished in order to provide a meal. It is not surprising that he refused the post of drawing master to the Royal Family.

Everyone who came into contact with Blake was struck by the peculiar distinction of his personality. His manner and conversation were alike unforgettable. His wide open eyes, were bright with the illumination of some internal radiance, burning and piercing into the very soul of those they looked upon. He was in the highest sense of the word a good man, proud and independent in spirit yet humble and mild in his private life, revolutionary in his theories, yet orderly in his conduct, poor and bound down by the necessities of his daily labour and at the same time rich in his visionary treasures and happy in his supernatural existence. There was a time when visions would come at his call and many of his poems were thus "dictated" to him. A story is told of his introduction to a patron of art as "the Divine Blake who has seen God, sir, and talked with angels." Apart from his walks round London, the only occasion on which Blake visited the country was when he and his wife spent three years in the little seaside village of Felpham, in Sussex, in order to be near a friend who had given him a commission for some engravings. "Our cottage," he writes, "is more beautiful than I thought . . . Heaven opens here on all sides its golden gates." He began some of his greatest works here—the "Jerusalem" and the "Milton" and was annoyed when Hayley, his friend and patron, would come and give him some mechanical piece of work to do. The climax came when he was asked to paint a fire screen for a lady. This he absolutely refused to do. He told Hayley that he was "determined to be no longer pestered with his genteel ignorance" and went back to London. But the long walks on the seashore had filled his spirit with new visions which were to inspire some of his grandest creations. His home was a room in Fountain Court, Strand, in which he and his wife, worked, cooked, ate and slept. The large sash

window overlooked a court beyond which might be seen the Thames and the distant downs of Surrey and Kent. There seems to have been a second room "kept for receiving visitors."

Of his best known works the "Songs of Innocence" and the "Book of Job," the former was hand-printed and illustrated in water-colours when he was thirty-two, the latter was not finished until he was seventy. This was the work which was chiefly to occupy Blake after his return from Sussex.

The Book of Job attracted him early. Its contents became his favourite and his greatest theme, the designs are full of his deepest thoughts and imagination. Mr. Wicksteed points out that according to Blake, Elihu rebukes Job, not for sin as the other friends did but for the importance he attached to his own struggles after an isolated perfection. The attempt to find life's purpose in the saving of our single souls is to be blind to the universal spirit. Thus aroused Job realises that his single personality is not the *goal* of life for him but rather its *key*, and in the eighteenth design we see his own earthly life symbolised by a sacrificial flame soaring up into the Divine life which has become a white sun of pure light. The two lives, in virtue of the complete loss of self in love of his fellow men and of every creature in the divinely human universe, are thus united in Job himself.

As Mr. Laurence Binyon says, the Job series alone suffices to show what a master of imagination Blake was, a poet when he painted as when he wrote. There is no one who has depicted fire and flame as splendidly as he. He loved to give to his figures the rushing movement of wind. He communicates the sense of movement so vividly that we seem to share it. Wonderful too, is his apprehension of the vast and starry spaces of night.

Blake had a passionate love for his native country and when in later life he came to invent his own mythology, "Albion" stood for "the Chosen People" in whose land "Jerusalem," his "Ideal City of the Imagination" was to be built.

> I will not cease from mental fight,
> Nor shall my sword sleep in my hand
> Till we have built Jerusalem
> In England's green and pleasant land.

It is nearly a hundred years since Blake died, almost unknown save to a small circle of admirers. To-day his work is sought and valued perhaps more than that of any other artist or poet. "The crude charge of insanity which used to be levelled against him is surely almost dead," says Mr. Wicksteed. A charming story on this point is told of a young man asking a friend of Blake if he did not think him cracked. "Yes, sir," replied the friend, "but his is a crack that lets in the light."

[Institute librarians might like to read of : "Blake and His Poetry" in the "Poetry of Life" series, 1s. 3d. and "Blake's Vision of the Book of Job," by Joseph Wicksteed, 10s. 6d., illustrated with Blake's designs.]

> Think not thou canst sigh a sigh,
> And thy Maker is not by :
> Think not thou canst weep a tear,
> And thy Maker is not near.—BLAKE.

What W.I.s did in 1944

Illustrations for the following brief summary of the thousand and one activities of the Women's Institutes were taken from the Wartime Work Calendar for 1945 published by the Buckinghamshire Federation and drawn by Mrs. E. A. Holme.

SUPPOSING someone said to you, " Yes, I know Women's Institutes make jam, but what else do they do ? " How would you reply ? Well, here are some of the things you might say about W.I. doings last year.

There were 5,835 Institutes last month with a membership of 288,300. Each County Federation has a number of Voluntary County Organizers, about one for every ten Institutes, and last year the N.F.W.I. trained 59 new V.C.O.s. Many of these travel 20 or 30 miles to visit an Institute. A Warwickshire V.C.O. has bicycled 1,258 miles on her visits, and a Denbighshire V.C.O. uses an auto-cycle, " James ", to reach mountain-side hamlets. Even those who have cars and enough petrol don't find V.C.O. visits in the black-out a soft job. Nevertheless a minimum of 30,000 V.C.O. visits are paid every year and probably twice that number would be a more accurate figure.

WATER SUPPLY

Although there was no Annual General Meeting last year, the resolutions of 1943 gave the N.F. Executive plenty of work to go on with. One resolution stated that water and sewerage should be a national responsibility; acting on this, the Executive water questionary was sent out and answered by over 3,500 W.I.s. **It was the first time Institutes had been asked to supply facts and not only opinions,** and also the most ambitious survey undertaken. Moreover, it was the first time Institutes in many counties had formed a village committee of men and women to ascertain facts often not known to half the inhabitants, nor even to the local authorities. The summary (*obtainable from the N.F.W.I., price 3d.*) was well reviewed in the Press. 4,824 copies were sold, and the publication coincided with the discussion in the House of Commons on the Rural Water Supplies Bill. How far local M.P.s are supporting a better water and drainage service is one of the things W.I. members will want to know from Parliamentary candidates at the next election.

Two other 1943 resolutions urged that all children should have an equal chance of a good education, and that W.I.s should take an active interest in vacancies on local authorities. The N.F.W.I. held 23 county conferences to discuss the Education Act and local government. Many of the conferences had an educational expert or a local government official as well as an N.F.W.I. speaker.

The Questions of the Day School, held at Radbrook College, Shrewsbury, was about Home and School. Fifty students from 26 English (but alas ! no Welsh) counties attended.

In the same week an International Conference on Freedom from Want was attended not only by our own members but by foreign guests (paid for by N.F.W.I. funds) representing more than a dozen different countries.

The Annual General Meeting gives the N.F.W.I. mandates (that is, instructions for action) on questions in which Institutes have already been actively interested and sometimes on questions which Institutes have never considered before, the latter being the case with the resolution that men and women should receive equal pay for equal work. Institutes are now taking part in the battle for equal pay waged by other women's organizations for the past thirty years, and are represented on the Equal Pay Campaign Committee, of which Mrs. Tate, M.P., is chairman.

Ever since 1922 W.I.s have been urging the Government to appoint more Women Police, last year with a measure of success. Following a meeting in London held jointly with other women's organizations, Mr. Herbert Morrison, the Home Secretary, insisted on a number of local authorities appointing Women Police, and announced his intention of appointing a Woman Inspector.

The N.F.W.I. is represented on the Council of British Societies for Relief Abroad, and undertook during 1944 to be one of the four principal organizations for distributing wool for children's garments for liberated Europe. Five tons a month is the quota, and some of the garments made by W.I. members are already being worn by the children in Greece; 2,071 fur coats and hoods have been sent to Russia in 1944 under the Aid to Russia scheme.

One of the best ways of getting to know about people in other countries is the Letter Friend scheme, which now totals 6,874. There were 523 new partners last year. Another link with countrywomen overseas has been forged by the Rural Thrift Craft Exhibition organized by the British Council. W.I.s supplied 20 crafts to tour the British Empire.

Women gladly seized the opportunity to learn new crafts during last year, when 131 Guild of Learners members took their " A " test, compared with 57 in 1943. Meanwhile seven centres achieved 2,500 potato baskets, in answer to a special appeal from the Ministry of Agriculture. Service to the troops has included hot baths and day and night work in mobile canteens.

SCHOOLS

" What else do they do ? " Let's take a look at the schools provided by the N.F.W.I. Cotton printing, farm accounts, household jobbery, press reporting, gloves, the Social Half-hour and many others. Then the committees on which the N.F.W.I. is represented. Housing (the Dudley Committee on Design of Dwellings, the Hobhouse Committee on Rural Housing, the Housing Centre and the Housebuilders' Registration Council); village halls; music and drama (Carnegie committees); the British Film Institute; the National Coal Board; the League of Nations Union; the Sankey Committee on Adult Education; the County Gardens Produce Committee; Woman Power Committee; Nursery Schools Association; and 36 others.

FOOD PRODUCTION

Many are the demands that have been made upon the N.F.W.I. by the Ministries of Agriculture and Food; W.I.s have stood the strain well and good humouredly. There were 1,174 preservation centres set up last year, and Headquarters supplied everything from preserving bottles to string, as well as nearly 50,000 fruit bushes in 1943-44, 35,734 collections of vegetable seeds, 3,702 packets of tomato seed and 2,207 packets of haricot beans. Culinary and medicinal herbs, especially foxgloves, have been collected for the Ministries of Food and Supply. Marketing is a side of W.I. work which has made a great advance in 1944. There are now 319 recognized market stalls and 60 of these were opened during 1944. Conferences for Market Officers were held in London, Shrewsbury, Carlisle and Bath.

CICELY McCALL

THE HOUSE

ON THE TERRACE

A DAY AT DENMAN COLLEGE

THE A.G.M. BROADCAST

(Above) COMMON ROOM
(Below) HERBACEOUS BORDER

THE FOUNTAIN

"A GREAT day—the fulfilment of so many hopes"—thus one W.I. member to another in the crowd gathered at the Denman College on April 29, when 640 of the A.G.M. delegates, mostly from long-distance counties, were taken from London in 20 motor coaches to have a first glimpse of the countrywomen's college they had asked for in 1945. Crowd—yet it scarcely seemed so. House and grounds expanded in welcome to their owners, offering hospitality, it seemed, not only to these but to all other W.I. members represented by the day's visitors. Coaches drew up at the drive gate—their loads a bit tiff from the drive. No. 3 party had been badly shaken by an accident to their coach—the only one to break the order of a movement bearing a strong military flavour, suggesting the mind of a W.I. husband.

The impression that remains of the house is of shapely rooms made alive by the explanation of their future use given by indefatigable stewards; made colourful with exquisite flowers arranged by our second gardener, Miss King. Miss Bucknell's beautifully lettered notices guided the visitors through house and gardens; members eagerly sought the bedrooms to be furnished by their counties. Staffordshire's gift of crockery was on view in the dining room; the common room showed Lady Denman's gift of embroidered chairs, Lady Brunner's soft gold curtains and the grand piano, from Mrs. Hopkinson of Cambridge, draped with Oxfordshire's patchwork cover. Parties emerging from the kitchen end were busily writing notes to take back to their Institutes—and asking about courses— how soon, how many—and how long ?

Anyone who had been in the gardens during the past months was disposed today to blink and rub her eyes—was it possible that Miss Clarke had made this productive order out of the wilderness into which she came ? The cordon fruit trees, the satisfying lines of early vegetable sowings, irises—of all flowers the most pleasing in a walled

garden—Raspberries, Norfolk Giant, immense in their health, and glimpses of joys to come in the hot houses. Further afield some walked to the park and warren. Many bought posies, or carrots, radishes and asparagus at the produce stall ; others carried away photographs, postcards and pamphlets from the literature stall. All gathered at the house in the early afternoon to hear the broadcast version of the Albert Hall meeting.

Some members, as they grouped to catch their buses, appreciated having been looked after. Others would have preferred to wander oblivious of time and party—but stairways in the house, gateways and paths in the walled garden and other strategic narrows could not take congestion without spoiling the day for many. And the refreshments, so carefully planned to refresh at vital moments—no, the caterer's wife was not a W.I. member, the caterer had not benefited by military experience in "movement control". But W.I. stewards came to their rescue in cutting and spreading and washing up, and only hoped that no one else went home quite as hungry as themselves.

All thanks to them for this happy first view of our college. One only wished to be in all places and talking with all people at once— our Warden, Miss Christmas, serene and smiling, somehow could.

JOAN YEO

*   *   *   *

ON THE TERRACE (see above): l. to r.—Miss Tennant, Miss Farrer, Lady Denman, Lady Albemarle, Miss Tomkinson, Mrs. Neville-Smith, Lady Brunner.

THE PICTURE MAP on the front cover, showing the locality of Denman College and nearby landmarks of interest, was specially designed for HOME AND COUNTRY by Freda P. Nichols. We hope it will serve as a useful guide to members who are planning to visit the college for their summer outing.

Our Royal Members

by Inez Jenkins
formerly General Secretary of the N.F.W.I.

THE members of our Royal Family have a love of country pursuits. They spend such time as they can in the country. They like country ways and country people. This may well be one reason why the Institutes, being country women's organizations, have come to enjoy the personal interest of the Queens and Princesses of England.

The Institute movement has now existed and flourished in three reigns. Very early in its history comes the first mention of a Queen's interest in its achievements. In the summer of 1917 there were no Federations, National or County. There were only eighty Institutes started and supervised by the Agricultural Organization Society with Lady Denman as Chairman of its W.I. Sub-committee, Mrs. Nugent Harris as its Honorary Secretary and Mrs. Alfred Watt as its Organizer. The country was at war and a National Economy Exhibition was being staged in Hyde Park. To this the Institutes sent a tiny produce and "something out of nothing" exhibit— jams and bottled fruits, home-made bread, stuffed and wooden toys, the first fur gloves, odd examples of thriftcraft. This exhibit attracted the special attention of Queen Mary who visited the Exhibition. In particular she was interested in a child's dress made from old stockings and a home-made mackintosh. "Your Institutes are doing splendid work" she said to Mrs. Nugent Harris who was in charge of the exhibit. "I shall do all I can to foster the movement." Fifteen months later—there was a National Federation now—the Institutes held their own first Exhibition in London in the Caxton Hall. It was organized by Miss Alice Williams, then Honorary Secretary of the National Federation and first Editor of HOME AND COUNTRY. The Queen, bringing with her the Princess Royal, came to see how W.I. work was progressing. This was an Exhibition not of handicrafts only, but of all that the Institutes were making and growing. The story goes that an unrehearsed but lively incident was a game of hide-and-seek in and out and under the stalls when a family of high spirited rabbits made their escape. Fortunately the chase was over before the arrival of the Royal visitors.

Four months later still, at Queen Mary's express wish, an organizer— Mrs. Watt—was sent to talk to the village of Sandringham about starting an Institute. Both the Queen and the Princess Royal were present at this propaganda meeting. On March 6, 1919, Sandringham W.I. was formed as the eight-hundred-and-eighty-sixth Institute and Queen Mary was then elected its first President.

The Queen was a frequent attendant at meetings whenever she was at Sandringham. She took a keen personal interest in the development of the young Institute and was responsible for some of the detailed suggestions which added to the friendliness of the Social Half-hour. Her own effective salesmanship at certain of the early Jumble Sales is well remembered. But her interest and knowledge of the movement went beyond her own village. A cutting from *The Times* of April 13,

1923, records how when King George V and Queen Mary visited the Royal Agricultural College at Cirencester, which was then concerning itself in village social development, the Queen seized the chance of giving a propaganda talk to the Principal on the value of Institutes to Gloucestershire villages and the importance of their democratic basis.

Queen Mary, whose memory is just now so vivid for us all, was herself a notable needlewoman and honoured the Guild of Learners by becoming an honorary member. To her the Handicraft Exhibitions of the Institutes always made a special appeal. She visited most of those which were held in London and her quick, informed interest in all that she saw will not readily be forgotten. At one Exhibition the Queen was presented with an embroidered dress for her small grandchild, our present Queen. Two years' later when making the tour of another N.F.W.I. Exhibition, Queen Mary gave an instance of that wonderful memory for which the Royal Family is famed and brought delight to the heart of a steward by her sudden, smiling recognition: "Why *you* made my granddaughter's little dress —it is wearing very well." At the Exhibition of 1929, Queen Mary accepted a linen counterpane which Institute craftswomen from every county in England and Wales had shared in em-

This historic picture shows Queen Mary and the Princess Royal at the very first exhibition held by the N.F.W.I. at the Caxton Hall, London, in October, 1918. Miss Alice Williams, our Founder Editor, and Mrs. Alfred Watt, who introduced W.I.s into this country, are on the extreme right. This picture appeared on the cover of the first issue of Home and Country, March, 1919

broidering. This was the occasion when the Queen, on arrival at the entrance to the Imperial Institute, discovered that she had forgotten her Institute badge. Recognizing a fellow-member from Norfolk in the crowd, Queen Mary quickly greeted her and "borrowed" her badge. It was also the occasion when Lady Denman recalls that she was advised by the Lady-in-Waiting that the Queen should spend at most an hour and a half at the Exhibition. *After three hours* an exhausted Lady Denman found herself curtseying her farewells to a Queen as fresh and full of enthusiasm as when she first arrived!

*   *   *   *

Queen Elizabeth the Queen Mother also joined Sandringham Institute and when she became Queen was elected Joint-President with Queen Mary. She remains the Institute's President today, and since her election has never missed its New Year Meeting. When she was Duchess of York she visited the National Handicraft Exhibition of 1935; as Queen she visited the exhibition of 1938 upon its opening day and there exists a delightful photograph of the Queen watching a spinning demonstration by the late Miss Somerville of West Kent, where it seems doubtful whether spectator or demonstrator is enjoying the occasion more.

It is common knowledge that the Queen felt particular sympathy with the war-time problems of women. Her understanding of the difficulties both of policy and practice which were faced by the Institutes at the start of the war is written between the lines of the message of goodwill which she sent to her fellow-members in the spring of 1940. This was a moment when the Institutes were meeting

above: **The Duchess of Gloucester, visiting the W.I. Market at Olympia, was delighted to see the soft cheese made on a farm near her home.** *left:* **The Duchess of Kent inspects the W.I. House at Olympia in 1951**

"When we have won through to peace, a great page in the history of Britain's war effort should be devoted to the country women in this dear land of ours." So said the Queen, in 1943 at the Annual General Meeting

criticism because the organization had not turned itself wholly over to war work. There was misunderstanding of the motives which led the movement to cling determinedly to its own programme of activities. But the Queen in her message recognized and praised the help which Institutes were giving in the evacuation scheme and their co-operative work for the services; and she made special mention of the monthly meetings held under difficulty. These she said were proving "a welcome source of strength and refreshment".

The Queen kept in touch with the development of the Institutes' war effort. She visited canning and jam making centres in Buckinghamshire and Surrey. When the National Federation presented a complete canning unit to Reading University, for use by Institute members on two days a week, the Queen, as an Institute member, inspected the unit and herself packed, sealed and initialed a can of plums for despatch to Mrs. Roosevelt in America. In 1943, delegates to the one Annual General Meeting held during the war, arrived to find the Queen there to speak to them and to thank them for the "magnificent contribution" that the Institutes were making towards the winning of the war. The Queen came again to the first Annual Meeting held after the war and again addressed the delegates. And when in 1946 drama, dance and music groups were brought together in the Combined Arts Festival in London, the Queen attended one of the final performances —a delighted member of that large and happy gathering.

above: **In November 1946, the Queen Mother, as Queen, visited the finals of the Combined Arts Festival in London. Here she is shown talking to some of the performers**

below, far left: **The Princess Royal, member and President of Harewood W.I., examines handicrafts in the W.I. tent at the Great Yorkshire Show in 1952.** *centre:* **On the opening day of the National Handicraft Exhibition in 1938 the Queen Mother, as Queen, watches a spinning demonstration by the late Miss Somerville of West Kent.**

right: **The can of plums which the Queen Mother, then Queen, packed, sealed and initialled when she visited the canning unit presented by the National Federation to Reading University during the war. The can was then sent to America to Mrs. Roosevelt**

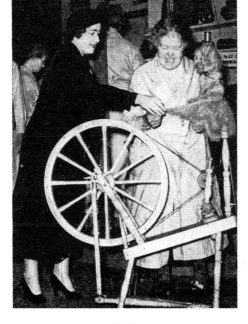

The Queen, as Princess Elizabeth, accompanied by the Duchess of Gloucester, watching a cotton printing demonstration in the W.I. tent at the 1951 Peterborough Agricultural Show, where the work of the Hunts and Northants W.I.s was exhibited

Princess Margaret, accompanied by Lady Brunner, leaves the W.I. "Ideal" Home at Olympia in 1951 after seeing over the house

The Princess Royal appreciates, as did her mother, the handicraft work of the Institutes and is herself an energetic knitter and embroiderer on canvas. She takes particular interest, however, in the produce side of the movement and never fails to visit the National Federation stands at Chelsea and the Royal Agricultural Show or the Institute tent at the Great Yorkshire Show. The Princess Royal is a member and President of Harewood Institute in Yorkshire; the Duchess of Gloucester belongs to Barnwell W.I. in Northants and the Duchess of Kent to Iver Village W.I. in Bucks. Both Duchesses take pleasure in the dramatic activities of the Institutes—on one occasion the Duchess of Kent sat through the non-stop performance of four Institute plays. Both Duchesses also associate themselves with leading events in their County Federations and have visited and spoken at rallies and exhibitions.

* * * *

Our present Queen, Queen Elizabeth the Second, is also an Institute member. She joined the Sandringham Institute in 1943 as did Princess Margaret three years later. Then the Institute could boast that its membership included three generations of the Royal Family. Since her accession to the Throne, the Queen has accompanied the Queen Mother to the January meeting of Sandringham Institute and HOME AND COUNTRY's own exclusive photographs, taken at the time and reproduced in this issue, are a particularly delightful and intimate commentary on the occasion.

Although as yet the Queen has had but few public contacts with the movement, she is knowledgable as to its work and progress. Her interest and pleasure were evident when at the time of her

A Countrywoman's Book, the wedding gift from the Women's Institutes to Princess Elizabeth, which was presented to her personally at Clarence House. Each of the then 58 County Federations was responsible for a section of the book

marriage, she received from the hands of Lady Albemarle, then National Federation Chairman, the movement's wedding present,—an Institute book to which every county had contributed a page symbolizing its particular beauties and traditions. In 1951, as Princess Elizabeth, she visited the Institute tent at the Peterborough Agricultural Show and was fascinated there by the demonstration of printing on cotton. This year, as Queen she paid a visit to the Women's Institute Market, which was a special feature of the Ideal Home Exhibition at Olympia and accepted an Institute-made coronation group—a king and queen of gilded ginger bread! At the Annual General Meeting which followed the Queen's accession to the Throne, the National Federation of Women's Institutes, assembled in conference, addressed to Her Majesty a message of loyalty and devotion. This Loyal Address was beautifully inscribed and decorated by a Devonshire member in red, black and gold. In it the Institutes thanked the Queen for her interest in their work.

* * * *

The Coronation of our young Queen is a great, a solemn and a moving occasion. Upon her are centred the love, the loyalty and the hopes of a commonwealth of nations. In no hearts and thoughts does she hold surer place than in those of Institute members. We are proud to think of her as one of our own number—our Sovereign Member.

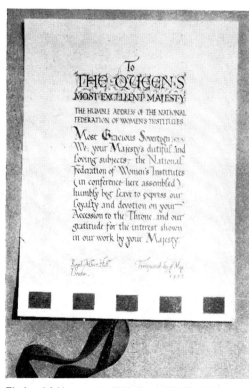

The Loyal Address sent to H.M. Queen Elizabeth II. from the Annual General Meeting held after her accession to the Throne

The photographs on this page of H.M. The Queen and H.M. Queen Elizabeth the Queen Mother at a meeting of Sandringham W.I. on January 21, 1953, were taken exclusively, with Royal permission, for HOME AND COUNTRY for reproduction in the Coronation issue.

H.M. The Queen, about to pour out tea, shows a member that she is wearing her W.I. badge on her lapel. Although Her Majesty has long been a member of Sandringham W.I. (she joined in 1943), this was the first meeting she attended as Queen

Shining silver, fine china and a gay cloth set the scene for afternoon tea, as the Queen Mother chats with Sandringham W.I. members

Inspecting the competition entries of rock cakes and potted hyacinths. Their Majesties seemed much interested to learn from the judge what qualities she would look for in a rock bun

But, before tea, business must be dealt with, and the Queen Mother, President of Sandringham W.I., takes the chair. Queen Elizabeth sits on her right

End of an exciting afternoon. Their Majesties say goodbye to their fellow members as they prepare to return to Sandringham

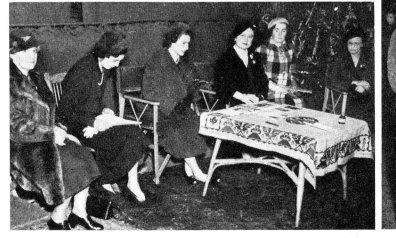

THE LADY DENMAN, C.B.E.

CHAIRMAN OF THE NATIONAL FEDERATION OF WOMEN'S INSTITUTES

From the Bishop of Chichester's Address at the Memorial Service to Lady Denman at Balcombe Parish Church, June 9th, 1954.

A GREAT company of people, of all classes and views, meet here this afternoon in remembrance of Lady Denman. For nearly the whole of her married life she lived in Balcombe Place. Her influence and fame went far beyond this parish's borders, through the work she did for over forty years in the service of women. But it was here that she made her home, had her own people about her, and received her friends and fellow-workers from far and near. It was here too that she thought out her plans, as the centre and the headquarters of her many activities. It is here, therefore, in Balcombe, that those nearest to her have asked that a tribute of remembrance might be paid. . . .

In her public life there was one great motive by which her work was directed—the determination to do everything she could to help the women of her country. She sought, so far as it lay in her power, to prevent them from being trampled upon. She was also resolved to secure that, with the help of a sound education and in other ways, they should have every opportunity for the development of their gifts, and for making their full contribution to the life of the community as citizens and country women, as wives and mothers. . . .

There were three special interests, amongst many, with which her work was most closely linked.

One was the Family Planning Association, founded in 1930. Lady Denman was convinced that, since the family was the foundation of national life, far more thought should be given to its making and maintenance than it commonly received. She was particularly alive to the evil consequences, especially in poverty, misery and physical and mental disease, which a disregard of the need of planning involved. This is not a popular or an easy subject. It needs great human understanding, and ethical insight, as well as statesmanship. But it was Lady Denman's firm conviction that if the nations were to wrestle successfully with the problems of war, starvation, destitution and ill-health, rightly-directed family planning was a necessary condition of the advance, and perhaps even the survival, of the race. . . .

The second special interest in which Lady Denman played a leading part in both World Wars was the Women's Land Army. . . . Lady Denman was its moving spirit and Director-in-Chief.

Without her immense driving power, without her determination to get what she was convinced members of the Land Army needed for their work, however hard the battle she had to fight against prejudice or bureaucracy, and without the confidence which women all over the country had learned to place in her disinterestedness, courage and integrity, the Women's Land Army could not possibly have achieved its immense success. . . .

I have reserved to the last that special interest which was in fact the first and greatest of all. Lady Denman entered the Women's Institute movement at its very early beginning, in 1916, at the age of 32. From 1917 to 1946 she was Chairman of the National Federation of Women's Institutes. She saw in the Institutes a means not only of helping women in domestic science and homecraft, but also of training them to take their part in the affairs of the community, to understand contemporary trends and issues, and to help in the solution of some of the problems of contemporary life. Under her leadership the movement grew in a quite remarkable way. From the very first her main concern was to safeguard its democratic and independent character. Non-party political, and non-sectarian, it drew and draws together women of all classes. It helped and helps them to develop their capacities, in all sorts of ways, domestic and social in the largest sense; in craft work; in the kitchen, the farm, the garden and the market stall; in music, dancing and drama; and even in the better understanding of other nations, by its relation to rural women's organizations of many countries. In all this Lady Denman was the teacher, and the driving force. She was not only an incomparable Chairman at the Annual General Meetings in the Albert Hall, with her mastery of procedure, her zest and her humour, but she was also the far-seeing leader, as Chairman of the Executive Committee, in decisions of policy and the very human friend of the ordinary individual member. . . .

To the end of her life she was valiant for the truth which she saw, and set an example in her human love, her service to others, and her concern for justice, from which all who knew and loved her may profit. She has left a name behind her which will not be forgotten.